LANDSEER

LANDSEER

THE VICTORIAN PARAGON

CAMPBELL LENNIE

HAMISH HAMILTON
LONDON

First published in Great Britain 1976
by Hamish Hamilton Ltd
90 Great Russell Street London WC1B 3PT

Copyright © 1976 by Campbell Lennie

SBN 241 89432 8

Printed in Great Britain
by W & J Mackay Limited, Chatham

FOR ISABEL

CONTENTS

ILLUSTRATIONS

THE INFANT APPRENTICE

Finding a scrap of paper and a pencil in my pocket I made him sketch a cow.

—John Landseer of his son, Edwin

IN THE early part of last century the area within a half-mile radius of Queen Anne Street (shortly thereafter Foley Street) in Marylebone was probably the nearest thing London has ever had to an artist quarter. The district abounded in artist-residents including Turner, Fuseli, Benjamin West, B. R. Haydon, James Ward, Flaxman, Northcote, Mulready, Leslie, Collins, Alfred Chalon and Stothard. Martin Archer Shee, a future President of the Royal Academy, lived in Cavendish Square, in a house once occupied by Romney. Hazlitt was then busily engaged in painting portraits in nearby Great Russell Street; and Newman Street was said to throng with artists and sculptors. Had anyone carelessly thrown a stone in those welldoing though not excessively plush environs the chances are that the figure doubled-up in pain would have been a painter, a sculptor or an engraver.

By means of a leisurely stroll several of those eminent artists would find their way to a house in Queen Anne Street East (soon to be 33 Foley Street) where dwelt a man of almost equal eminence, John Landseer. It was there, allegedly on March 7th 1802, that Edwin Landseer was born. However, the Landseers were poor on dates. Doubt had already surrounded the birth of John Landseer himself: two early authorities differed by a cool eight years and 130 miles, F. G. Stephens believing him born in London in 1761 and C. M. Monkhouse at Lincoln in 1769. The doubts surrounding Edwin's birth are less extreme. The popular year is 1802; but in the record of *Baptisms solemnised in the Parish of St. Mary-le-Bone in the county of Middlesex, in the year One Thousand Eight Hundred and Twenty-One* his year of birth was entered as 1803, which would have made the future child prodigy prodigious by one more year. However, when a child is baptised at the age of eighteen (or nineteen) human memory is apt either to err or flatter. Eighteen-o-two is the more favoured year, solemnised by inscription on his coffin-plate. So much for the doubts. The certainty is that Edwin was born into art and design as other children were born into the theatre or the circus; for John Landseer was a leading engraver of the day and himself the son of a jeweller.

The art of engraving was, of course, a natural extension of the jeweller's craft. Jewellers and goldsmiths were the first to use the graver and the needle on metal. Holbein and other well-known artists had designed jewellery; and Hogarth had begun by engraving household plate before graduating to the copper etchings that made his name. In John Landseer's youth engraving was very much a career with a future; and the boy's jeweller father was obviously anxious to develop as far as possible his son's evident eye for design. One of his friends was the wealthy Soho jeweller, Peter Romilly, whose son, a boyhood playmate of John's, became Sir Samuel Romilly, the noted lawyer and politician. Romilly senior it was who persuaded Landseer senior to apprentice John to William Byrne, one of the best instructors of the day. Byrne and the equally illustrious Hearne had produced a famous series of engravings, *The Antiquities of Britain*. Byrne's views of such diverse topographical subjects as the Lakes of Cumberland, the Falls of Niagara and the scenic delights of Italy were hardly less popular. Neither Landseer senior nor, in turn, his son John could be accused of settling for second best for their boys.

The high quality of English engravings in the late eighteenth century was reflected in the popularity of handsome illustrated editions the English classics. This led to considerable rivalry between the of major print publishers of the time, particularly between the businesses belonging to Alderman Boydell and Thomas Macklin, each of whom had his own gallery. Macklin had begun life as a cabin boy before becoming a picture-frame gilder, from which he graduated to print and picture dealer. He was discerning enough to take on the young John Landseer, whose first works for him were vignettes after de Loutherbourg landscapes intended for his ambitious illustrated Bible. *Macklin's Bible* was his reply to his great rival's *Shakespeare*, the Bible being the only artistic concept capable of outdoing the complete works of the Bard. One of painters approached by Boydell in the great art race had been Sir Joshua Reynolds who, although the leading portraiturist of the day, seems to have been regarded (erroneously) as a likely painter of historical subjects. Sir Joshua's enthusiasm for Boydell's epic scheme cannot have been great; but, like many another artist, he seems to have been impressed by the inside of the Alderman's purse.

This no-holds-barred rivalry inspired Macklin himself to approach the eminent President of the Royal Academy to commission from him a handful of biblical subjects, for one of which, *The Holy Family*, he paid Reynolds 500 guineas. The young John Landseer must have watched the forceps birth of such masterpieces with suitable awe. But it was a less spiritual family group by Sir Joshua that doubtless claimed his chief interest. This was *The Gleaners* (otherwise known as *The Cottagers* or as *Macklin's Family Picture*). It represented a scene of improbable rusticity with the print-publisher's wife and daughter and a miscellany of farmyard poultry. The group included a third person—a dear and pretty family friend, Miss Jane Potts, soon to become the bride of John Landseer. Little is known about the charming round-faced girl standing in bucolic bliss with a sheaf of corn on her head. She was born in 1874. The couple met at Macklin's house while he was executing plates for the *Bible*, and they were married in 1893. Only seven of their fourteen children survived infancy, hardly an unusual pattern for the times; but repeated childbearing, and the deaths of so many young ones, obviously contributed towards a resigned and recessive character.

As a young woman, however, she clearly inspired John Landseer. It was at the time of their courtship that he began to exhibit at the Royal Academy, the official sign that a young engraver had arrived. He made his debut in 1792 with *A View from the Hermit's Hole, Isle of Wight*. It would be pleasant to record a long record of success with that body, but for which, as Collins said, 'artists would be treated like journeymen'. But John had already been taught disillusionment with the Academy at the hands of his own mentor William Byrne. The cause was the refusal to accord full academic status to engravers. Associate Engraver of the Royal Academy was the most exalted title they could claim; and it was a distinction which the best engravers, many of them prosperous and influential, found difficult to accept. In practical terms it meant that the best engraver in the land could only show two of his prints at the Annual Exhibition while even the most mediocre Academician artist had the right to exhibit eight drawings, paintings or sculptures. Byrne, along with several other eminent engravers of the day including Woollett and Pye, refused to consider the 'half-honours' of Associateship. His resentment took root in John Landseer, influencing the course of his career and, one feels, affecting his character; tingeing it with iron but also with bitterness, depriving it of expansiveness but also of complacency.

As with most of the best controversies, there was much to be said on either side. The exclusion of engravers dated from the foundation of the Royal Academy in 1768. The Scottish engraver Sir Robert Strange believed that the real motive had been originally political,

as he had been excluded from full membership because as a young
man in Scotland he had engraved a banknote for Prince Charles Edward the Pretender. But the reasons for assigning to engravers a
lower status than to artists, sculptors and even architects was mainly
artistic. Sir Joshua and many other artist-academicians felt (with
some justification) that engraving did not require true creative or in-
ventive powers. The Academy's attempt in the second year of its
existence to half-redress the wrong made things even worse. The
air of patronage about their decision to admit six engravers to the
secondary rank of Associate merely angered the engravers and united
them in their opposition to the Academy. For some time no engraver
could be persuaded to put his name forward; though, in due course
and inevitably, a few of the less distinguished shuffled forward cap-
in-hand to claim the associateships going a-begging. The issue was
further confused by hypocrisy. The eminent engraver Bartolozzi was
appointed full R.A. after submitting an original painting, though the
nature of his true profession was never in any doubt. Not every Aca-
demician-artist supported the deliberate down-grading of engravers—
David Wilkie and several others were heartily opposed to it. Sir
Joshua's original argument about lack of creativity may have held
some water; but the growing dependence of artists on engravers for
the spread of their reputations was painfully obvious, as indeed was
the high standard of British engraving. And at a pinch the engravers
could always fall back on the Old Masters. This fact no doubt
boosted their resolve not to settle for second-best.

In 1802, the year of Edwin's birth, John Landseer was in the thick
of the controversy; pressing for four engravers to be made full
Academicians, for the award of medals to encourage young student
engravers, for the assignment of a place in the Academy's exhibition-
rooms for *unpublished* engravings only. That same year a vacancy had
occurred among the Associate Engravers, but the pariah place remained unfilled. However, in 1806, by now convinced that he could
fight more effectively from within the Academy, Landseer put his
name forward. He was elected by ballot. Doubtless many of his
fellow-engravers who still held aloof allowed themselves a knowing
smile as they watched their young stormy petrel hop into the gilded
cage. But John Landseer was as good as his threats. He continued to
press for full Academic status, for the institution of a professorship
in engraving; bombarding the Academicians with printed addresses
on the subjects. His lectures on the Art of Engraving delivered that
year were eagerly attended. He aggrandised his craft by describing it
as 'sculpture by incision', a definition adopted by other engravers. He
was a forceful orator: one of his audience at a later lecture-series

found him 'animated in his style, but his animation is produced by indulgence in sarcasm and emphatic diction. He pronounces his words in *italics*, and by colouring strongly he produces an effect easily'—the style of today's political orators, in fact. Never a man to distinguish between a personal and an artistic grudge, John Landseer included several disparaging references to his erstwhile employer's rival, Boydell, accusing him of palming-off inferior plates on the public. It was in many ways an unfair accusation to make, especially about a name as powerful as that of Boydell. Although the Alderman himself had died two years before, his nephew Josiah decided that the time had come to spoke a wheel that appeared to be running away with itself. Landseer, who had had his scripts vetted for slanderous content by his old friend Sir Samuel Romilly (now Solicitor-General) was confident of staying the course. But a hastily-called 'hole-in-corner' meeting of the Committee of the Royal Institution abruptly terminated the series of lectures halfway through. John's characteristic response was to publish them in the following year, taking good care to underline and annotate all the more offensive parts. For many years they remained the standard text on the subject. Meantime, the Prince Regent had been handed the reins of state. In 1812 Landseer forcefully petitioned that somewhat unlikely gentleman on his rights as a sculptor by incision. Like the engravers' later appeals to Parliament in 1826 and to King William in 1837, it fell on deaf ears.

In the interim John's graver had not been idle. He continued to turn out plates of vigorous merit by Turner and Ibbetson among others: his largest series was *Twenty Views of the South of Scotland* by James Moore. Nor did he confine himself to landscape art. His engravings from animal drawings by the Dutch masters, Rembrandt, Rubens, Snyders and others, were not only skilled but prophetic. Continuous controversy had, however, taken its toll, as did the repeated rebuffs of the Royal Academy. Years later he complained about having received from Sir Martin Archer Shee and others 'a very great deal of illiberality and was finally repulsed in the most ungracious way'; but even at the time injured dignity had begun to replace his old free-hitting sarcastic style. His disillusionment extended to his work as a teacher. At least one of his pupils complained of being 'not well used by Him, in respect of instruction. Landseer employed much of his time in writing letters, and sent Him with them'. The same pupil, Berenger, also repeated to Joseph Farington R.A. that the engraver was 'warm in his temper, though he does not appear so out of doors, and is not liked by those of his profession'. But Farington was a confidant of Landseer's who, like many compulsive diarists, could repay friendship and trust in rather dubious ways; and who, as

Lawrence Gowing noted, 'wrote down everyone's opinion in the hope
of developing his own'.

His instructor John Byrne had noted John's passion for letters;
and it was to writing and another early love, archaeology, that the
disenchanted engraver turned. He was a percipient art critic and
commentator who had very early on espied the genius both of Stubbs
and Turner, commissioning views from the latter of the Isle of
Wight and other localities. In 1808 he launched a new quarterly,
Review of Publications of Art, that was almost alone in praising Turner's *Battle of Trafalgar* as 'a new kind of Epic Picture' that had
'suggested the whole of a great victory . . . Perhaps no landscape
painter has ever before so successfully caught the living lustre of
Nature itself . . .' Turner himself was perceptively likened to one of
'those few musicians of transcendent skill, who while they expose
much less than others the extremes of the compass of their instruments, produce superior melody'. The *Review* ceased publication after
the second number, at a loss to Landseer (according to Farington's
intelligence-service) of £400. A similar fate befell his much later
weekly periodical, *The Probe*, in which, to Redgrave's mind, 'the
artists were sharply handled'. The writing-off of such ventures seemed
to argue a fair degree of affluence on John Landseer's part, partly the
legacy perhaps of his father's successful trade in expensive baubles.

Some commentators have blamed John's Landseer's espousal of
writing and archaeology entirely on his treatment at the hands of the
Academy; but the formula seems a little strong, especially since he
did not publish his first archaeological tome, *Observations on the
Engraved Gems brought from Babylon*, until ten years after his bitterly
ironic *Lectures on the Art of Engraving*. This was a scholarly attempt
to show that the gems known as the Babylonian cylinders had been
used not as talismans or amulets but as royal signets. Six years later
he produced his *Sabaean Researches: Essays on the Engraved Hyro-
glyphics of Chaldea, Egypt and Canaan*. Apart from his own interest
in such esoteric subjects, their publication perhaps also indicated a
desire on John Landseer's part to poke a stick in the eye of the eminent Academicians who had stood against him and whose only skill,
after all, was their ability to wield a paint brush. Not all his grand
projects achieved completion. *Antiquities of Dacca*, begun in 1816,
was never finished; whilst a later commentary *Description of Fifty
of the Earliest Pictures in the National Gallery*, though it terminated
on the assurance *End of Vol. I*, never had a successor.

If anyone benefitted from the unreasonable strictures placed on
engravers, it was Edwin and his brothers and sisters. Had John Landseer met with a sympathetic reception at the Royal Academy; had

his plea to institute a Professorship of Engraving (with himself as the most likely candidate) been heard; his young family might have seen much less of their father. But he now had plenty of time to devote to his children; they at least could profit from the far-seeing advice to which the artistic establishment paid such scant attention. The surviving children were three boys and four girls: Thomas, the eldest brother, was supposedly born in 1795,* Charles in 1799, and Edwin three years later. The eldest girl was Jane who later married the animal painter Charles Christmas and died of her first childbirth; Emma, the youngest became Mrs. Mackenzie; Anna Maria and Jessica never married. All, however, attained some proficiency in drawing or engraving or in both. John Landseer's studio was clearly an open house where his children were concerned. It is difficult to imagine him sending them off with a flea in their ear for interfering with engraving instruments or plates, papers or inks.

Young Edwin, naturally, began to draw 'as soon as he could hold a pencil with some steadiness'. It was to his mother that he first turned for instruction, but she only ever gave him one of two objects to draw —a shoe or a currant pudding. Even in his tenderest years, the boy obviously foresaw a limited artistic future in portraying just these two items. Accordingly, at four years old, he approached his father, who at first was scarcely more helpful, setting him a candle to draw and giving him his first taste of the iron of discipline: 'Now you must finish it tonight before you go to bed!'. Later, however, he became more expansive. 'Nature is the best teacher, my boy!' he would say. It was, besides being a cliché, only a half-truth. In the young, imagination is also a great teacher; but imagination was the very quality which Sir Joshua (with some justification) had found wanting in engravers. The impossible battles, the prehistoric monsters, the raging floods and fires and torrents, the collisions of worlds with other worlds, and all the other extravagant flights of fancy in which infant artists are wont to indulge (usually to their own vocal accompaniment) seem to have been largely denied the young Edwin. Almost as soon as he could walk, he was lifted into fields beside domestic animals and encouraged to draw them, not as creatures of wonder, but as the kind of exact representations which made the Victorian era the spiritual as well as the temporal mother of photography.

In those far-off days fields stretched almost interrupted from Marylebone to Hampstead. One one occasion, as an old man walking with his friend William Howitt, John Landseer stopped at a point near

* Again, in the 1821 Marylebone Baptismal Register, Tom's birth-year (though blurred) looks like 1798. Charles's is given as 1800, and the eldest child Jane's as 1795.

Frognal on what is now the Finchley Road. 'These two fields were Edwin's first studio,' he told his old friend. 'This was a favourite walk with my boys, and one day when I had accompanied them, Edwin stopped by the stile to admire some cows and sheep that were quietly grazing. At his request I lifted him over, and finding a scrap of paper and a pencil in my pocket I made him sketch a cow. He was very young indeed then—not more than six or seven years old. After this we came on several occasions, and as he grew older this was one of his favourite spots for sketching. He would start off alone, or with Thomas or Charles, and remain till I fetched him in the afternoon. I would then correct his work, and make him correct defects before we left the spot.'

The repetition of the words *make him* and *made him* is perhaps significant. There was a good deal of the Spartan in John Landseer, and Edwin clearly was expected to draw for his supper from an early age. As against this sketchbook discipline, however, there was his father's openly expressed contempt for the schoolroom. Edwin's sister Emma later remembered him as 'always running away from school and always drawing'. If his father didn't encourage this truancy, he certainly winked at it. In the Victorian writer Allan Cunningham's view John Landseer shared with Sir Thomas Lawrence's father 'an opinion that ordinary education was unnecessary, if not harmful, to boys who were destined for artists. Of regular schooling, Edwin Landseer had none, so that he could not write until well after the ordinary age'.

John Landseer's rejection by the Academy obviously had something to do with his determination to make at least one of his boys, and preferably all three, into established artists, to capture if only by proxy the magic initials, R.A. Although not the kind of man to show favouritism, he was soon aware that Edwin was outpacing his older brothers, whose talents were of a more painstaking order. When Edwin was only five he made a study from life of a foxhound which was, as Cunningham remarked, 'quite marvellous'. Before he was ten he had proved his ability to draw every species of domestic animal not only recognisably but with such an eye for detail that a farmer or a stockman could have told a great deal from them; as well as, in many cases, the temper and disposition of the animal. When he was eight Edwin executed a series of finished engravings from his own work: these included the head of donkey (with an oddly articulated neck), the head of a shorthorned sheep (whose horns show a remarkable grasp of foreshortening) and an excellently detailed head of a boar.

Even the weather, it was said, could not dampen the boy's compulsive urge to draw from the life. On one rainy day sudden cries of frustration rent the household. Edwin had, apparently, been sketching a horse standing at the Foley Street cab-rank, when the driver arrived to remove the cloth from the animal's back. This unwitting interference with his composition had caused him to explode with annoyance. The imperious cries of youthful rage were perhaps prophetic—Edwin never quite reached the age when he was too old to throw a tantrum.

At the age of seven Edwin was already supplementing his study of domestic animals with sketching visits to the menageries. His first ever etching was of the head of a lion, which, of course, became his third favourite subject among the animals. Of the two collections of wild beasts in London at the time, one was the Tower Menagerie and the other Polito's, in the Exeter 'Change, not far from Edwin's home. The latter was a somewhat dilapidated building in the Strand that housed a fair number of wild animals confined in cramped cages round the walls. It was a notoriously unpopular spot with cabbies and carters, since the roaring of the lions and tigers would habitually panic the horses in the street below. Edward Cross, the menagerie's owner, soon developed a great interest in the little curly-headed boy who seemed dwarfed by his sketchbook, and allowed him every facility. The early drawings, however, showed the boy to be as much influenced by contemporary illustration as by the live models: his portrayal, aged seven, of a lioness and two cubs, though full of spirit, was as far removed from reality as the garish jungle vegetation with which the menagerie walls were liberally daubed. The Tower was another obvious haven for would-be animal artists, wild beasts having been kept there since the thirteenth century. Once again Edwin was able to ingratiate himself, especially with one kindly keeper whose wife was one day badly mauled by a lion. When Edwin went to express his regrets, the distraught keeper reassured him: 'Go on with your drawing, lad, and never mind me.' Both the apology and the reaction seem to indicate an extremely likeable and engaging youth. Edwin continued to haunt the Tower Menagerie until 1834, when the animals were removed to the Zoological Gardens at Regent's Park.

The great painter-anatomist George Stubbs had died only a few years before, and his example probably impressed on Edwin the importance of dissection to an animal artist. One of the young artist's companions on his visits to the menageries was the future water-colourist, John Frederick Lewis, who had been born two years after Edwin in the same street* and was also the son of a well-known

* It has been suggested that J. F. Lewis was born in the same *house*, the Landseers having presumably moved to another address in the same street; but, according to

engraver. Lewis's nephew records that his uncle and the young Landseer 'were great chums as students, and used to buy carcases of foxes and game, etc., and take them home for dissection and study, keeping them under their beds in daytime, which was never discovered'. Nor were the lessons of Polito's lost on Lewis: his studies of lions and other animals were masterly, and Sir Thomas Lawrence later employed him to add animals and sometimes landscapes to his portraits, but with Lewis's departure for Spain and North Africa some twenty years later the paths (and the artistic interests) of the 'chums' diverged. The skull of a pointer, drawn about the time Edwin was secreting carcases under the bed, was a finely-observed little study; and his interest in the clinically bizarre was shown in his portrayal of a *lusus naturae*, an extra pair of ill-formed legs and a tail growing from the shoulder of an otherwise perfectly proportioned young bull.

Edwin had soon acquired a local reputation as an artistic prodigy, which several later commentators have done their utmost to enhance. Today some of the claims (like the early drawings themselves) have a somewhat old-fashioned look. Extremely precocious as an artist he certainly was; whether such precocity amounted to prodigy is another matter. True prodigy defies comparisons; but many of Edwin's youthful drawings could equally be the work of a competent artist not many years older than himself. Much of it is therefore only prodigious on learning the age of the artist; without such prior knowledge it is unremarkable. It is obviously unfair to denigrate youthful works of art, but these do manifest a great deal of what it is the artist's business to hide—the tongue-in-cheek concentration that went into them. The art that conceals art is in notably short supply —'See how I have achieved this clever piece of foreshortening!' some seem to say; and others, 'Mark the realistic detail on the snout of this boar!'. The drawings are as much a credit to John's determination as to Edwin's ability, reflecting the highly professional background from which the boy had emerged. Some of the earliest drawings and etchings, lovingly annotated by John, are in the Victoria and Albert Museum; they reflect a thorough if rather limited training in art. But there were lurking dangers in a more refined artistic education. C. M. Monkhouse later gave pious expression to what John Landseer himself may have felt. 'His study was in the fields,' said Monkhouse, 'and the subjects which he drew . . . were such as are congenial and wholesome to the minds of all healthy boys, and were not likely to

---

Emma Landseer, the house in which Lewis was born was a smaller one that had been occupied by John Landseer *before* his marriage.

encourage the morbid activity of the intellect so often the fatal accompaniment of youthful prodigies'.

Edwin first blossomed forth as an exhibitor in 1813 when his animal drawings earned him the silver palette of the Society of Arts. In the following year both he and his eldest brother were awarded the Isis silver medal of the Society, Edwin for his drawing of a *Hunting Horse* and Thomas for an oil painting of a *Farmer's Horse*. Two of the young artist's most interesting productions of that year were the humorously contrasting *French Hog* and *British Boar*; the first of almost greyhound gauntness, the second of prosperous and complacent rotundity. Remembering the parlous state of Anglo-French relations at the time, one is left in no doubt as to their satirical intention. They were Edwin's first attempt at satire; he would try, try and try again, but success in the genre always eluded him. His first posed portrait outside his own family circle had been drawn the previous year—*C. Simmons Esq.*, a portly old gentleman on a pony, was only a copy, but said to have been a good likeness of the likeness. He also began to introduce human figures into his drawings, usually to reinforce the animal action, as in *Sheep Shearing* and *Ringing the Pig*.

These were farmyard scenes he had probably witnessed in Essex, when he went on his holidays to Beleigh Grange near Maldon. It was the home of family friends, the Simpsons, who remained friends into Edwin's adult life; Mrs. Simpson writing him long, fussy and prolix letters to which her husband would append a few droll and pertinent remarks. At the Grange Edwin made a fine sketch of a Persian cat which he presented to a servant girl Lucy Potter. Many years later, when Lucy became a housemaid in his own establishment, the elderly artist annotated the drawing: 'Sketched at Maldon by the little boy Edwin when ten years old, and now Sir E. Landseer, an old boy, 1866'. The most significant pictures made at Maldon, however, were the two that marked his debut as a Royal Academy exhibitor in 1815. *Portrait of a Mule* and *Head of a Pointer Bitch and Puppy* were both sub-titled, 'the property of W. H. Simpson, Esq., of Beleigh Grange, Essex'. It was proud distinction for a boy of thirteen, though it has been said that the Academy were always on the lookout for something different, hence earlier curiosities like George Morland's picture drawn with a poker, flower-pieces executed in human hair and so on. Edwin was recorded in the Catalogue as 'Master E. Landseer, H, 33 Foley Street'; the *H* standing for Honorary, in reference to Edwin's tender age. By a misprint in the same catalogue, the boy's first offering was entitled *Portrait of a Mute*, arousing much previous speculation as to how any artist, even one of the precocious

Landseer clan, could convey in graphic terms the inability to speak.
The critic of the *Sporting Magazine* later found the lop-eared animal
to be 'neatly drawn, well foreshortened and staring us in the face'.

Exhibiting in the most important gallery in the country at such an
early age was doubtless a proud distinction. John Landseer must
have seen it as the just reward of application and industry, his own
and Edwin's. It was hardly a time to ask whether it had all been
worth it: the answer would have been self-evident. And yet there
seemed to have been little of play and relaxation in Edwin's childhood. Among all the serious, and often laboured, studies of animal
life only one drawing of childish fancy appears to have survived . . .
The Tournament shows a rabbit-headed demon stabbing a devilish
knight in armour. It is a typical child's drawing—crude, spirited,
speedily-done—but for Edwin it was unique.

George Morland, who had died when Edwin was two, had likewise
had a father who was an artist, an engraver and a disciplinarian. The
resemblance to John Landseer was hardly complete—Henry Morland had been a much sterner, less volatile man than Edwin's father.
But he had set out in the same selfconscious way to achieve the same
result. Young George had been debarred from associating with other
boys; had been set endless exercises in drawing. At the age of ten he
was already a Royal Academy exhibitor, though forbidden to attend
the Academy schools because of the temptations of the metropolis.
Articled to his father at fourteen, the discipline became even more
constant and unbending. Every hour not spent by George at his easel
was in Henry Morland's opinion wasted. The effort was, to say the
least, counter-productive. At the age of nineteen the former child-
prodigy savagely freed himself from his intolerable disciplines. His
life thereafter was a descent into dissolution, debt and drunkenness:
his art, despite its popular success, scarcely fulfilled that early
promise. He died aged forty-one in a spunging-house, having earlier
written his own epitaph: 'Here lies a drunken dog'. 'Poor George
Morland', unable to leave home for fear of arrest by bailiffs, having to
imagine many of the animals he painted or have pigs scurrying
through his own apartments, spending his nights in a drunken stupor
on the floor, was a whispered by-word among artists around the turn
of the century. As a walking morality-lesson, he was doubtless known
to John Landseer, who naturally must have seen himself as a much
more civilising influence than Henry Morland. Yet Edwin, too,
would later react against a childhood that was basically incomplete;
and against a professionalism that had been instilled in him rather
too early for his own good.

Ironically enough, it was around the time of his debut at the Royal

Academy that a rare cameo was presented of Edwin at play. A would be patron who had been much impressed by the boy's mule called at the Landseer home to enquire about the picture. Through the garden gate he saw some boys playing with hoops. 'Does the artist Mr. Landseer live here,' he asked, 'and when can I speak to him?' 'You can speak to him now,' said the tiny boy with the hoop. 'I am Mr. Landseer.'

CHAPTER TWO

ENTER B.R.H.

The first moment I awoke my glorious Art darted into my Brains.
I arose elastic like a bow and set to work.
                                        —Benjamin Robert Haydon

IN 1815 John Landseer approached the painter Benjamin Robert
Haydon.
'When do you let your beard grow and take pupils?' he asked.
'If my instructions are useful and valuable, now,' replied
Haydon.
'Will you let my boys come?'
'Certainly.'
So began the Landseer brothers' brief but revealing relationship
with a remarkable man. It was immediately arranged that Thomas
and Charles would go every Monday, when Haydon would set them
work for the week. Edwin was to study the painter's dissections of
the lion, made in 1810; and to follow Haydon's advice to learn
anatomy by dissection. 'Lent young Landseer my Anatomical
Drawings, John Bell on the Bones, Anatomy of a Lion, Plates &C' he
noted in his diary not long after. Though he was never a regular
pupil of Haydon's, the future animal painter became the subject of
much comment, both enthusiastic and acrimonious, in Haydon's
Journals, a wonderfully boisterous and irreverent collection unfortunately published too late to assuage their author's perpetual
impecuniousness.
Haydon was a man of many and grievous faults—he was vain,
egotistic and boastful, a shameless borrower, a wayward companion
who would praise to heaven one month and damn to hell the next and
who finally confessed, 'I have not a friend in the world. I have worn
them all out'. His hatred of institutions and authority was at times
almost paranoic. He suffered from something bordering on persecution mania—if a patron or a sitter thought badly of him, he had been
'tampered with'; if a man lent him a horse it was to see him thrown.
Conceptually he was a great artist; but his technique usually failed to
match his grandiose ideas, partly because since boyhood he had

suffered from an eyesight deficiency that made it difficult for him to achieve depth of perspective. Yet Haydon had one great compensating virtue. His love for art, his commitment to it, were total and absolute; whatever his shortcomings as a painter he was an artist through and through. In that sense at least, he was a living rebuke to the douce businessmen-painters of the Victorian era. Five of his eight children died young, largely through the circumstances created by his singleminded pursuit of art. Yet it is hard to withhold affection from a man who could write in his *Journal*:

> I have not a pound in the World at this moment—yet I never passed a happier morning. Mary came to me for some money to pay for mangling. I said 'don't talk to me about mangling, look at that background', at which she kissed me with all her soul in her sweet lips & went away laughing.

or:

> The moment I opened my window a magnificent white cloud was passing. I rushed in for my palette, & dashed it into my Picture before it had passed. It does exactly.

When the Landseer boys first came to him Haydon was twenty-nine, a historical painter who confessed to feelings of ungovernable excitement when there was a large empty canvas in the house. His own philosophy of painting he summed-up in repetition of the grandolinquent phrase High Art, which he used both to exalt his own work and disparage other people's. His two artistic obsessions were the Elgin Marbles and the Cartoons of Raphael, both of which he spent hours studying and copying. Naturally, he encouraged his newly-acquired pupils to do the same.

Haydon had been one of the most spirited spokesmen for the Marbles, brought from the Acropolis in Athens by the 7th Earl of Elgin to prevent their destruction by the Turks. The rescue operation had been regarded in some quarters as sheer vandalism; others, with tidy and practical minds, begged leave to question the value of anything so chipped and broken. In 1810 Lord Elgin justified his actions in a lively pamphlet: in the following year the fragments from the Parthenon frieze went on display in Burlington House. Yet the government and the public remained sceptical. Several artists, including the sculptors Flaxman and Nollekens, called on the government to purchase the magnificent relics. Haydon threw himself with characteristic verve into the controversy, and his famous letters to the *Examiner* and *Champion* newspapers were equally effective in publicising the Elgin Marbles and Benjamin Robert Haydon.

Finally, of course, the stones carved by Phidias and his pupils four
hundred years before the birth of Christ were bought for the nation
in 1816 for £36,000—hardly a generous figure, considering Lord
Elgin's personal outlay of more than £50,000. Though his espousal of
the Marbles had made him something of 'lion', Haydon's reverence
for them was touchingly genuine. He would contemplate them for
hours on end, often moved to tears by their grandeur and beauty.
'The last words I should wish to utter in this world,' he declared, 'are
Elgin Marbles! Elgin Marbles!'—and he liked to recall the tribute paid
them by a thoroughbred horse on entering the studio which started
back and neighed on beholding a plaster cast of the horse's head of
Selene. What Edwin derived from his study of the Marbles is difficult
to say. At least in his horses he avoided the notorious 'flying gallop'
much affected by sporting artists of the time. Photography later
exposed the myth of this ridiculous posture, showing that in the
moment when all four hooves are off the ground they are gathered
under the horse instead of being extended back and fore. In Western
Europe the cliche was handed down from father to son like some
family heirloom. But the ancient Greeks had known better.

Haydon's other love, the Raphael cartoons, also involved him in
controversy. The cartoons were kept at Burlington Gardens, and
their use for copying was confined to Royal Academy students.
Haydon, quite rightly, found such an arrangement both arrogant and
parochial in view of the timeless significance of Raphael's work; he
launched himself into a campaign to have them made available to
his own and other pupils. Soon there would hardly be a time when
Haydon wasn't quarrelling with the Academy, to which he became,
by his own description, 'a perpetual indigestion'.

'My object is to found a School, deeply impregnated with my
principles of Art, deeply grounded in all the means, to put the clue
into the hands of a certain number of young men of genius that they
may go by themselves.' Haydon's ambition was to re-establish the
principles by which the old masters had been taught, and it is plain
from his *Journals* that John Landseer's approach to him was a
significant event in his life. The 'young men of genius' who formed
the nucleus of his school were the Landseers, Bewick, Chatfield,
Lance, Prentis and Harvey. Charles Eastlake, later to become renowned more as administrator than painter, had been with Haydon
since 1813. The apostle of High Art always made great play with the
fact that he taught his pupils free 'without one shilling of payment'.
It was perhaps only technically true. Eastlake, whom 'I educated
for 3 years without payment' frequently found himself out of funds
by the arrangement. Haydon once invited him to the theatre four-

teen evenings in a row, each time airily leaving his pupil to pay for the tickets. Later, harassed by creditors, he persuaded two former pupils, Bewick and Harvey, to put their names to bills amounting to six hundred pounds. He was afterwards himself deeply ashamed of this transaction; though Bewick never lost his admiration for Haydon's peculiar resilience. While painting the figure of Lazarus into one of his epic canvases he was repeatedly bedevilled by bailiffs. 'Bewick,' he remarked with admirable understatement on returning from one such interview, 'if I am called again it will be impossible for me to go on; that is the third time this morning that I have been arrested.'

In his *Journals*, however, it was usually overstatement. On January 31st 1819 Haydon announced: 'On Saturday last was the proudest day of my life . . . This day was the most glorious in reality & in promise for the historical painting of England that had ever happened'. The occasion was the opening of the exhibition of eight cartoons by Tom and Charles Landseer and Bewick for which Haydon wrote an accompanying text, *Description of the Drawings from the Cartoons and Elgin Marbles by Mr. Haydon's Pupils*. Haydon was severely rapped for his pretensions. He was mercilessly guyed as the self-appointed 'Director of the Public Taste' and the opening of his exhibition savagely caricatured as 'St. James' Street in an Uproar, or the Quack Artist and his Assailants'. Bewick remembered the humiliation of the occasion, which must have been shared by Tom and Charles. Edwin, however, stood notably apart from the furore, and from that time dates the High Artist's disillusionment with his most talented pupil. At Christmas in 1818, Haydon's son Frederic recalls:

> The whole family of the Landseers, father and children—with one marked exception I regret to say, that of Edwin—wrote and sent him a joint letter . . . begging him to accept their cartoon drawings for his forthcoming exhibition as a mark of their gratitude and regard. The terms in which the letter is expressed are highly honourable to both pupils and teacher. 'We bear in mind,' they say, 'your offer of payment, but we bear in mind also the instruction, &C, which our family has received at your hands, of which we request you to accept the drawings as an acknowledgement, not as a compensation.'

Although such a letter must have been highly gratifying to Haydon, on receipt of it he immediately penned the wounded note:

> Edwin Landseer, though under as great obligation to my instruction, and more for bringing him forward in the world—for I sold his first picture—did not sign, for fear of the Academy.

Edwin had joined the Royal Academy schools in 1816, in itself
something of a blow to his erstwhile tutor and his ambition to
establish 'a better and more regular system of instruction than even
the Academy offered'. It was possibly a little churlish of Haydon to
blame a highly-talented boy of fourteen for wanting to attend the
leading place of instruction in the country. John Landseer himself
had clearly connived at the move. Although, like Haydon, a born
rebel against monolithic systems, he knew better than any man the
power of the Academy and the long-term penalties of opposing its
will. When he saw Haydon caricatured as the 'Quack Artist' and
'The Director of the Public Taste', his sympathies were no doubt
with the protagonist of High Art; but he must also have secretly
applauded his own good sense in gently removing his sons from under
the somewhat dubious protection of Haydon's defiantly-flapping
wings.

The picture Haydon claimed to have sold for Edwin was *Fighting
Dogs Getting Wind* painted in 1818 and shown in the exhibition of
the Society of Painters in Oil and Water Colours. Some might have
said that it sold itself. The *Examiner* rapturously acclaimed 'our
English SCHNEIDERS' and went on: 'Did we but see the Dog's
collar, we should know that it was produced by no common hand, so
good is it, and palpably true. But the gasping and cavernous and
redly-stained mouths, the flaming eyes, the prostrate Dog, and his
antagonist standing exultantly over him . . . give a wonder-producing
vitality to the canvas'. It might be supposed that such a review
would sell any work of art, but the picture and its painter later became the subject of a disgruntled entry in Haydon's *Journal*:

> The higher a man is gifted by nature, the less willing he is to
> acknowledge any obligation to any other being, however just or
> decent.
>
> This applies to Edwin Landseer particularly. He is a young man
> of most extraordinary genius, but his genius was guided by me, &
> first brought into notice by my enthusiastic recommendation of
> him . . . When he began to shew real power, I took a portfolio of his
> drawings to Sir George Beaumont's one day at a grand dinner, &
> shewed them all round to the nobility, when they retired to their
> coffee. When he painted his Dogs, I wrote Sir George & advised
> him to buy it. In short, I was altogether the cause of bringing him
> so early into notice. These things are trifles, but when one sees a
> youth strutting about and denying his obligations to me, I may as
> well note them down.

Sir George Howland Beaumont, skilled landscape painter and

patron of the arts, paid 30 guineas for the picture. After disagreeing
with Sir George over a commission, Haydon found him the kind of
patron 'who wishes to have the reputation of bringing forward genius
without much expence. He is a man of rooted meanness of heart, who
would as soon have blood wrung from him as money—and this he
tries to conceal from the world, by wishing to appear a liberal patron
of Art'. Turner was another painter who might have echoed the
opinion. Sir George seemed to regard Turner's unexpected success as
a personal reflection on his own taste and judgement: his reaction was
to indulge in personal attacks on the great painter and his followers
like Callcott. However, by his purchase of *Fighting Dogs*, though
'without much expence', he played a significant role in the emergence
of the young Edwin as a professional artist.

At the Academy schools, Landseer came under the direct influence
of another great man, Fuseli, who was then Keeper. Edwin's reputation had preceded him. 'Where is my little *dog-boy*?' the Swiss painter
would call out, looking round his class. Again, it is difficult to discern
the teacher's long-term influence on his pupil's work. Most of the
Keepers were perhaps too immersed in their own painting (and their
own thoughts) to fill the role of dedicated tutors: Fuseli himself was
never seen without a book in his hand. C. R. Leslie wrote of Fuseli's
'wise neglect' of his pupils, and of the Keeper's belief that 'Art may
be *learnt*, but cannot be *taught*'. Normally a rather brooding little
figure, he clearly took to young Edwin who already displayed the
blend of artistic ability and engaging charm that would later prove
both blessing and curse. He was ambi-dextrous with the ability to
correct work with either hand, depending on how he stood at the
time (an ability on which Edwin later rang the changes). Less
admired by his students was his habit of correcting their work with
his thumb-nail which, being long and sharp, often damaged their
drawings beyond repair. His views of his contemporaries could be as
scathing as those of Haydon. Thus his opinion of the unfortunate Sir
Martin Archer Shee—'The vorst painter God ivver made'—was probably topped by Haydon—'The most impotent painter in the solar
system'. He took issue with the Hanging Committee on Haydon's
behalf when one of the latter's paintings was placed impossibly high
at an R.A. Exhibition—'My God, you are sending him to hivven
before his time!'. Fuseli's own work shows no great empathy with
animal art, and his rarefied style was hardly one that a strapping
young outdoors painter might be expected to emulate; but he doubtless allowed Edwin plenty of scope for natural development. He was
an undogmatic teacher: Linnell recalled the invariable conclusion of
his advice, '. . . but you know best'. His liberality extended to class

discipline. One day he surprised a student mimicking him in front of the class. 'It is very good,' was his only comment. 'It is better than I could have done it myself.' One can imagine why Blake described him as 'The only man that e'er I knew/Who did not make me almost spue . . .'.

Edwin's curly-headed good looks had already attracted attention to him in another capacity, as a model. He had been the subject of *The Cricketer*, by 'Master J. Hayter', shown at the Royal Academy in 1815. In the following year, he reappeared in *The Death of Rutland*, a Shakespearian piece by C. R. Leslie, as the hapless young victim about to be murdered by Clifford in *Henry VI: Part 3*. Although he posed as 'the pleading boy with a rope around his wrists' there seems to be no Shakespearian precedent for the rope.

When he was sixteen, Edwin produced a picture that pointed to a possible future career. *White Horse in a Stable*, painted for R. H. Pierrepoint, had neither animation nor subject-matter: it was a straightforward horse-portrait of the kind produced by the journey-men-painters of the day who travelled from Hall to Manor immortalising the gentry's prize livestock. It was an assured career. As the sporting artist Ben Marshall had said, 'Many a man will pay me fifty guineas for painting his horse who thinks ten guineas too much for painting his wife'. James Ward made the same discovery, when a Mr. Thorpe approached him to paint his favourite racehorse and his three pretty daughters—in that order. The English passion for horse-paintings had bemused the eighteenth-century French critic, Monsieur Rouquet, perhaps more inclined to look on horses as one of the pleasures of the table:

> As soon as a racehorse has acquired some fame, they have him immediately drawn to the life; this for the most part in dry profile; but in other respects being a good resemblance: they generally clap the figure of some jockey or other on his back which is but poorly done.

Nor was the vogue confined to horses: bulls and oxen and prize boars were all candidates for portraiture, usually with their better points exaggerated out of all proportion, so that a prime animal like the 560 stone Bradwell Ox looked rather like a giant bovine balloon about to take-off and float away over the fields. Edwin's early acquaintance with farmyard animals had obviously suited him to be this kind of travelling professional, and the *White Horse* indicated that, had he so wished, he had this type of vocation in his pocket. It was perhaps not very well paid to begin with. The *White Horse* had an odd career in that it went missing and wasn't found until twenty-four years later in the hayloft where it had been secreted by a dishonest servant. The money-modest forty-year-old Landseer charged for it in 1842 what had been his going rate in 1818, ten guineas. Subsequent paintings within the next few years for Lord Henniker underlined Edwin's marked ability to paint horses in 'dry profile'; and the sixteen-year-old boy no doubt gave established horse painters like Ferneley and Ward a bit of a shock.

All in all, Edwin was now beginning to feel like an established professional painter himself (and slightly patronising with it), as shown in a letter to his generous Essex host, Mr. W. H. Simpson:

Foley Street
August 12 1818

Dear Sir

I must beg to apologise for detaining the pictures so long, but hope you will now receive them safe, and that you will like the 'Brutus', as it has been generally admired, and thought the best thing I have done on so small a scale. I am exceedingly obliged to you for your kind invitation, but am doubtful whether I shall be able to avail myself of the pleasure this season.

I remain
Yours truly
Edwin Landseer

The Cat Disturbed, later engraved as *The Intruder*, was Edwin's most important exhibit of 1819. This painting, of his favourite canine model Brutus surprising a cat in a stable, consolidated rather than advanced his reputation. In the following year, however, he began to apply to good effect two of the principles taught him by Haydon— never to fear a large canvas and to learn by dissection. The three Landseer brothers were already familiar with Haydon's expansive approach to epic subjects. There were even hints that Edwin had helped the painter on at least one picture. This was *Christ's Entry into Jerusalem* which seemed to the *Examiner* in 1820 'in our humble judgement the best individual picture that has yet proceeded from a British hand'. Certainly it boasted an all-star cast—Haydon's friends Wordsworth, Keats and Hazlitt had sat for some of the portrait heads. But other critics were less than enthusiastic. A much later article in *Fraser's Magazine* savagely asserted that 'the only part of the picture decently executed was the jackass; and since that great success Mr. Haydon has been known in the profession as the Jackass Painter'. But it was another twenty years before the long-standing rumour was finally committed to print in an American magazine: 'the

ass on which the Saviour rides is inimitably fine. When the picture
was painted, Sir Edwin Landseer was a pupil of Haydon's; and 'they
say' that the young man was permitted to paint in the animal'.

The case for authentication of the authorship of the Saviour's
donkey perhaps rests with modern art-detectives, since the picture
now hangs in an Ohio seminary. The rumour was certainly a distant
echo of Wilkie's comment on the 1818 Royal Academy Exhibition,
'young Landseer's jackasses are very good'. However, we know that
Haydon made extravagant preparations before committing his
donkey to canvas. 'Dissected the fore half of an ass,' he wrote in his
Journal of 1818, '& gained immense knowledge. My head now beginning to be cleared of my ignorance of the animal.'; and the following
day: 'I got the half of an ass and set to work with fury'. At the same
time he was deeply immersed in Stubbs' anatomical drawings of the
horse. He also liked later to relate the story of the villager at Pet-
worth who, after enquiring if he was the painter of *Christ's Entry*,
said: 'Ah, sir, that was a picture—that was a picture—and what a
donkey!'. Haydon's pleased reaction was hardly typical of a man who
owed the rather disparate element by which his epic picture was best
remembered to the efforts of his star-pupil. That is not to say that
young Edwin, with all the precocity of his sixteen summers, did not
give his advice to the historical painter; or that Haydon failed to take
it. And the High Artist may even have been sensible enough to turn
his back long enough to let Edwin add a touch or two of his own.

In dissection, too, Edwin was beginning to wed theory with
practice. The year 1820 produced an unexpected bonus in the inert
and tawny shape of a lion that had died at the Exeter 'Change. The
management kindly made over his dead Majesty to two of their most
regular customers, Edwin and his friend Charles Christmas, who
trundled the cadavar in triumph round to their studio. The dissection
of the carcase led to several new pictures. *Lion Enjoying his Repast*
and *Lion Disturbed at his Repast* were painted in 1820 and shown at
the British Institution in the following year: *Prowling Lion* was
exhibited at the Royal Academy in 1822. The canvases were large,
up to six feet by eight. Nor were his dissectory efforts confined to the
lion. He made numerous studies, mainly in black and red chalk, of a
horse's head and of dogs and cats that revealed both a keen scientific
curiosity and a remarkable understanding of animal anatomy. Edwin
would later be accused of having a morbid obsession with dead
animals. Certainly his efforts of that year reflected a little of the
youth's rather wide-eyed fascination in the presence of death. He
spent a lot of time in local slaughter-houses; and drawings like *The
End of All Labour* show his familiarity with the fate of old horses who

have outlived their use. *The Vulture's Prey*, an imaginative picture of a dead horse lying contorted on some rocks beneath a circling vulture, was also based on careful studies made in the knacker's yard. In *Seizing the Boar* the animal is very much alive and protesting; but the picture reflects, again, a kind of fascination with man's tyrannical and often savage dominion over the animals.

The same year marked Edwin's first attempts at book illustration, when his father's essay on *Carnivora* became the text for a volume entitled *Twenty Engravings of Lions, Tigers, Panthers and Leopards*. Tom Landseer engraved the plates for his brother's drawings, which included one of a couchant lion with its paw resting regally on a sceptre, a rather improbably *Contending Group* of lion, tiger and leopard fighting over the carcase of a fawn, and *Tiger Tearing the Carcase of an Indian Bullock*. These scenes were highly fanciful, but his *Lioness and Bitch* was an authentic partnership: the lion-cub Charlotte had been picked up in Africa by some sailors and suckled by a dog-bitch, the inseparable pair becoming one of the main attractions of Cross's Menagerie. *Twenty Engravings* linked Edwin's name with those of Rubens and Stubbs, as well as the lesser lights Reydinger and Spilsbury.

The magazine *Annals of Sporting* now began to publish Edwin's illustrations engraved by Tom, notably *Pointers To-Ho*, a study of gun-dogs at work, very much in the sporting genre of the time. It became popular far beyond its actual merits. The truth was that a new section of the public had suddenly woken up to Edwin's existence. The practising connoisseurs of sporting art had to be very much led by the hand. To a large number of racecourse enthusiasts only a painting of a thoroughbred with a jockey on its back could be great art. In the same way, the country gentlemen who went out shooting over turnip-fields were suddenly alerted to the presence of a young man capable of holding up a mirror to their activities—a *real* artist for a change! *To-Ho* was a revelation. It was shown at no less than three of Edwin's galleries—the Royal Academy, the British Institution and the Society of British Artists—and the engraving by Tom became immensely popular.

One of Edwin's earlier models had been Lion, a huge St. Bernard or Alpine Mastiff, as the breed was then more accurately known. It was the largest animal of its kind in England; six feet four inches long and two feet seven in height at the dip of its back. Edwin had espied the enormous brute exercising a manservant in the street one day and had followed the pair home, asking the owner in his irresistibly polite and charming way if he might draw the canine phenomenon. Permission was granted, and the result had been *Alpine*

Mastiff, exhibited at Spring Gardens in 1817 but painted a year or two earlier ('From a drawing by my brother Edwin, aged 13' ran Tom's note to the engraving). So realistic had the portrait been that, according to the *Examiner*, it had produced an 'exciting effect . . . upon a canine judge admitted to the room'. Some human art-experts were equally impressed. The drawing, accurate, strong and vigorous though overly anatomised, caused the normally level-headed F. G. Stephens to jump overboard: 'It is really one of the finest drawings of a dog that has ever been produced. We do not think that even the artist at any time surpassed its noble workmanship'.

This earlier drawing had previewed a work exhibited at the British Institution in 1820. *Alpine Mastiffs Reanimating a Distressed Travel-ler* attracted more attention than anything the young artist had previously done. It showed the two dilettantish St. Bernards, Lion and his son Caesar, posing as the real thing, one of them pawing at the snow and licking the face of the prostrate traveller, the other howling for help, as the monks hasten to render aid. *Annals of the Fine Arts* (Volume V) greeted the picture with unconcealed rapture: 'Snyders never painted better than the heads of these dogs, could not have painted the dying traveller near so well, and never gave half the historical interest and elevation to any of his pictures, unassisted by Rubens, as this possesses'. There was more than a touch of chauvin-ism in the criticism, which was sufficiently intemperate even to embarrass a doting father. *Annals* had already declared of Edwin's pictures in the previous British Institution Exhibition that they 'placed him at once as the first animal painter of the day; he is not to be spoiled by such merited praise; he will do better things than he has done, but what he has done is better than any other person can do; he sees deeper into Nature than any of his pictures have hitherto displayed; he must improve, because he will never be able to equal his ideas'.

John Landseer, a keener and less emotive critic, was moved to protest (though doubtless with inward delight) that the *Annals* were over-exposing his boys. 'Is there not a little too much about my sons in it? I am afraid there is, considering they are youthful students, but let that pass.'

'We differ from Mr. Landseer,' retorted the Editor. 'We have not mentioned them oftener than they deserved, and we shall continue to notice them as long as we think they merit it.' This, unfortunately, was not long—since the *Annals* closed with the next issue. John Landseer later engraved *Alpine Mastiffs*, unable in his capacity as a *litterateur* to resist the addition of an accompanying pamphlet, *Some Account of the Dogs of the Pass of St. Bernard*, which explained how these sagacious animals worked in pairs to bring succour, alcoholic and otherwise, to snow-blanketed travellers.

Despite the father's obvious concern to keep his youngest son's feet attached to the ground, it is unlikely that Edwin considered himself overpraised. These were, in fact, heady days for the young artist, who was now widely known both to the animal-loving and the sporting fraternity. His name had already been linked with that of the great animal painter James Ward, thirty-three years his senior, whose powers were already on the wane. Time, it seemed, was entirely on his side. Throughout his youth most of the established competition among sporting and animal artists had been obligingly dying-off— George Morland and Francis Sartorius in 1804, George Stubbs in 1806, Sawrey Gilpin in 1807, John Boultbee in 1812. In 1821 he was able to look back with evident satisfaction though with occasional hesitancy of spelling on his personal success. In a document headed *List of pictures that I have painted which I have been paid for*, he named and priced the works he had sold to date. The list, of course, included *Fighting Dogs* to *Sir Bomont* for £31. 10/–. Other items among many were a *Poney and Dog* to a Dr. Baker for £4. 4/–, *Plummer's Dog* for £21, as well as *Alpine Mastiffs* to one of the Russells for £180. The list ended on the somewhat rueful footnote, 'Not paid for: £30. 0'; but the sum total was impressive for an artist still in his teens and working in Regency London—£1,030.

It is not difficult to discern the peremptory hand of John Landseer in the preparation of the list. The artistic establishment may have rejected him, but he was determined that it would open its portals wide to receive his precociously talented son.

CHAPTER THREE

AND SO TO BEDFORDSHIRE

I am forced from time to time to read over my papers of holy
orders to prevent myself from admiring her too much.
—The Rev. Sydney Smith of Georgiana, Duchess of Bedford

EDWIN WAS only eighteen or nineteen when, in his capacity
as an emergent painter of the English school, he first went to
Woburn Abbey. It was the prove the most fateful introduction of his life.

In residence at the time were the 6th Duke of Bedford and his
second wife Georgiana (the name also of his unfortunate and neglected first wife). Opinions of the 6th Duke varied. The stuffed-shirt
diarist Greville found him 'a good-natured, plausible man without
enemies, and really (although he does not think so) without friends
. . . a complete sensualist and thinks of nothing but his own enjoyment'. He had certainly been a wild spender since youth; but he was
sensitive enough to include the fine arts among his extravagences.
Few painters would have quarrelled with Haydon's verdict 'a good
kind friend to all artists' and 'the only man in a tight corner'—the
last referring not to the Duke's sagacity but to his evergreen ability
to be tapped for a few pounds. He was among the first of the stately
home owners to phase out the old masters in favour of contemporary
painters. The practice made the collection of pictures on the whole
much more immediate and interesting. One met the artist and commissioned the portraits or the scenes one desired: one could discuss
one's own intentions as well as the artist's effects, and therefore
claim a hand in the finished product. Besides, the owners of the great
houses were doubtless aware at times of the inbred nature of their
acquaintances and interests—estate administration, agriculture,
travel, sport. Artists and writers provided an interesting diversion, a
useful cross-fertilisation of ideas. In Landseer's case, the fertilisation
went further.

Georgiana, a great beauty, was the youngest daughter of the 4th
Duke of Gordon. The 4th Duchess had been a matchmaker of
perseverance and resource, convinced that the ducal status was one

from which there could be advance but no retreat. Having married off Georgiana's two elder sisters to the Dukes of Richmond and Manchester, she had begun to engineer a match with Francis, 5th Duke of Bedford. Francis, however, seriously overtaxed himself on his indoor tennis court, and died in March 1802 after an operation for a strangulated hernia. To the formidable Duchess of Gordon such a setback was only temporary. She now set about convincing Georgiana and the new Duke, the recently widowed John, that they were made for each other. Georgiana's affection for both brothers had perhaps not been entirely spontaneous. She had conceived a deep but hopeless passion for Napoleon's stepson, Eugene de Beauharnais; and although she now seemed ready to temper passion with reason, she never stopped looking for the dashing young lover who would sweep her off her feet. That romantic figure was hardly the rather staid-looking 6th Duke, who was 36 when she married him in 1803, Georgiana being twenty-two.

At the time of his second marriage, the 6th Duke already had three sons—Francis, Earl of Tavistock (who was to succeed him), Lord William Russell and Lord John Russell (a future Prime Minister). Their enthusiasm for their stepmother was at first unbounded. There were 'no end of jolly rows' recalled one of them, referring to Georgiana's unerring ability to liven-up the sedate gatherings at Woburn, previously inhibited by the Duke's shyness and their mother's delicate health. Georgiana's parties may have begun in traditional style, but they frequently developed into bun and cushion fights; fruit was also for throwing and furniture was overturned if it got in the way. There were unsophisticated party-games like blind man's buff, and unaccustomed shrieks of laughter rang through Woburn's stately corridors.

The Duke bestowed on his second wife the attentive adoration he had failed to show towards his first, buying or renting for her a beautiful cottage in Devonshire, a Kensington villa, a winter home in Brighton, as well as the Doune, in deer country near Rothiemurchus, a late-summer retreat for the whole family.

Georgiana's energy was apparently boundless; producing ten children of her own, looking after three stepsons and a husband seemed to leave her with plenty to spare. Her husband was properly appreciative. As they grew up, however, the feelings of her stepsons changed. Their delightful little half-brothers and sisters gradually began to assume the aspect of minor monsters. Wild and boisterous some of them certainly were—but it was no doubt the invasion of their territory by a gang of little strangers, the feeling of being muscled out of their heritage, that affected the three brothers most of all. And the fecund brood-mare was Georgiana. With their marriages, their resentment against their stepmother was complete. Georgiana was the kind of woman any stepdaughter-in-law might be expected to dislike—she was lovely, bold, outspoken, able to be calculating. Lord William's wife Bessy took an especially virulent dislike to her; a dislike strongly tinged with sexual jealousy. William had been the favourite among her three stepsons, and Georgiana had frequently soothed away his adolescent troubles by cradling his head on what, under the circumstances, was more a pair of breasts than a motherly bosom. Bessy later imputed an intimate relationship between her husband as a boy and the stepmother who was, after all, only nine years his senior. Lord William's later description of her children as 'little savages, with minds not elevated above the grooms' may therefore have had more complex strains in it. The eldest boy Francis, who had a very good nose for looking down, spoke scathingly of 'the Duchess and her belongings', whilst even the more temperate Lord John deplored his father's being 'under the influence of a wicked woman'. There is no doubt that Georgiana's unresolved relationship with her French aristocrat left a large gap in her sensuous nature. The amiable 6th Duke obviously had many qualities; but he was hardly God's gift to women. There were clearly times when Georgiana saw herself as God's gift to men.

When Edwin appeared on the scene, Georgiana was already the mother of eight 'little savages'. He was then a handsome rather soft-faced youth whose wavy hair flopped engagingly over his brow. The charm of manner was already well in evidence, as was the conviction that, having been a successful exhibitor since the age of eleven, he must one day become a famous painter. But the precocity was in his art more than in his manner. He was still, no doubt, overawed by the splendour and magnificence of places like Woburn, by acceptance among one of the wealthiest families in England. We may assume that he was not quite ready to seduce a duchess, but that the Duchess seduced him—and without much preamble. Precautions were also lacking. The present Duke of Bedford acknowledges that Landseer was the begetter of the last two of Georgiana's ten children—Alexander, born in 1821, and Rachel, born in 1826.

Although Edwin's subsequent portraits of the two children were to display a tender, wistful and intimate quality missing from most of his other portrayals of children; he began, in fact, with the Bedford animals. His first noteworthy picture was the *Old English Bloodhound* of 1821, 'taken' as Algernon Graves notes, 'from a dog at Woburn'.

The intimacy was to last, on and off, until the Duchess's death.

For some years it went almost unobserved by the outside world. Haydon, of course, with his unerring ear for gossip, was one of the first among Edwin's fellow-artists to know. Increasingly harassed by creditors, much of his life was passed in a sick agony of apprehension. In the attempt to settle his parlous financial affairs, he 'flew about the Town like an Eagle', constantly accosted by petty officials saying, 'Sir, I have an execution against you!' Inevitably, his morality came under attack—not from Edwin. But it was Edwin who, in his *Journals*, became the whipping-boy:

> I never . . . degraded myself, or disgraced my Patrons by becoming the pander to the appetites of their wives.

After being excluded from a gathering (not by Landseer) on account of his 'moral character', the name of his most brilliant pupil was again indignantly invoked:

> I never seduced the Wife of my Patron and accepted money from the Husband while I was corrupting his Wife & disgracing his family.

Despite all attempts at discretion, the more scurrilous periodicals later began to make play with the story. Thus, *The Satirist* in 1833:

> The Duchess has been suddenly taken ill in Ireland. Strong draughts were resorted to which relieved the patient. Edwin Landseer is her Grace's draughtsman.

The 6th Duke seems to have been the very model of a complaisant husband. Doubtless he was much preoccupied with the extensive Woburn estates, and the consequences of his extravagance which he tried to correct with small economies—like having the marker of his tennis-court serve at table. The eldest son who succeeded him knew him as a man 'without the power to hold his hand when money was within his reach'. Much of his Grace's energy was also engaged in trying to keep the peace between his sons and their wives on the one hand and Georgiana on the other. Lord William's wife Bessy, her most implacable enemy, had already made an impact on the diarist Thomas Creevey:

> I have never seen a woman that I hate so much as Lady William Russell, without knowing her or even having exchanged a word with her. There is a pretention, presumption and laying down of the law about her that is quite insufferable.

Bessy's hatred of Georgiana, whom she described variously as 'vulgar-minded', 'coquette comme la lune' and 'a complaisante of the lowest kind', finally resulted in her exclusion from Woburn. The formidable hostess, Lady Holland, a neighbour of the Bedfords both in the country and in town and a great friend of the Duke's, was another who took a dislike to Georgiana—stretching the Duke's resources as a mediator even further. Whatever his preoccupations, his friendship with the young painter did not waver—a comment perhaps on the rather negligent morality of the times. In the midst of a political crisis in which the Duke's son, Lord John Russell, was involved, William found 'the Duke and Landseer *tête à tête*, not bitten by the frenzy of London (parliamentary), but quiet and almost indifferent'. The Duke's letters to Landseer were mainly on the subject of commissions, some of them involving the Duchess. In August 1827 he rebuked Edwin for undercharging for a portrait which the painter probably felt had already been paid for in other ways:

> The price you name for the portrait of the Duchess is quite ridiculous, and you must allow me in this instance to place my judgement in opposition to yours, and consequently to pay 50 pounds to your account in Messrs. Gosling (which I have already done) instead of the sum you have named.

Other letters from the Duke had a bumbling and innocent air:

> Do you know any good Bird Stuffer who could improve my Ptarmigan? I wish it to represent what that bird really is, and it now wants the strong characteristic of the red round the eye. It is now at Mr. Harcourts . . . Hanover Square, and if you know of an intelligent stuffer, he may take it from there and improve it under your instructions.

Such letters suggest possible oblivion on the part of the Duke; a man obsessed with the trivialities of the day, busily engaged in increasing his predecessor's debts from £200,000 to half a million, welcoming into his house the smart but devious young painter who, in Haydon's words 'undoubtedly adorned the forehead of his Grace'. It was in its way a proud (if clandestine) distinction for the twenty-year-old from Foley Street not only to have acquired a Duke for a patron and a Duchess for a mistress but to have (arguably) fathered a peer as well.

Despite his exalted friendships, Edwin continued to establish his reputation in the London galleries. His *Rat Catchers*, showing three of his favourite dogs, Brutus, Vixen and Boxer patiently waiting for a ferret to raise a rat in an old stable, was exhibited to much praise at the Royal Academy in 1821. The French painter Géricault on a visit to London wrote enthusiastically of 'the animals painted by Ward and by Landseer, aged eighteen years; the Old Masters have produced nothing better of this kind'. It was, however, his painting of Brutus surprising a cat in a well-stocked larder that gave him perhaps his most tangible encouragement to date. *The Larder Invaded,* the original for which had been drawn on a schoolboy's slate, was shown at the British Institution in 1822, and gained him a premium from the Directors of £150—a sum, half of which Haydon quickly dispossessed him. The historical painter called on the Landseers to beg an urgent loan of £75, pointing out that the young Edwin did not immediately need the money. John Landseer gave him what he asked, going through the ritual of accepting Haydon's post-dated cheque, which became a family heirloom. Many years later, when Haydon's name came up in company, Edwin turned to his sister: 'Jessy, bring me Haydon's dishonoured cheque'. By that time, however, he had himself acquired Haydon's monumental work, *The Judgement of Solomon.* Admiration and bitterness were strangely intermingled in the relationship between Landseer and his one-time mentor.

In his early twenties Edwin produced several pictures which later exposed him to charges of sadism. *Mischief in Full Play* was a small picture painted with all the concentration and care of a Dutch masterpiece, a remarkably controlled work for a painter of twenty-one. The Dutch tranquility was, however, notably absent. The picture shows a boy on a donkey mercilessly belabouring it with a stick, although its foreleg is tied and it cannot go forward. In *The Dancing Lesson*, a boy lashes a performing monkey with a whip, the fear and distress on the dressed-up animal's face being exactly rendered. Whatever his feelings at the time, Landseer later regretted this picture. It was engraved against his will by J. C. Zeitter; and the painter subsequently bought up and burned every copy he could get his hands on. It was, however, *The Cat's Paw,* shown at the British Institution in 1824, that seemed most obviously to reflect an obsession with cruelty and violence. A cunning monkey has his eye on some chestnuts aromatically roasting on a hot stove: unable to touch them himself he has bodily seized a screaming and writhing cat whose paw he uses to dislodge the chestnuts from their red-hot resting-place. This was the first picture Edwin sold for three figures. It was bought from him for £100 and sold a few days later for £120 to the Earl of Essex, a great patron and also a great philosopher who once said, 'The secret is to be content with the little one has. The Duke of Bedford and Lord Egremont, with all their wealth, are not happier than I am'. Forty years later Edwin estimated the value of the painting, still in the Essex family, to be about £3,000.

There were many other pictorial lapses into animal terror, distress and torture. With Landseer's later penchant for dead and dying game, they were often quoted in illustration of his morbid and latently violent streak. It was, however, possible to make too much of these depictions of cruelty, relating as they did much more to the painter's youth than to his Victorian middle-age. The Victorian era would later adopt a selfconsciously humanitarian attitude towards animal suffering, but in Georgian times when Landseer was a youth public exhibitions of cruelty were an aspect of everyday life. It was, in fact, accepted that some creatures, human and animal, would suffer, and that others would enjoy the interesting diversion of watching them suffer. The early morning executions of criminals at Newgate were popular with sightseers on their way to work. Jeering at the inmates of Bedlam and other such institutions—gibbering, half-naked and often in chains—formed many an enjoyable Sunday outing. The visitor to Tothill Fields could choose from a wide range of organised violence and cruelty. Prize-fights were not confined merely to the male sex. F. M. Redgrave* remembered seeing two 'Amazons, stripped to the waist, their long hair tied tightly under a handkerchief, beat one another into a disgusting state, seconded by two of their own mild sex, and hounded on by friends and acquaintances'. He also recalled matches with dogs pitted against bears; and one man running eagerly forward 'to feel the tendons of the bear's forepaws, when Bruin had seized one of his canine tormentors and was hugging out his life'. As late as 1825 at Warwick, George Wombell staged a Dog and Lion Fight, in which a lion called Wallace killed every bulldog thrown into its cage, carrying the last around in his mouth as a terrier does a rat. Dog-fights with heavy betting on the participants were, and remained, a popular spectator-sport. The *Sporting Magazine* featured a picture by Chalon of a famous animal owned by Lord Camelford that had killed three other celebrated fighting-dogs in its time and had never been beaten. Cock-fighting wasn't declared illegal until 1849, and the 12th Earl of Derby (who gave his name to the race) kept 3,000 fighting cocks on his estates.

Landseer himself, though a relatively sensitive individual where dogs were concerned, never lost his enthusiasm for watching fur and hair fly. He later owned a tiny terrier, little bigger than its intended victims, that was an accomplished ratter. Frederick Goodall, R.A.,† described a fight in a servants' hall where this canine midget was matched against a huge rat which it held at bay for twenty minutes: a larger dog was finally introduced to despatch the rat, but only after both toy-dog and rat had been badly bitten. Landseer also kept

---

* *Richard Redgrave C.B., R.A., A Memoir* 1891.
† *The Reminiscences of Frederick Goodall, R.A.* 1902.

hounds for hare-coursing in later years. Bull-baiting, fights between dogs and monkeys, the brutal business of ringing a farmyard
boar; these subjects and many more figure in early Landseer pictures.
They serve to remind us that Edwin was middle-aged before Victoria
came to the throne; his social education, his morality, his view of
cruelty may have passed through the pious (and suppressive) cleans-
ing process of Victorianism, but their roots were in the Georgian era.

About 1825, however, Edwin began to design and etch highly
decorative Game Cards on which the shooters at Woburn and in
Scotland could record the extent of their bag. A closer look at some
of the thumbnail pen-and-ink drawings was slightly disquieting—
the arched contortions of a hare in the instant of being shot, a
feebly-twitching grouse expiring among stalks of corn, a snipe
frenetically wing-beating its last. Animal portraiture was, of course,
a familiar theme, as were the dead game birds and animals much
affected by still-life artists. Before long, however, it was being
suggested that young Edwin had invented a new art form—the
portrayal of animals that were neither alive nor dead.

CHAPTER FOUR

DISCOVERY OF THE HIGHLANDS

*He will make himself very popular, both with the master and
mistress of the house, by sketching their doggies for them.*
—C. R. Leslie on Landseer's introduction to Sir Walter Scott

IN 1824, almost against his will, Edwin was persuaded to take a
place of his own. Until that year he had lived with his father
who, as F. G. Stephens* observed, 'managed his son's affairs,
settled the prices of his pictures, received the money and treated
Edwin in his twenty-second year as he had done when he was twelve
years old'. For a young man with an aristocratic mistress and a
burgeoning career, such tight parental control must at times have
been irksome. However, he seemed to lack the outright will to break
away from it. He was, after all, the favourite in a large and closely-
knit family, and cannot have lacked for any home comforts. He did
have the lease of a studio in the Fitzroy Square area, described by
some as small and cramped; though at the half-yearly rent of £40 it
must, for those days, have been perfectly adequate. It was the dealer
who had negotiated the sale of *The Cat's Paw* who suggested that the
time had come to move. 'Why are you in this place,' he asked, 'without a carpet, a table and proper chairs? You should have a place
where you can keep a dog or two and have a garden and so on.' The
thought had obviously occurred to Edwin; besides which, no appeal
to his incipient snobbism was ever entirely lost. Yet even then he
hesitated. He had his eye on a cottage and garden on the west side of
Regent's Park; but on discovering that a premium of a hundred
pounds was required he called-off the deal, almost with relief. However, his adviser again took him in hand, offering to lend him the
money without interest and repayment whenever it suited him.
Thus, still in two minds, Edwin left home, for the house which subsequently became 1 St. John's Wood Road, and where he was to live
for just under fifty years—after reimbursing his mentor in twenty
pound instalments.

When he bought the place it was a simple cottage with a three or

* *Sir Edwin Landseer*, 1883.

four acre garden and a large barn that was subsequently converted into a studio. The garden's most dominant features were a huge mulberry tree and a long rose walk: it sloped gently towards a canal, at that time limpid and clear, though it later became something of a sewer. Neighbours remembered it as a wildly beautiful and natural place ruined by Landseer's future alterations as a large white mansion in a vaguely Italian style rose from the rubble of the attractive cottage and the picturesque old barn. But such 'improvements' were still some years away. Meantime Edwin retained his Fitzroy Square studio, for at least another two years, and acquired some of the trappings (and the habits) of the well-doing young bohemian. As Haydon tartly observed in May 1826: 'E. Landseer keeps a gig, though he has not paid for his room'. Nor did the move entail any break with his family, who visited him regularly, his sisters alternating at keeping house for him. As far as opening up St. John's Wood as a kind of artists' and writers' colony went, Landseer was something of a pioneer, if a hesitant one. When he moved there the district had a somewhat dubious reputation, as the haunt of kept women and high-class prostitutes. Two years after he had taken up residence, an unsavoury scandal broke in the newspapers and by a printer's error Landseer's address was quoted as a centre of sexual intrigue. Naturally, his friends made as much as possible of the joke.

The gesture of independence inherent in this removal was, however, the lesser of two singular and significant events of 1824. In that year Edwin made his first visit to Scotland. He went there with the painter C. R. Leslie, who was hoping to paint a portrait of Sir Walter Scott. They sailed from London and disembarked at Leith, where they were joined by G. S. Newton. Finding that the great novelist was away for a few days, the three artists decided to see something of the country for themselves. From Glasgow they went to Loch Lomond and Loch Katrine, crossing the mountains on foot to Loch Earn. After being rowed down the loch by a fey boatman who beguiled them with stories of the magic wrought by the Highland fairies, they went to St. Fillans to view the traditional pot-pourri, of muscle, undervests, tartan, piping, caber-tossing and greensward in the Highland games. Edwin was completely captivated. The scenery (though he was yet to see the grandest of it) was both more beautiful and more forbidding than he had ever imagined. He would return to the Highlands autumn after autumn, sometimes twice in the year, even after he no longer had the strength to cope with the hills, the long days in the bogs and the heather and the whiplash winds.

He had also looked forward eagerly to his meeting with Sir Walter

Scott at Abbotsford. 'He will make himself very popular, both with
the master and mistress of the house, by sketching their doggies for
them,' Leslie had predicted, with accuracy. Sir Walter himself became a Landseer enthusiast, writing of an exhibition two years later:
'Landseer's dogs were the most magnificent things I ever saw, leaping
and bounding and grinning on the canvas . . .'. On later reflection he
found the young painter 'one of the most striking masters of the
modern school'.

Sir Walter, of course, was a great lover of dogs. He was, said
Leslie, 'never seen unaccompanied by two *at least*'. There were
usually a small troop of them. Although not otherwise a notably
demonstrative man, the laird of Abbotsford almost compulsively
caressed and fondled and even kissed his dogs; and in 1825, faced
with bankruptcy and the prospect of losing them, he was clearly on
the edge of an emotional breakdown: 'It is foolish—but the thought
of parting from these dumb creatures has moved me more than any
of the painful reflections I have put down—Poor things, I must get
them kind masters. There may be yet those who loving me may love
my dog because it has been mine. I must end this or I shall lose the
tone of mind with which men should meet distress. I find my dog's
feet on my knees—I hear them whining and seeking me everywhere
—This is nonsense but it is what they would do could they know how
things are . . .'.

Surrounded by his beloved dogs, it is difficult to avoid seeing Scott
almost as a kind of Landseerian creation; and indeed they were fated
to suffer perpetual comparison. *The Times* later dubbed Edwin 'the
Walter Scott of painting', while the *Daily News*, in a posthumous
notice, took the theme further:

> His method of composition was remarkably like Scott's, except on
> the part of the early rising of the latter. Landseer went late to bed
> and rose very late—coming down to breakfast at noon; but he had
> been composing perhaps for hours . . . His conception once com-
> plete, nothing could exceed the rapidity of his execution (which
> was) quite as marvellous as Scott's.

Edwin's first visit to Scott lasted a week, in which he was very
much the slightly agog junior painter. In fulfilment of Leslie's
prediction, he sketched most of the family tykes. The one that impressed him most of all was Maida, a deerhound so large that experienced trackers would sometimes mistake his footprints for those of
some beast escaped from a travelling circus. When Landseer first saw
Maida, the dog was already aged and infirm, dying six weeks later.
He became nonetheless the inspired progenitor of all the deerhounds

Edwin later painted. His sketches subsequently resulted in *A Scene at Abotsford* in which the unfortunate Maida is subjected to the attentions of a much younger and vigorous dog. Landseer had come upon Scott one day laughing at the persistence of a collie puppy anxious to play with the giant deerhound, for whom life had lost all savour. The picture was exhibited as *Crabbed age and youth can never agree* (possibly with apologies to Shakespeare). Capturing Maida's likeness was always something of an achievement: he hated to be drawn or painted and would offendedly get up and leave the room immediately he saw an artist set up his materials. Leslie discovered that Sir Walter himself occupied much the same kind of category as a sitter: 'Yesterday he only gave me a quarter of an hour, and then carried me off in his *sociable* . . . to see the Yarrow, famous in song, as indeed, are all the Scottish rivers'.

In both Scott and Maida's case, Landseer profited from his rapidity of execution. His small oil portrait with its sketchy surrounds (now in the National Portrait Gallery) would always rank as one of his best. Scott's portraiturists tended to make him larger than life, gazing nobly into some distant horizon. Landseer's portrait, complete with a bilious green coat that only adds to its charm, shows much more accurately the shrewd Lowland Scot who has nonetheless overreached himself; a man already beset by worries and disastrous business deals, whose life as a country laird was paid for by health-corroding work, and who had already begun to write his way out of £100,000 worth of debts.

Despite his many distractions, Scott was able to help Edwin secure the introductions necessary to a young painter with his eye on society, and in 1824 he wrote to the Duke of Wellington himself:

> My Lord Duke
> Will your Grace permit me to ask in behalf of my young friend Mr. Landseer, whose talents as a painter are probably known to you, permission to look at your Grace's valuable collection of paintings with a view to his improvement in his art.

It was a fruitful introduction, Edwin receiving his first commission from the great soldier only two years later.

The two men remained friends until Scott's death in 1832; and they met and corresponded from time to time. Most of the correspondence touched on Landseer's illustrations for the Abbotsford edition of the Waverley novels. It is said that Maida was the inspiration for the hound Bevis in *Woodstock*: if so Edwin must have used his imagination to picture the great dog, well beyond its strength and vigour when he first saw it. The illustrations for *Waverley* and *The*

Antiquary also showed beyond all doubt that Landseer could have
enjoyed a successful career as a book illustrator. But, of course, the
money (and the social kudos) were elsewhere, and he contributed only
occasionally to books and periodicals. In 1828 he produced several
drawings for the banker-poet Samuel Rogers' *Italy*, in which he
shared the honours with Turner. As well as contributing studies of
hunting and deer, one of a St. Bernard dog and another of *The
Cardinal and his Cat*, Landseer also added figures and animals to
landscape drawings by the greatest of English painters.

There had been another reason behind Edwin's desire to see
Scotland: the artistic prodigy had been forced to admit to a chink in
his armour—a weakness on scenery and backgrounds. Most painters
would have taken the lack philosophically, especially when they had
as wide a range of other subject-accomplishments to crow about.
Anyway, some of the very best artists made pictorial deals, either
feeing other painters for figures or animals or backgrounds, or
exchanging their talents on a mutual aid basis. Edwin had been
heavily conscious of the music-hall theatricality of his background to
Alpine Mastiffs Reanimating a Distressed Traveller, although it had
been a brave attempt for a youth who, as Monkhouse noted, 'had not
yet seen a mountain either in Switzerland or elsewhere—always
excepting Primrose Hill'. In 1822 he had been forced to invoke the
help of the landscape painter Patrick Nasmyth for the background
to *The Bull and the Frog*. Although he later made sparing use of
fellow-artists like Lee and Roberts for scenery and architecture, he
was clearly determined personally to lick the problem. Before he
visited Scotland he already had at least one picture with an unfinished background. This was his portrait of an enormous Newfoundland called (as monster dogs so often were) Lion. When Edwin
saw him, it had been artistic love at first sight. Lion was an animal of
great dignity: on one occasion, whilst he sedately walked by the
canal, a bargee had prodded him with an oar, which Lion had
promptly seized, dragging his tormentor into the water. Another
time, as it sat for Edwin, the young artist had pushed a live mouse at
the huge dog which he promptly snapped-up in his capacious jowls,
gobbling and slavering with apparent enjoyment. However, when
Lion opened his jaws a little later the mouse popped-out completely
unharmed and scurried off. Lion himself presented Edwin with no
difficulties (few animal-subjects ever had); but he decided to defer
completion of the picture until he had been to Scotland to observe
some rugged scenery, which certainly added authenticity to the great
dog's portrait. Much later, incidentally, the same picture narrowly
escaped being used as part of a barricade in the 1848 Revolution,

having crossed the Channel in a stout packing-case for a Paris exhibition.

Landseer's most eager hope, however, had been to see the red deer in their true surroundings. By 1820 he had already pictured deer in some English park (perhaps Woburn); but these had been strangely vapid and spindly creatures, uncertainly drawn and clearly incapable of standing at bay. *Tired*, a picture of a stag pursued by a hound made in the same year had attracted some tart critical comment— Edwin's lack of sufficient knowledge to provide a background had moved the *Art-Journal* to remark that the deer appeared to be leaping over a chasm. His first sight of the wild red deer was doubtless a moment of intense excitement, and he lost no time in tracking them down. The *Chronicles of the Atholl and Tullibardine Families* recorded that 'during the time of September, 1824, Mr. Landseer, the celebrated painter, spent ten days with his Grace to obtain some studies of deer. Mr. Landseer repeated his visit in 1825 and 1826 during which time he made portraits of some of the hillmen and afterwards painted his well known *Death of the Stag in Glen Tilt*'.

From the mid-1820s Landseer went to some trouble to cultivate the acquaintance of the great Highland landowners, and was soon welcome at some of the biggest and best of the (often treeless) 'deer forests'. At least one of these meetings was accidental, like the one in the Glen Feshie forest described in his *Reminiscences of Life in the Highlands* by the Earl of Tankerville, then Lord Ossulston:

We soon ensconced ourselves behind a heathery knoll within a few yards of our poacher, to watch his proceedings before we finally pounced upon him. He was a little, strong-built man, very like a pocket Hercules, or 'Puck' in the 'Midsummer Night's Dream'. He was busily employed gralloching* his deer. This he did with great quickness and dexterity, not omitting to wash the tallow and other treasures carefully in the burn and deposit them on the stone beside the deer. He next let the head hang over so as to display the horns, and then squatting down on a stone opposite took out of his pocket what I thought would be his pipe or a whisky flask: but it was a sketch book!

Seeing that we had mistaken our man, I came into the open and found myself face to face with my friend of many years to come— Landseer.

In the Scottish mountains Edwin found a new lease of art. To a young urban painter, rapidly acquiring a not entirely enviable reputation as a painter of dogs and little else, the Highlands provided

* Removing the innards from.

a new direction and impetus. He was already beginning to be beset by wealthy ladies waxing lyrical over the virtues of their pets and begging him to paint them, and a future as a parlour-painter of lapdogs may not have seemed inconceivable. In that sense his discovery of the Scottish Highlands was almost a reaffirmation of his manhood.

His touch to begin with was nonetheless uncertain. He was still largely bogged-down in one of Haydon's favourite premises—that all great art had a historical setting. Early studies like *A Hunting Scene* and *Taking the Buck* had an almost idyllic quality, a cross between Rubens/Snyders and the Parthenon frieze. All tended to combine the same elements of nobly struggling stag, snarling and expiring hounds and a handsome young huntsman about to deliver the *coup de grâce*. Some, like *The Duke of Atholl with Foresters*, attempted to blend action and portraiture in a rather farcical way, with the nobleman posing rigidly for his portrait while, inches away, a stag thrashes in its death-throes with his gillies. It was several years before Landseer could altogether prise his deer-stalking pictures loose from the influence of the Old Masters; but his *Return from Deer Stalking* of 1827 suggested a partial recognition that all need not be frenetic activity—that, in fact, the chase could be observed in tranquility, with two tartan-clad Highlanders, two deer-laden ponies and three dogs creating a successful tableau out of an old chieftain's weary return after a fruitful day on the hill.

Meantime, however, Landseer had not deserted the vein of sentiment that was later to blight much of his work. *The Widow*, shown at the Royal Academy in 1825, pictured a duck mourning the death of her handsome husband. Even today the masterly portrayal of both birds is partially lost in the inference of a state of holy matrimony between two wildfowl. At that time Landseer and his engravers were already embarked on the course of sentimental titles that would provide his future detractors with a plentiful supply of ammunition. Judged purely as a nature painting, as a picture of a duck displaying consternation over the death of its mate, it has much to recommend it.

In the following year, Landseer was elected an Associate of the Royal Academy. He was twenty-four, the youngest age at which such an honour could be granted: only a few other artists achieved such early distinction including Lawrence, Turner and, later, Millais. As a regular exhibitor at the Royal Academy since 1815, having missed only the year 1816, Edwin was no doubt in line for the honour. However, the picture which clinched the matter was *The Hunting of Chevy Chase*, a large painting in the romantic mould which showed the influence of Sir Walter Scott, Haydon, the Elgin

Marbles, Rubens and perhaps Delacroix and was correspondingly unsatisfactory. The appearance of his masterpiece had been signalled in
the previous year when he had painted the mournful oil on panel,
Chevy Chase, showing a dead knight, his dead horse, dead deer, dead
and dying dogs, a howling hound, a grieving widow, a praying monk.
Landseer had seen and been impressed by a similar scene based on
the bloody old border ballads sketched by Edward Bird and hung at
Abbotsford, and his own earlier painting seemed to echo both this
work and Delacroix's *Massacre of Chios*. However, the much larger
(almost 6′ × 7′) *Hunting of Chevy Chase* no doubt fulfilled both in its
impressive size and in its heroic theme the qualities required of a
young artist in pursuit of an Associateship—no matter that it was
considerably less inspired and satisfactory than many a much smaller
Landseer work. The subject had been suggested to Edwin by a visit
to Chillingham Castle, the seat of his friend the Earl of Tankerville.
The ancient ballad itself had recalled the bitter rivalry between the
Earls Percy and Douglas which had come to a head after Percy, out
hunting, had pursued his stag onto Douglas territory: in the subsequent battle both leaders and most of their followers were slain.
Typically, since he was rather wary of battle scenes, Landseer chose
the hunting episode, with a stag in trouble, baying, snarling and dying hounds and the Earl Percy mounted on a fine plunging horse.
The large oil on panel had been a commission from the Duke of Bedford: today the painting hangs in the Birmingham Art Gallery. It
might have been subtitled *Much Ado about a Deerhunt*, having the
decided air of straining at an epic. Dogs flee (and perish) hither and
yon: a huntsman from an idea by Rubens blows his horn with all the
dramatic intensity of sounding the last trump. Even some nineteenth
century commentators refused to take it altogether seriously. Monkhouse for one pointed out that the bow of the warrior waiting to get
in a shot at the much-beleagured stag was so loosely strung that the
arrow when released would have dropped at the archer's feet.

   Whilst *The Hunting of Chevy Chase*, his sole Royal Academy
exhibit of 1826, confirmed Landseer's place in the artistic establishment, he sent seven pictures that year to the British Institution;
almost a personal record, though in 1833 he would show eight. The
British Institution for Promoting the Fine Arts in the United Kingdom had been founded in 1805, staging its first exhibition in the
following year. Its unstated purpose was to shake-up the Royal
Academy which was certainly not immune from either smugness or
lethargy. Being controlled by patrons, however, its administration
had a dilettantish air and its influence was never strong; although it
could claim credit for introducing the One Man Show, with the

Reynolds exhibition in 1813. It became Edwin's second most important showcase. Except for a long period between 1845 and 1858
broken only by one appearance, he continued faithfully to exhibit at
the lesser gallery, eighty-one pictures in all from the age of sixteen.
His contributions were said to have been instrumental in staving-off
the Institution's constantly-threatened collapse, which finally
occurred in 1867. Five of the seven exhibits in 1826 were Highland
scenes, a measure of the strength of his new-found fascination: another, *The Dog and the Shadow*, showing the dog of the fable about to
drop its meat when it beholds its own reflection in the water, was
much praised, as the kind of cosy subject-picture just coming into
vogue.

The Monkey Who Had Seen the World, a Royal Academy exhibit of
the following year, was an obvious candidate for charges of 'quasi-
humanising'; though, as with *The Cat's Paw* and *The Dog and the
Shadow*, the source was *Gay's Fables* rather than Landseer's imagination. The subject of the picture, a kind of local monkey made good, is
dressed as a Regency buck in cocked hat, cravat, square-cut coat,
satin breeches, silk stockings and buckled shoes: his naked stay-at-
home fellow-monkeys regard him with drop-jawed envy and wonder,
one of them sampling his ornate snuff-box. It was thought to be
extremely clever at the time, though today the effect is merely
embarrassing. What was interesting (and in some ways prophetic)
was Edwin's apparent advocacy of the posturing dressed-up monkey
and his dismissive contempt for the dowdy stay-at-homes. The entire
disconcerting question of the relationship of monkeys to humans was
at that time a subject of much speculation. In 1827–28 Edwin's
brother Tom produced a series of twenty-four etchings from his own
drawings called *Monkeyana, or Men in Miniature*, presenting
monkeys in a variety of human roles, as dandies, drinkers, gossips
and so on. They evidenced a genuine feeling for satire, and have often
been quoted in support of the view that Tom's originality and skill
as a draughtsman was unfairly eclipsed by his duties as an engraver,
particularly of Edwin's work. Though it has been suggested that
Edwin helped on the drawings, their style is defiantly Tom's own; a
rather bizarre and fanciful style which also emerged in his strangely
overripe but extremely vigorous representations of gnus, giraffes,
hippos, hyaenas, tapirs and other exotic animals. As zoological likenesses the studies leave much to be desired; as drawings they are
enormously impressive—almost more interesting than the beasts
themselves.

While Tom's almost exclusive habitat was London, Edwin continued his annual jaunts (sometimes twice in a year) to the Scottish

Highlands. One of the chief attractions was the presence of Georgiana, Duchess of Bedford. The Duke, whose general tastes favoured the more gentle scenery of England (and bird-shooting rather than deerstalking) did not always accompany his wife and family to their late summer holiday retreat of the Doune in the forest of Rothiemurchus, Inverness-shire. At nearby Glen Feshie (otherwise rendered as Glenfeshie, Glen Fishie and Glenfishie), Georgiana leased some land once owned by the Dukes of Gordon and created her own Highland paradise, a collection of huts described by the deerstalking writer Lt.-General Crealock as 'a kind of sporting village of bothies'. Glen Feshie itself was 'a wild and beautiful glen, with some magnificent old fir trees in it'.

In the 'Twenties the children accompanied their mother to the summer place which, in Scott's words, 'the Duke has taken to gratify the Duchess's passion for the heather'. Sir Walter had known the Duchess when she was the beautiful young Lady Georgiana. In November 1827 he dined with her at Edinburgh's grandest hotel, the Waterloo, recalling her 'fine family, two young ladies silent just now but they will find their tongues or they are not right Gordons'. He was most impressed with Alexander (whom he called *Alaster*): 'A very fine child . . . who shouted, sung and spoke gaelic with much spirit'.

On the following day Georgiana was still on his mind: 'I used to think her Grace *journalière*. She may have been cured of that fault or I may have turned less jealous of my dignity. At all events let a pleasant hour go by unquestioned and do not let us break ordinary gems to pieces because they are not diamonds'. As an afterthought he added, his eyebrow only slightly raised: 'I forgot to say that Edwin Landseer was in the Duchesses train'.

Whether in the Highlands, in London or at Woburn, Landseer remained in the Duchess's train. He taught her to use the graver: between 1825 and 1832 she etched several of Edwin's simpler drawings with a fair degree of assurance and skill, mainly scenes of family life around their Scottish home. Throughout the 'Twenties and 'Thirties the artist painted numerous portraits of Georgiana's brood, sometimes accompanied by their pets. Her Grace's eldest daughter Georgiana, afterwards Lady Charles Romilly and unkindly described by the diarist le Marchant as 'a dull dowdy', was shown in the saddle as was the galloping *Lord Cosmo Russell on his pony Fingal* (1825), in Highland dress and accompanied by the inevitable running dog. In the same year *Lady Louisa Russell feeding a Donkey* was the first of many studies of Georgiana's second oldest daughter, the future Duchess of Abercorn, who remained a lifelong friend of the painter's.

A few years later, now an attractive young woman, Landseer portrayed her in cool profile in *Cottage Industry*: she is crocheting, a carefully strayed wisp of hair shows the effort involved. It was one of several private Bedford family portraits that enjoyed great public popularity. Two years later Edwin showed her, married now, as *The Duchess of Abercorn in Fancy Dress*.

There were several portraits of his own alleged children. *The First Leap* in 1829, with the young Alexander jumping his pony Emerald over a fallen tree trunk at Woburn, celebrated a kind of initiation rite apparently familiar to the upper classes; one to which Alexander's eldest half-brother Francis had many years before subjected his own younger brother. 'Tavistock' Lord John had recorded, 'made me leap some places that I was afraid of.'

Edwin's brush always dealt very tenderly with Lady Rachel. *Little Red Riding Hood* showed his reputed daughter peeping out in beguiling fashion from her fancy-dress hood. It was obvious that Rachel loved dressing-up. In 1832 Edwin again portrayed her, aged six, as *The Little Actress at the Duke's*, attired beyond her years in a bonnet and shawl and leaning on a stick—one can almost hear the gales of doting family laughter that must have greeted her performance. A picture of the same year that gained immense popularity was *Lady Rachel Russell feeding a Pet Fawn*, whose name (doubtless for the benefit of fawn-historians) was recorded as Harty. In *Lady Rachel Russell Reading*, the future Lady James Butler has the look of a grown-up young lady who has put her previous frivolities behind her and is now intent on improving herself. This portrait was, according to Landseer, afterwards 'drawn on the stone by the French governess'.

Between 1823 and 1839 Edwin produced a great many portraits (some posed, some quickly sketched) of the Duchess and her family. The first formal portrait in 1823 showed her dressed resplendently off-the-shoulder as though for receiving guests; another, some seven years later had her in much more sober and matronly habit. Whatever Georgiana did, wherever she went, Landseer's sketchbook was apparently always there—the Duchess of Bedford on a pony, with a chimney sweep, at a Glen Feshie reception, arriving at a Highland ball, with the Duke, with her various children, holding one of her granddaughters. Many, including one interesting seated sketch from the back, featured Georgiana's swan-like neck and almost vertiginously sloping shoulders, considered marks of great beauty and features which she herself displayed to the full.

In the Highlands with his new-found family Edwin knew enjoyment and relaxation. The Gordons were a handsome and spirited breed. There was much to admire in the elderly yet active 4th Duke of Gordon who made some sort of deerstalking history by shooting a huge stag of seventeen points at Gordon Castle in his eighty-fourth year. He was also skilled in hawking, and a keen breeder of falcons (a theme that would soon make its appearance in Landseer's painting). Nor did he allow age to keep him out of the saddle. In 1825, two years before his death, Edwin had sketched *The Duke of Gordon's Favourite Hack*. The old Duke was a man of many parts: he composed at least one popular Scottish song, *Cauld Kail in Aberdeen*. Edwin was not to meet Georgiana's mother—she had died, estranged from her husband, when the artist was only ten. Jane, however, had been universally known as 'the beautiful Duchess of Gordon', and the source of Georgiana's beauty was therefore no secret. The old Duke was succeeded by Georgiana's brother, George, the legendary Cock of the North, soldier extraordinary and founder of the Gordon Highlanders. The handsome 5th (and last) Duke, who died in 1836 without issue, was featured in Landseer's oil on panel, *Deerstalking in the Highlands*, along with Georgiana and Lord Alexander. The date ascribed to it is *circa* 1828, though from the sprat-like size of Alexander it must have been painted a few years earlier than that.

That Landseer should have emerged from his Highland jaunts as a skilled chronicler of deer-stalking was, of course, no surprise to anyone. What was much more unexpected was the free and spontaneous artistic rapport he established with the Scottish scenery. His response had been almost immediate: the first ever true landscape had been his *Highland Valley* in 1824. In another few years Edwin was painting landscapes with assurance, affection and skill. Scotland, as one early critic had observed, 'taught him his true power—it freed his imagination: it braced up his loose ability; it elevated and refined his mind: it developed his latent poetry: it completed his education'. This was nowhere more true than in the new freedom of execution he found in his former *bête noire*, landscape. It was a genre that he himself never took entirely seriously: it could never have been said that he 'studied' it. The interest in landscape had been born of the consciousness of his inability to add a convincing background to his animal portraits and his refusal to accept the fact of this gap in his artistic skill. It had been a frustrating gap, one that had threatened his artistic pride. Some years later, in the *Harvest in the Highlands* of 1833, he would accept the help of a landscape painter, Callcott, to add a background, whether for reasons of expediency or a pressing deadline or of plain comradeship. But by that time the threat had passed. Landseer had already overcome his problem by himself, and without formality or selfconsciousness or fuss. As a mere accessory to the main trend of his art, the Highland landscapes were delightfully free from the heavy hand of obligation, and the over-detailed finish, that marred so much of his work. He had no reputation to maintain as a landscape artist; no eager queue of patrons waiting to snap-up his next study of the Highland lochs, rivers and mountains. Perhaps he did not yet realise it himself, but these were the conditions under which he functioned best.

Edwin considered his oil on board, *Scene on the River Tilt*, good enough to be exhibited at the British Institution in 1826. Each autumn produced more studies not altogether perfectly composed, but usually interesting, often full of atmosphere and always painted in a wonderfully free fashion. *The River Teith, Perthshire* was a scene rather less rugged than the kind which most inspired him. *Spearing Salmon* showed Highland fishermen at work in a jaggedly-rocky river with lowering skies over the mountains beyond. *Landscape in Scotland with Waterfall*, reputedly of the Pot of Gartochan, Drymen, showed a characteristic, winding and boulder-toothed river at close quarters. By 1830 Edwin had found his touch in landscape. *Highland Landscape in the Cairngorms* of that year was a magnificently dramatic study, full of atmosphere and impending incident, capturing not only the grandeur but the morosity of mountains and weather. Loch Avon inspired a number of landscapes, including the colourful *Encampment on Loch Avon* and the Tate Gallery's *Lake Scene: Effect of Storm*, a view across the loch of Shelter Stone Crag.

At least one contemporary artist has found these landscapes both a revelation and an inspiration. Derek Hill in the Royal Academy's 1961 Landseer Exhibition catalogue described the impact of his first sight of *Lake Scene: Effect of Storm*:

> I had accepted the then current opinion, that Landseer was the epitome of all that was most boring and tiresome in Victorian painting, without questioning it. The revelation that came on seeing the Tate panel gave me much the same sensation that Corot must have felt when he first saw a Bonington in a shop window in Paris. A sensation that in Corot's case made him abandon his job and devote the rest of his life to painting—'This is how a landscape should be painted'.

The value Landseer placed on his own landscapes was not great. He had shown none at the Royal Academy, depending mainly on studies of animals and Highlanders. Nevertheless, his election as a full Royal Academician in 1831 came as no surprise to anyone. It was an almost automatic honour, assured by his success, his national reputation, his regularity as an exhibitor and the high tone of his patrons. The name Landseer was all too familiar to the Academy, but a cloak of establishment respectability had fallen even over John Landseer with his appointment in 1826 as an engraver to George IV. By tradition Edwin had to present a picture by himself to the Academy, which was acknowledged by the presentation of the diploma of membership, duly signed by the sovereign. Edwin's diploma picture, painted in the previous year, was *The Faithful Hound*, showing a dead knight in armour pillowed against his horse, his loyal bloodhound howling its anguish. James Manson* deplored Landseer's choice of such a gloomy theme for what was, after all, a celebratory occasion. This picture, indeed, was sometimes confused with *The Dying Warrior*, but that was the offering of his brother Charles many years later. Doleful diploma pictures apparently ran in the family.

Landseer's approach to Academic honours had been unusually smooth, without being unduly precocious. Although elected A.R.A. at the earliest possible age, seven years had elapsed before his election to R.A.—the gap between had only been two years in Fuseli's and Wilkie's case, three in Lawrence's and Turner's, though Constable and Millais each had to wait ten. Edwin was a mature twenty-nine— Lawrence had only been twenty-five, Wilkie and Opie twenty-six and Turner twenty-seven. Nevertheless many another aspirant no doubt watched the animal painter's progress with envy. The letters *R.A.* had an almost magic significance. Some painters looked on the status as a kind of tropical island paradise onto which they could sink blissfully after battling for years through the storm-tossed seas. Accordingly an artist's work sometimes suffered after election—'as if he had undergone chemical transmutation' was Haydon's opinion; while Linnell complained of the 'heartburnings, calumnies and injurious conduct (that) beset everyone struggling in that direction'. Certainly the occasional leaning on oars after election was nothing to the frenetic activity beforehand. George Clint, who withdrew altogether from the Academy, protested to a parliamentary committee of the way Associates were compelled to go about like vassals cap in hand from door to door, humbly begging for the privilege of being allowed to see those who could shortly decide their fate, whilst the Academicians themselves were canvassing urgently on behalf of their own relatives and friends. Competition, lobbying and petty jealousies were certainly rife. The newly-elected Etty who in the final ballot of 1828 had defeated Constable by 18 votes to 5, gleefully wrote to his brother Walter comparing himself to one of the latter's ships:

* *Sir Edwin Landseer R.A.*, James A. Manson 1902.

This is to inform you that your good ship the *William Etty* arrived safe and came to anchor in the bay tonight at half past ten; after being beaten about for so many years in the *Arte* (not Arctic) ocean. After being nearly wrecked on the coast of Italy we put in to Venice and were there well caulked with Venice turpentine. After combating many hard gales from Cape Difficulty and being nearly upset on Rejection Rock, on nearing land a *Constable* got on board some of the Royal ships, and came out with five or six guns (swivels). But a broadside of eighteen long forties sent him to the bottom.

R.A. elections tended to inspire puerility of this sort among grown men. Constable's own elevation to Academic honours was inexcusably tardy, though it did not prevent him from actively opposing his own direct rivals like Linnell. It was not, of course, long before Landseer found himself being lobbied, and he doubtless on occasion had the lofty manner to go with it. As Constable wrote to his friend Leslie in 1832:

Linnell spoke long to Landseer in Regent Street with his hat off all the time—I should not have wanted any other reason not to vote for him—no more did Landseer himself—he gave him a snub almost.

Linnell, however, was one of the few who did not suffer financially from the lack of initials after his name, leaving a healthy £200,000 behind him when he died. Constable, on the other hand, at the height of his fame was making about £800 a year, the kind of money many lesser artists were realising for a single picture.

Thought Constable became a loyal Academician, he seemed to retain the bitterness that sprang from long rejection and lack of recognition. His attitude to his rivals could be splenetic. He never quite forgave his naval victor of the 1828 elections, noting that a certain exhibition contained 'nothing but some women's bums by Etty' and dismissing a picture by another of his pet hates, Collins, as 'a landscape like a large cow turd'. Landseer's easy passage to honours meant that there was little competitive iron in his soul: he seldom had a harsh word to say of a fellow-painter. He was also spared the specialist rivalries that frequently reduced artists to the status of heavyweight boxing contenders, being firmly established as an animal painter before his potential rivals came on the scene. Indeed, he would be more bedevilled by the flattery of imitation than by the bitterness of contention.

The varnishing days, in which the painters put the finishing touches to their pictures before each annual exhibition, were a mixed social and professional occasion. It was the time when the great Turner was most in his element, moving among the other artists to give them the benefit of his advice. As Landseer later declared: 'I have seen him detect errors during the days when we met at the Academy after the pictures were placed; and whatever he suggested, was done without question, and it was always an improvement, whether in proportion or chiaroscuro, or anything else'. Indeed, he once touched up a painting by T. S. Cooper* which, to the cattle-painter's astonishment, a stranger bought for £300 sight unseen, with the comment, 'No matter; Turner would never have touched it if it had not been worth it'. Landseer was one of the few who ever touched a Turner painting. *Mortlake Terrace* is dominated by the figure of a small black dog. While Turner was out of the gallery, Edwin fashioned the little dog, cut it out and stuck it on the terrace itself as a joke. When the landscape painter returned he was not in the least put out. Instead, he adjusted the alien cut-out slightly, varnished it over and assured the intruder a place in posterity.

Turner and Landseer were associates on the committee of the charitable Artists General Benevolent Fund. Edwin and his fellow committee-member John Lucas were greatly amused by the way in which, when the three shared a cab on returning from meetings of the Fund, Turner would insist on alighting some way from his home in Queen Anne Street rather than risk the detour that would involve him in paying his part of the fare. Turner equally enjoyed guying Landseer's pomposities. When the animal painter inflatedly entitled one of his deer pictures, *Coming Events cast their Shadows before them*, Turner riposted with his watercolour showing a night sky with bursting rockets over a Swiss lake, *Coming Events cast their Lights before them*. Like his father, Edwin never made the mistake of under-estimating Turner, whose later work was a standing joke among certain other artists: Haydon himself loved to relate the story (later foisted on Picasso) that the landscape painter's works were often hung upside down or sideways. 'I should think no man could be more accurate in his observation,' Edwin said of Turner. 'He was thoroughly grounded in everything, and, without exception, I should say, the best teacher I ever met with.'

The two men, nevertheless, treated each other with a certain amount of circumspection. After one annual banquet at the Royal Academy Turner asked Cooper 'to give me his arm down the stairs, which I willingly did. Sir Edwin Landseer and Lord John Russell, then Prime Minister, were in conversation together near the entrance,

* *My Life*, 1890.

and I heard the former say to Lord John as we passed: 'There is Cooper leading out the "Nestor" of the Royal Academy.' 'Never mind them,' said Turner to me—'Never mind them. *They* shan't lead me out.'

Yet Edwin was present at Turner's last public appearance, following his funeral cortege. 'Landseer told some of his best stories,' Redgrave recalled, 'and in our coach . . . it was often necessary to sit well back to hide a face not quite characteristic of a mourner.'

CHAPTER FIVE

THE HIGH LIFE BECKONS

I have an exquisite gratification in painting portraits wretchedly.
—Benjamin Robert Haydon

'COMPARE AND contrast' pictures were, of course, to become a feature of Victorian art. In 1829 Landseer had painted two famous little companion pictures, *High Life* and *Low Life*, which contrasted an elegant and aristocratic deerhound with an un-gainly and roly-poly butcher's dog. *High Life* is a fine little composi-tion, the rather disdainful deerhound admirably done, the background of armour and battlements reflecting the romantic influence of Scott's novels that would soon become a national obsession. *Low Life* is too obviously its opposite. Its intentional vulgarity moved Ruskin to comment in his tangential style:*

> Cunning signifies especially a habit or gift of over-reaching, accompanied with enjoyment and a sense of superiority. It is associated with small and dull conceit, and with absolute want of sympathy or affection. Its essential connection with vulgarity may be at once exemplified by the expression of the butcher's dog in Landseer's *Low Life*.

Whether or not it was a case of great minds thinking alike, the most significant fact about *Low Life* was that with it Edwin bade a resounding *farewell* to low life. He had reached a stage in his own life where he did not wish to be associated, however obliquely, with vul-garity of any sort. Henceforth (with occasional later exceptions like the popular *Jack in Office*) he would eschew animals of lowly birth and confine his subjects mainly to the upper classes. The same broad rule would apply to his human sitters. He would certainly find some inspiration in the Highland shepherds, crofters, poachers and drovers (whom he doubtless saw as *nature's* aristocrats); but, as his contacts with the nobility grew, the rich and seamy animal scene of Georgian London entirely lost its appeal. His nose now seemed fixed too high in the air to allow him to appreciate the paintable life going on all around him.

* *Modern Painters* Part IX Ch. vii.

There had been great promise in such as *The Dustman's Dog* and the differing versions of *The Rat Catchers*, pictures with youthful faults but with enormous vitality. The eighteen-year-old Landseer had even drawn a poodle about to explore an effluent pipe; *The Expectant Dog* being appropriately dedicated to the Hon. Frederick Byng, Metropolitan Commissioner of Sewers. Such raunchy themes would soon give way to subject-titles like *The Pet of the Duchess* and *Waiting for the Countess*. This rather selfconscious departure from artistic democracy, this rejection of all dogs that might conceivably harbour fleas, was an obvious failing that did not escape the attention of later commentators. A correspondent complained to the *Illustrated London News* of Landseer's 'keen eye for cleanliness. His animals are always combed, brushed and polished as if they were intended for a world of Sundays'. Increasingly the painter himself would 'groom' his own paintings and engravings, heightening the gloss on a coat or, in best beautician fashion, removing unwanted hair.

However, on his autumn migrations to the Highlands, Edwin was still able to set up his easel without too much social forethought. The *Illicit Still* (painted for the Duke of Wellington and now in Apsley House) was a fine manly portrayal of a deer-hunter who has called at the place, shouldering-off his dead booty long enough to throw back an illegal drop of 'the cratur'. Landseer himself no doubt sampled the raw and fiery product of those clandestine shebeens, the Highlanders' understandable attempt to benefit from their own national heritage without reference to the hated exciseman. *The Illicit Still* was shown at the Royal Academy in 1829, in the same year as *The Fireside Party*, a conglomerate of shaggy terriers basking in the firelight of a bothy (said to be the originals of the 'Peppers' and 'Mustards' of Scott's *Guy Mannering*). The latter was much praised, and rightly, for Edwin's masterly handling of the terriers' hair; though the number and shagginess of the dogs might make it too obviously a virtuoso performance for everyone's taste.

The Illicit Still foretold a series of intimate Scottish scenes, featuring a variety of Highland worthies. They were a different make of servitor from those Landseer had known in England: he grew to respect their independent cast of mind: in much the same way as Victoria was later to find in her faithful retainers like John Brown and John Grant the opposite of the traditional fawning courtier. *Highland Music* (Royal Academy 1831) showed a crofter playing the pipes within the confines of his bothy, much to the consternation of his dogs, one of which is supplying its own mournful chorus. It was the forerunner of several more Highland interiors, which showed the drab undecorated earthen-floored innards of those comfortless peat-reeking bothies. None of them was totally satisfactory—their unlit dinginess was perhaps too closely allied to Landseer's doubtful colour sense which would always be, as the Catalogue of his posthumous R.A. Exhibition observed, 'the weak point in his harness, through which the enemy shaft reaches home'. 'Unsuffused,' that colour sense indeed was most of the time, 'by the rich glow of life.' Again, there was more toil and heartbreak behind the spartan crofting existence than the painter wished to see. Edwin's contemporary, Thomas Faed (whose enormous reputation has been even more totally eclipsed than Landseer's), was at least partly aware of the terrible human cost involved in the consecration of thousands of acres to a sporting gentry rather than to working people: pictures like *The Last of the Clan* showed he knew something about the Highland clearances and the cruel break-up of families through depopulation and emigration. Yet Landseer's accomplished *Highland Interior* of 1831 contrasted without comment the picturesqueness of the Highlander's dress and the drabness of his abode. *The Breakfast Party*, exhibited in the same year at the British Institution as *Too Hot*, showed a Highland lad feeding his dogs from the characteristic large dish on the floor. 'They seem to move and chatter/Over the scalding batter' twittered *The Amulet* who published the engraving, grateful for the glimpse into the life of the deserving poor in Caledonia. One would think more of the Highland interiors were the props not always so depressingly the same. Three years later there appeared *A Highland Breakfast* (Royal Academy 1834) which rather coyly juxtaposed a Highlandwoman breast-feeding her baby and the crofter's dogs, one of them suckling puppies, gathered round the by now inevitable communal platter on the floor.

In 1831, a rabidly Highland year, there also appeared '*How to Get the Deer Home!*', which pictorially posed the head-scratching problem of being stuck out on the hill with an illegally shot deer, as well as *Poachers Deerstalking* and *Poacher's Bothy*, the latter a kind of corollary to the first, being a dark but spirited portrayal of a slightly satanic-looking poacher who has manhandled his carcase into the box-bed in his bothy. He still seems unsure of how to conceal the dead deer completely as he awaits the gamekeeper's knock on his door. Not that his reaction is likely to be fawning or apologetic: the Highland poacher was a creature of independence and spirit. In his book *Wild Sports of the Highlands* (1846) Charles St. John remembered one of his acquaintance:

A finer specimen of the genus Homo than Ronald I never saw. As he passes through the streets of a country-town, the men give him plenty of walking room; while not a girl in the street but stops to look after him, and says to her companions. 'Eh, but yon's a bonnie lad!' . . . As he walked into my room followed by his two magnificent dogs, he would have made a subject worthy of Landseer in his best moments . . .

'The life of the Highland poacher is far different from that of an Englishman following the same profession,' averred St. John with just a suggestion of chauvinism. 'Instead of a sneaking night-walking ruffian . . . the Highlander is a bold fearless fellow, shooting openly by daylight, taking his sport in the same manner as the Laird, or the Sassenach who rents the ground.'

This description is somewhat at odds with the subjects of *Poachers Deerstalking* (otherwise known as *Waiting for the Deer to Rise*); three poachers on the hill at night, one holding the mouth of their terrier to restrain him. Nevertheless, one wishes Landseer had had sufficient original sin in him to persevere with such promising artistic strains as the poachers and the illicit stillmen. Yet he supped too often at the groaning board of the rich to spare much more than passing (and secretive) sympathy for the presumptuous fellow who saw the deer as as much his heritage as the landowner's and who walked tall down the streets of the Highland townships in his plain grey kilt (being a master of protective coloration) with his dogs weaving round his legs.

Of equally independent mien were the Highland drovers who took their herds of sheep and cattle over the drove roads to sell in England. T. S. Cooper who painted them in the Cumberland Fells, the route they took to avoid paying the tolls, found them refreshingly unimpressed by the practice of art. One of them, looking over his shoulder as he painted, searched for some words of comfort before observing patronisingly that 'We must take different drifts, for we cannae a' be drovers!'. Cooper had wanted to paint the same Highlander's fine sheepdog, wondering if it would lie still for long enough. 'Oh, yes, mon,' said the slightly surprised drover, 'he'll do anything I say to him.' The dog meantime had disappeared, dragging his master's rain-sodden plaidie. The drover whistled for him, but the dog didn't appear. When the two men went looking they discovered him in the kitchen, carefully holding up his master's wet plaid in his mouth to dry before the fire. 'What a subject it would have been for Edwin Landseer,' sighed Cooper.

Drovers Departure: a Scene in the Grampians of 1835 was one of Landseer's most successful Highland scenes. Although not huge, it is an extremely crowded canvas, showing the drovers about to set out with their flocks and herds on the long journey southwards. The

1(a) Self-Portrait of Edwin
Landseer as a Boy

1(b) John Landseer, by his son
Edwin

2(a) Benjamin Robert Haydon,
by G. M. Zorlin

2(b) Fighting Dogs Getting Wind

3 Edwin Landseer, by Sir Francis Grant

4 Georgiana, Duchess of Bedford

5 The Old Trossachs Inn

6(a) Sir Walter Scott

6(b) John Gibson R.A.

7(a) Sleeping Bloodhound

7(b) Dignity and Impudence

8(a) Van Amburgh with his Animals (reproduced by gracious permission of Her Majesty the Queen)

8(b) Shoeing

drawing of the innumerable animals is masterly, though it illustrated the trouble Landseer always had in blending a large number
of disparate elements. 'Every picture ought to have a look-there!'
the genial painter John Varley had wisely said: in canvases like
Drovers Departure there is much to admire but little that irresistibly
claims the eye, unless it be the figure of the elderly drover who is being fortified for the journey with a dram. John Landseer posed for
this figure, hence a somewhat refined and scholarly-looking drover.
The picture was admirably etched by James Watt, who shrewdly
bought the copyright for two hundred guineas. Nevertheless, it became Landseer's most popular engraving to date, paving the way for
a future fortune in engraving rights. The original now hangs in the
Victoria and Albert Museum. So crowded, indeed, was the canvas
that it produced some offshoot pictures—*The Tethered Rams* was
apparently suggested by it, as was *Protection—Hen and Chickens* and
the grazing white Highland pony can also be seen in the Wallace
Collection's *A Highland Scene*.

Throughout the 'Thirties Edwin continued paying somewhat circumscribed court to Georgiana. With the children growing up, Landseer and the Duchess were sometimes alone, except for a couple of
servants, at the Doune in Inverness-shire. The painter would stalk
and sketch, encouraging Georgiana in her own efforts to draw and
etch. When the bad weather kept them indoors, they would experiment with cooking, one of these experiments reputedly resulting in
the invention of *Pommes Duchesse*.

In her Campden Hill town house and at Woburn, Edwin was
equally in evidence. A room at Woburn had been converted into a
fully-equipped small theatre for Georgiana, a keen amateur actress.
To play opposite her in these theatricals, she would import leading
men from the London stage, among them Charles Mathews, *the*
light comedian of the day. No effort or expense was spared; even the
programmes were of white satin. Edwin's duties both there and in the
court theatricals at Windsor were twofold—to make-up the ladies
and to paint the scenery. His reputation as a make-up artist perhaps
owed more to his exciting presence than to his skill. His friend Lady
Caroline Norton once wrote him of a report she had heard 'that the
Dram. Pers. of the theatricals held a great consultation whether they
should ever wash their faces again and so destroy what each considered your Chef D'oeuvre. I do not know what they decided, but
we have every hope that they remained happily unwashed and un-
washing, merely brushing the dust and cobwebs away'.

Scenery-painting was yet another artistic role which he apparently
essayed to perfection. A correspondent to the *Athenaeum* wrote

enthusiastically of a typical piece of Landseerian scenic art, partly showing the interior of a room opening onto a balcony:

> In the doorway stands a lady's dog, marvellously touched in, in a listening attitude, with one of the forepaws uplifted, exhibiting in a startling degree all the artist's wondrous power, even in the coarse and hasty manner incidental to the scene-painter's art.

He also painted outdoor scenes which included deer and human figures. The immobility of such figures (including the dog with the upraised paw) in a scene of any length can hardly have done much to further the play's air of authenticity; but doubtless it was part of the theatrical convention of the time.

Although he did not see the stage as a suitable career for a young lady, Edwin was fascinated by the theatre, and at one time had discussed going into theatrical management with Charles Kean, who would invite the painter to his performances. There is no record of Landseer as an actor: perhaps he shared the almost universal disability of wits, raconteurs and after-dinner lions in that particular art. However, he was a tenor of some accomplishment, and would sometimes sing duets with Georgiana, as he often did with his sisters and his brother Charles.

In her early fifties Georgiana's sense of fun remained as pronounced as ever. Sir David Brewster's daughter recalled 'her gay circle of fashion, of statesmen, artists and lions of all kinds'.* On one occasion when the Chancellor Lord Brougham was visiting at the Doune, he retired early, being indisposed. While he lay resting an animated discussion arose as to whether Lord Chancellors carried the Great Seal around with them on social visits. Georgiana determined to find out, and ordered a cake of soft dough to be made. A procession of lords, ladies and gentlemen was then formed with Georgiana in pride of place, bearing a silver salver with the lump of dough on it. The invalid Lord was summarily aroused from his slumbers with a demand to get up forthwith and exhibit the Great Seal. Though he refused to rise from his bed of pain Brougham ruefully asked for a strange-looking box to be brought to him, extracting from it the controversial object, whereupon he solemnly 'impressed the seal upon the cake of dough—the procession retired in order, and the Lord Chancellor returned to his pillow'.

Georgiana's gaiety and sense of fun, her mischievous readiness for any new adventure, had, of course, another side. She retained the same eye for a likely man she had possessed when the attractive young painter walked into her ken. By the mid-Thirties Edwin, like

* *The Home Life of Sir David Brewster*, Mrs. Gordon 1869.

many another lover of a married woman, had no doubt made the painful discovery that his mistress was betraying him with more than her husband. The diarist le Marchant had recorded in July 1833:

> The Dutchess of Bedford passed the day with us—a bold, bad woman—with the remains of her beauty . . . Lord Ebrington was also of the party . . . He has been one of the most handsome persons of the day and one of the most pleasing, as too many ladies know to their cost, and amongst others her Grace of Bedford.

Lord Ebrington's taste may have been more towards kept ladies— he had been one of the many exalted clients of the courtesan Harriete Wilson whose bribery-laden threats to publish her memoirs had elicited Wellington's famous phrase: 'Publish and be damned!'. However, Georgiana's roving eye was no more insistent on equals than was Lord Ebrington's. Three years later her arch-enemy, Bessy, Lord William's wife, was writing in gleefully acidulous vein to her friend, the Countess Lieven:

> Vouz verrez je crois le Duc et la Duchesse à Paris. Son amant actual n'est pas plus le peintre mais dit-on son valet de chambre suisse.

Landseer himself appears to have remained true in his fashion. In 1834 he produced a series of eight drawings called *The Mothers*, dedicated to Georgiana and etched by C. G. Lewis. Coming from any other source, a fastidious female recipient might have taken the gift somewhat amiss, since the mothers portrayed included a cow and a sow. The other animal dams with offspring were a dog, a horse, a donkey, a sheep and a goat. However, the key drawing, *Highland Nurse*, was of a human mother tenderly giving suck to her baby: it doubtless recorded moments of blissful intimacy that Georgiana and Edwin had sometimes shared. It also recorded the Duchess's well-known obsession with the young of any species. Now, however, with the childbearing years safely behind her, she seemed to have found a new (if relatively brief) lease of sexual life.

Edwin himself was discovering that he was the victim of his own versatility. Even apart from animals there seemed little (with the exception of architecture) that he could not successfully achieve in painting—at any rate, nine times out of ten. His first ventures into child portraiture had been almost accidental, an attempt to please Georgiana. Yet their popularity had extended well beyond the Bedford family circle. Some of them, thought Allan Cunningham's *Lives* quoting *Little Red Riding Hood, Cottage Industry* and *Lady Rachel Russell with a Pet Fawn*, 'are as well known as any of his pictures'. A majority of his child portraits showed the youngsters with their pets. It was, apart from all else, a useful form of double insurance—if the child's likeness fell short of perfection the pets seldom did. It was also a formula that proved irresistible; that could have kept him exclusively employed on child-animal studies for the rest of his life.

Yet it was an individual and rather unlikely child portrait that brought him most to attention. *The Naughty Boy* (sometimes called *A Naughty Child*) was apparently not of a boy at all, but a study of Lady Rachel Russell. Anticipating a conventional portrait, Landseer had found his daughter in a contrary and rebellious mood, and had made the best of a bad job by painting her thus, petulantly defiant in the corner to which she had been sent. Since child portraits (largely because of the high rate of infant mortality) were traditionally angelic, the idea of portraying a child as a sulky little horror was considered a highly amusing and original one, though one has to look very hard to see virtues in it today.

Nevertheless, after appearing at the British Institution in 1834, *A Naughty Child* was hailed as a minor masterpiece. The painter began to be inundated even more with enquiries and commissions from doting parents. 'Both my little girls are in painting condition', F. G. Egerton hopefully (and typically) informed Landseer in the following year. The subsequent portrait of Miss Blanche Egerton was certainly one of considerable charm, featuring a pretty little girl with long luxuriant hair, a cockatoo on her shoulder and her frilly drawers engagingly showing. It was later engraved for *The Children of the Aristocracy*, a publication of imposing presence and relentless snobbery.

It was, however, amongst the female aristocracy that the news of Landseer's coming of age as a child portraiturist was most breathlessly received. Much of it, naturally, was conveyed by word of mouth or by letter, the aristocratic network of tom-tom signals being second to none. Over the years a certain amount of twittering would often precede the commission. Thus Lady Bathurst (undated) to 'My Lady Dacre':

> I quite agree that £200 is a very moderate sum for what Mr. Landseer proposes . . . I suppose I have now only to wait patiently till I receive a summons to bring my children to him. I do hope they will be in better looks than they are at present. One is speckled like a little guinea hen and the other has one eye almost closed by gnat bites, but their misfortune will I hope not last many days. You do not tell me whether I am to go with a draft in my hand. I suppose this custom is universal—with many thanks . . .

Her patient wait and Edwin's attempts to ring the changes slightly on a heavily conventionalised subject resulted in the unremarkable *Children with Rabbits*.

Landseer's occasional attempts to cut down on the growing burden of his commissions were too half-hearted to meet with much success. The female aristocracy of last century was unused to rejections, cleaving through excuses and objections with a resolute prow:

Lady Oxford is grieved that Mr. Landseer cannot undertake to Paint her little Daughters at the present moment, but she hopes that when they return from the Continent that Mr. Landseer will have a little leisure to bestow upon them . . . It would give Lady Oxford great pleasure if Mr. Landseer could be persuaded to paint them (at) Wollaton when they return to that Delightful Place as the little girls will be seen to more advantage there amidst their favourite haunts & mounted on their pretty Ponies—but if Mr. Landseer will allow Lady Oxford to bring them to Mr. Landseer on Tuesday at *half* eleven o'clock on their ponies just to let Mr. Landseer see the Capability of Painting them after they return from the Continent it will give Lady Oxford great pleasure to take them to him . . .

His own reluctance to say no to an aristocratic client coupled with *their* reluctance to take no for an answer resulted in many more child portraits over the years, most of them politely professional rather than inspired. *Beauty's Bath* pictured the pretty young Miss Eliza Peel about to plunge her pet spaniel Fido into the suds: *On Trust* showed Princess Mary of Cambridge subjecting a large Newfoundland dog with a biscuit on its nose to the well-known parlour trick. 'Probably Landseer's best portrait picture' said Stephens of *The Sutherland Children*. Although his study of two youngsters with a garlanded fawn and a couple of dogs is too sickly sweet for modern tastes, it was immensely popular at the time, largely through a fine engraving by Samuel Cousins. Considerably more volatile was *The Hon. E. S. Russell and His Brother* (now in Kenwood House). Landseer had allegedly been discussing the eternal problem of the freshest way in which to pose the two young relatives of the Bedfords when the boys had given him his answer by racing past the window on their ponies. It is difficult now to comment on likenesses: the profile of the Hon E. S. Russell is perhaps rather flat, though creditably boyish and belligerent. The canvas nevertheless is a pleasing one. The hair of the black pony nearest the viewer is treated in masterly fashion, especially on the flank (a Landseer flank, in fact, could be almost as good as a Stubbs' haunch, and there is nothing in animal art better

than that). Another clever touch was to employ pictorially the insistence on a pecking order for which horses are notorious—the brown
pony has dared to push his nose ahead of the black pony, which lays
back its ears and rolls its eyes in a piece of disgruntled by-play which
clearly reflects the order of precedence between the brothers themselves. Landseer later returned to the tranquil pose with *Return from
the Warren*, showing the Hon. A. C. Ponsonby on his favourite pony,
an assured and beautifully-composed portrait that was among his
very best child studies. The dignified Ponsonby boy has much more
the appearance of an Hon. than the spoilt-looking whip-wielding E. S.
Russell—it is possible on occasion to suspect Landseer of tongue-in-
cheek.

The whole question of portraiture was a painful thorn in the flesh
of most serious painters. Often it represented for nineteenth-century
artists what advertising (ostensibly) represents for artists and writers
of our own day—a despised method of making a comfortable living.
The perpetually impecunious High Artist Haydon was moved to
occasional gasps of envy. 'Oh, how these portrait dogs get on!' he
would sigh, referring to John Lucas's recent acquisition of a four-
horse carriage. Yet the sighs were few, and the loathing was absolute.
In 1824 he had written to Miss Mitford: 'I question whether there be
in all the tortures of Hades, any torture equal to that of dragging
your brush over your canvas to copy the gaping idiotic vanity of some
nouveau riche . . .'. 'Finished one cursed portrait,' he confided to his
Journal at a later date, 'have only one more to touch and then I shall
be free. I have an exquisite gratification in painting portraits
wretchedly.' He suited his art to his words: in one portrait of a Mayor
of Norwich, Mr. Hawkes, the dignitary's hulking body was supported
on a representation of Haydon's own neat little legs. The historical
painter's advice to the portraiturist on making out his bill reflected
the depths of his contempt:

To two eyes at 10 gs. each	—	21. 0. 0.
To a nose	—	5. 5. 0.
To two lips (red &C)	—	6. 6. 0.
To two cheeks (fine complexion &C)	—	5. 5. 0.
To Lobe of the Ear	—	1. 1. 0.
To 1 Cravat	—	1. 1. 0.
To $\frac{1}{2}$ a Coat	—	1. 1. 0.
To 1 finger	—	1. 1. 0.
To a white cloud, table, & back of chair & bit of red curtain	—	5. 5. 0.
		48. 5. 0.

To altering the mouth to a smile,
& taking out two wrinkles in the
cheek and browning the grey hair   —   1.15. 0.
                                                     ─────────
                                                        50. 0. 0.

The arithmetic may be inaccurate, but there can be no doubts
about the strength of the sentiment which was echoed by many
another artist, including Barry, Watts and Uwins. 'Making old
women young and ugly women handsome is now my daily occupation,' Thomas Uwins had moaned in a letter to his brother in 1823;
and later: 'Could I get one third of the profit by painting other things,
I should think the tranquility of mind cheaply gained'. Fuseli hinted
at another reason for the growing popularity of having one's portrait
done: 'Every fool who has a phiz to expose and a guinea to throw
away, thinks by the expenditure of that small sum he becomes a
patron of art'. Some such patrons, of course, did not consider the
English school of portrait painting good enough, like the *nouveau
riche* lady quoted by Vernon Heath who airily announced that her
husband had promised to take her to Rome to be painted by the Old
Masters.

Landseer's own stance on portrait-painting had always been
ambiguous. Yet he knew both sides of that particular branch of art—
both the joys of an instant likeness and the gnawing agonies of a non-
likeness that would become increasingly an overpainted lump on the
canvas. His approach to portraiture had been as disinterested as his
approach to landscape had been indirect. The Duke of Bedford had
written to him in the mid-Twenties concerning his wife's likeness
and quoting Edwin at himself: 'As you say "It is the only regular
portrait you ever intend to paint" (which I am rejoiced to hear)'. The
young artist was, of course, hardly innocent of duplicity and decep-
tion where the 6th Duke was concerned, but no doubt he also had
Haydon's precepts and perorations still ringing in his ears. Almost
certainly Edwin did not intend adopting portraiture to any extent
before he began to be swept along on the social tide, with its fatal
undertow of flattery, obligation and favours returned for favours
given.

Landseer's first serious attempt at a celebrity portrait, apart from
Georgiana in 1823, had been his *Sir Walter Scott* of the following year.
It had been dourly unsuccessful—a florid and mournful physiognomy
and a stiffly-leaning plaid-covered body terminating in a hand like a
bunch of carrots. (The inability to portray hands and arms was a
feature of several early portraits, including the otherwise impressive
Georgiana, Duchess of Bedford, *circa* 1830.) However, while still in his

twenties, Edwin had proved his skill as a portraiturist with his fine
little later study of the great novelist seated at his desk. Several more
of comparable merit were to follow. Lord Melbourne was another who
seemed to inspire rather than intimidate Edwin's style. Landseer
had apparently met the statesman at Holland House, to which Lady
Holland had invited him 'to dine tomorrow' in language as bizarre as
her behaviour:

> You will meet Lord Melbourne who will be happy to submit his
> ear to your inspection. If you would like to stay all night you will
> have a room.

This commission from Lady Holland, an oval panel, was executed at
Woburn Abbey, and by many bequeathments passed to Earl Mount-
batten of Burma. Another Landseer portrait of Melbourne, probably derived from the same sitting, is in the National Portrait
Gallery; a good boldly-painted face though with the characteristic
vagueness as to drapery and background that would increasingly
earn so many of Edwin's pictures the definition of 'unfinished'. The
young Victoria's view of the portrait of her idol displayed slight in-
consistency of mind in an impending sovereign. It was 'like him but
too fat and though flattering is not in my opinion half pleasing
enough. It is very well done'.

Edwin's visits to Holland House also secured him the commission
to paint Dr. John Allen, the political and historical writer and long-
time librarian at the fashionable town-house. Allen was a Doctor of
Philosophy who preferred to be called Mr. rather than be inundated
with bleeding thumbs and coughing fits and requests to loosen the
stays of fainting women. His portrait was one of many that became
the subject of Edwin's shyness over money. Allen had to write the
painter in 1838 suggesting an additional fifty pounds for his portrait: 'Considering the universally acknowledged excellence of the
picture, the price you ask for it is too moderate . . .'. This accomplished study is now in the National Portrait Gallery.

Some of his aristocratic sitters intimidated him less that others. He
made a good small portrait of his friend the 6th Duke of Devonshire
(still at Chatsworth). The date generally ascribed to it is 1832 because
the book at the Duke's elbow is *The Hunchback* by Wilkie Collins
which came out that year—though it seems a slightly shaky premise
on which to date a picture, which does not appear to be associated
with a family picture including the Duke and shown in the same
year.

Among the most impressive of all Landseer's individual portraits
was his fine canvas of the Rome-based sculptor *John Gibson R.A.*

(Royal Academy), painted in the mid-Forties. 'He is a God in his studio, but God help him out of it,' his pupil Harriet Hosmer said of the absent-minded sculptor who was wont to alight at railway-stations and enquire not only where he was but where he had come from. The portrait admirably captured his grave, handsome and ascetic countenance, as well as the somewhat removed and un-worldly look of a man capable of falling in love with his own crea-tions, notably the *Tinted Venus*.

Occasionally Landseer was moved to portray a face from among those he met accidentally on his travels. In 1831 there was the attractive *Stone Breaker's Daughter* (she has brought his dinner to her father, who is engaged in this most soulless of nineteenth-century tasks); and *The Auld Guid Wife* of the following year, an ancient body whose roots were in Scottish history—'She'll ken fine Cul-loden's sad day'—and whom Landseer told Graves he kept alive with whisky while he painted her.

Lord Ronald Gower, whose sister Evelyn had figured in the famous *Sutherland Children* portrait, observed of Landseer: 'Like many great artists, when trammelled with a commission he seemed to lose power . . . commission is often the grave of talent'.* In Edwin's case it went further. Commissions would become the grave of his health and peace of mind. Whatever the inveterate professionalism of his early upbringing, he remained an amateur in the sense that he could only paint freely and well that which genuinely interested him. Results were therefore unpredictable. Sometimes an unpromising commission undertaken with a heavy heart would turn out well as he warmed to the subject, an interesting adult or an unexpectedly charming child: at other times a flattering proposal eagerly under-taken would plunge him into the depths of nervous depression. In fact, Landseer never learned to equate the acceptance of a commis-sion with his possible inability to satisfactorily carry it out. It was one of the symptoms of his perennial immaturity.

* *My Reminiscences*, 1883.

CHAPTER SIX

DANDIES TOGETHER

Would you please send me a dozen pairs of gloves of a dead leaf colour which can be bought from the Tyrolean glove sellers? Have them so that they will fit your hand (this is a compliment) and I will send you the cost (this is a lie).
—Count d'Orsay in a letter to a friend at Frankfort

ONE OF the most popular meeting-places of the leading writers, artists and politicians of the day was the successive London homes of Margaret, Lady Blessington—at St. James's Square, Seamore Place and (most renowned of the three) Gore House in Kensington. Edwin became a frequent visitor. Only the most emancipated ladies ever went there, however, because Lady Blessington had a 'past'. She had been born Margaret (or 'Sally') Power in the tiny village of Knockbrit in County Tipperary. Her father Edmund had been violent, domineering, intemperate and perennially hard-up, though a true Power in his handsomeness. Margaret's blossoming beauty did not escape the attention of the officers of the local British army garrison, in particular one Captain Farmer of the 47th Regiment of Foot. Farmer being rich as well as randy, Margaret's unscrupulous father sold her into marriage at the age of fifteen to a man who was (like Power himself) a sadistic brute. Three months later, disgusted by the excesses imposed on her by her husband, she fled back to the unwelcoming arms of her father. Now sunk deep in drunkenness, debt and squalor, Power's attempts to attract officers to his home through the charms of his two eldest daughters became even less disguised than before. In 1807 he was tried but acquitted for the brutal murder of a peasant boy. Badly frightened by her father's increasing violence, Margaret ran off with Thomas Jenkins, a cavalry officer, and settled fairly happily with him in Hampstead. Alas, the amiable Jenkins though an officer was scarcely a gentleman. He sold Margaret for £10,000 to Viscount Mountjoy, a widower, when she was twenty-five. However, the Earl of Blessington (as Mountjoy shortly afterwards became) was anxious to regularise the union, and a convenient fall by Farmer from a high window whilst in a drunken stupor removed the last obstacle to the match. The soiled plaything of the brutal and licentious soldiery entered society.

Society, of course, did not open its arms any too eagerly. Lady Blessington's reputation had preceded her, and no respectable woman would enter her salon. Always as ingenious as she was beautiful, the Countess made a virtue of necessity, inviting the most interesting men in London to her home. Over the years she became the close friend of writers like Dickens, Thackeray, Bulwer Lytton and Walter Savage Landor; painters like Lawrence, Wilkie and Landseer himself; theatrical figures like Macready; prominent politicians like Palmerston, Earl Grey and Disraeli. But her closest intimate was the French dandy Count Alfred d'Orsay, her partner in a notorious scandal involving Harriet, Lord Blessington's daughter by his first wife. Blessington's will had been an astonishing document, leaving Harriet his extensive estates in Ireland on condition that she married d'Orsay. The reluctant girl had accordingly been wed at the age of fifteen to the gorgeously-attired d'Orsay in Naples, after the horrified British minister in Florence had refused to countenance such a ceremony. Lady Blessington, doubtless recalling her own enforced nuptials, stipulated that there must be no consummation of the match until the bride was nineteen.

England was soon agog with the scandal, the interpretation of which the gossips found brutally simple. Lady Blessington and the Count d'Orsay were lovers. Together they had duped the incompetent and doddering Lord Blessington (who was to live only a few more years after d'Orsay's appearance) into signing the iniquitous will. Even the Countess's insistence on a four year moratorium on her stepdaughter's virginity had a selfish motive: she could not bear immediately to share her young French lover with another. D'Orsay nevertheless made repeated clandestine attempts to ravish his teenage bride. Such was the story relished by society—though much of its truth is now open to question.

D'Orsay first met Lady Blessington in 1821. He was twenty, a French army officer whose only assets were his aristocratic lineage, his looks and his charm: she was thirty-two. As a young fortune-hunting buck recently arrived in England, d'Orsay sought entry to all the best houses. One of these was Holland House, presided over by the formidable Lady Holland, the Countess of Blessington's sworn rival. At dinner, it is said, the great lady, seated next to the young French adventurer, began to find him unbearably self-possessed for a mere foreigner. Lady Holland's rudeness towards her guests was legendary, and on that occasion took the form of dropping things on the floor—first her napkin, then her fan, then her fork, then her spoon—in order to discompose her young guest. The ruse proved un-successful. D'Orsay each time bent down suavely to retrieve the fallen objects without once interrupting his flow of broken-English chatter. Finally, incensed by such whipper-snappery, Lady Holland swept her wine-glass from the table, whereupon d'Orsay turned coolly to the footman behind him. 'Put my couvert on the floor,' he said. 'I will finish my dinner there. It will be much more convenient to milady.'

This putting-down of her chief rival no doubt helped confirm the young Frenchman in Lady Blessington's affections, as well as in those of her husband who (not unlike some other aristocrats of the day) had an equal eye for male and female beauty. 'The general notion was that Lord Blessington and Lady Blessington were equally in love with him,' wrote Charles Greville in his diary. For d'Orsay, however, their interest meant the kind of life he craved. Having been bought out of the army by Lord Blessington, he travelled with the couple through Europe, passing some time with Lord Byron, about whom Lady Blessington later wrote a book.

It was, however, in London that Landseer and d'Orsay met. They became firm friends: d'Orsay was to call Edwin 'the finest artist of our day' and sign his letters to him, 'Your best friend, d'Orsay'. The effect of d'Orsay on impressionable younger men was notorious. The Frenchman was, as Carlyle described him, 'the Phoebus Apollo of dandyism', always free with his advice to the young bucks who strove to emulate him. He once forbade the Earl of Chesterfield to dress in anything but blue, from coats to ties, a suggestion which that mild young man somewhat shamefacedly followed for quite a time. We do not know what sartorial advice, if any, he gave to Landseer, but we can be sure that his effect on the artist one year his junior was considerable. Edwin began to dress in the height of fashion; to adopt foppish gestures and airy mannerisms; to assume the clipped tones of the gentry, droppin' the *g*s from the ends of words. D'Orsay could hardly be blamed for the accent—his own was outrageously French; but in the matter of peacockery (and subsequently in the matter of gambling and a generally conscienceless attitude about money) his influence on Edwin was decidedly baleful.

Landseer's liaison with d'Orsay was based partly on art. The Frenchman was himself a painter and sculptor, though with little claim to immortality. Thackeray's daughter, Lady Richmond Ritchie, who met him when a young girl, recorded her amazement over a drawing he kindly left for her: 'It was a very feeble sketch: it seemed scarcely possible that so grand a being should not be a bolder draughtsman'. He was also notorious for errors of perspective. To a critic who pointed out that in his portrait of Chesterfield the ear seemed grossly out of proportion, the ever-ready d'Orsay replied: 'Pardon, but it is ze picture of ze *ear!*'. He loved to visit professional artists, setting their teeth on edge by lounging about their paint-spattered studios in his immaculate and dazzling creations. 'Such dress,' wrote Haydon, 'white great coat, blue satin cravat, hair oily and curly, hat of the primest curve & purest water, gloves scented with eau de cologne, or eau de jasmine, primrose in tint, skin in tightness. In this prime of Dandyism, he took up a nasty oily dirty hog-tool & immortalised Copenhagen by touching the sky.' Copenhagen, which Haydon was engaged in painting, was the Iron Duke's favourite charger; and the thought of a Frenchman touching even the background to Wellington's horse was too much for a staunch English patriot. Immediately d'Orsay had gone he retouched the desecrated spot. Nevertheless, he obviously relished every visit by the dandy who 'bounded into his Cab, & drove off like a young Apollo with a fiery Pegasus. I looked after him. I like to see such specimens'.

D'Orsay's horses, like their master, were larger than life, and artists like Haydon and Landseer sought permission to sketch and paint them. Thackeray's daughter retained two infant impressions of d'Orsay—'the godlike beauty of his figure' and his 'enormous horse staring at us over the sunblind'. His carriage was no less impressive. A century and a half before the phenomenon was defined, he affected a psychedelic cabriolet, which was so instantly recognisable that proprietors of gambling-dens would allegedly pay the noted dandy substantial amounts of money just to leave his carriage standing outside their establishments for an hour or two. When he was twenty, Landseer had made a spirited oil sketch of *Count D'Orsay's Charger*, a fine light bay obviously very much on its toes. The picture, now in the Sheffield Art Gallery, is remarkable in that it is the only Landseer signed *E.H.L.*, the *H* standing for Henry.*

The Count was also a dog-lover, whose pets, too, were apparently more formidable than average. According to Frith, he possessed one fierce and class-conscious animal which insisted on travelling side by side with its master on the seats of a first-class compartment. Before the train left the station the guard would respectfully remind

---

* Edwin was apparently glorying temporarily in his new middle name. In a sudden access of piety all seven Landseer children had been baptised on May 23rd 1821, when most of them were young men and women. Edwin had been named after a member of the household, his Uncle Henry Landseer, a travelled artist whose only R.A. exhibit (in 1824) seems to have been *Morning—View near Aroche on the River Chanza, Andalusia, Spain*. However, John Landseer had advised Edwin that, professionally speaking, one Christian name was sufficient for an artist.

d'Orsay that the dog should be occupying the dog-compartment of
the guard's van. Equally respectfully d'Orsay would agree and
suggest that the guard remove him forthwith. The dog's massive
jaws would then snap shut on the air a mere inch from the extended
hand of the guard, who would hurriedly withdraw, leaving the
animal to travel once more in the style to which he had become
accustomed. D'Orsay also had a monster French poodle with a top-
knot like a judge's wig which Lord Lyndhurst, then Chancellor himself, one day remarked 'would make a capital Lord Chancellor'.
Landseer took the hint and sketched the animal for d'Orsay, his forepaws on the table (or bench) in accepted legal style, as *The Chancellor*. The pen-and-ink sketch later became the basis for a painting
bought by the 6th Duke of Devonshire called *Trial by Jury: or Laying
Down the Law*, representing several dogs gathered round a table in a
variety of pontifical poses, their would-be learned expressions intended to guy certain notabilities of the day. Before buying the
picture, the Duke insisted on the inclusion of his own Blenheim
Spaniel Boney, which Landseer felt constrained to do, squeezing-in
the canine afterthought in a way that did little for the composition
of the painting. (Alas, critics seldom allow for the whims of patronage!) *Laying Down the Law* was one of the paintings over which
Landseer was accused of unduly humanising dogs; but the intention
is clearly satirical rather than sentimental, and it is a little hard on
the painter to chastise him for falling short of a Hogarth or a Dean
Swift.

On his frequent visits to the artist, d'Orsay would make much of
the vivid appearance of the dogs that stood on the easel or around
the studio in a way that both flattered Landseer and amused himself.
'Keep the dogs off me,' he would call out before entering. 'I want to
come in, but they might bite me. And zat fellow in ze corner is growl-
ing furiously!' On one occasion, his handsome face wincing sympathetically, he asked Edwin for a pin 'to take ze thorn out of zat
dog's foot. Can't you see what pain he is in?'.

Edwin sketched d'Orsay several times, including one black and
white chalk caricature of *Count d'Orsay and the Artist Boxing*, which
exaggerates both Landseer's shortness and d'Orsay's height (he was
six foot three). It also emphasised the fact that d'Orsay was far from
being the conventional fop: he was a fine and heedless horseman and
his handshake was said to be bone-crushing. Nonetheless, his dress
proved him to be a narcissist of no mean order; and it seems likely
that, far from being Lady Blessington's lover and the rapist of his
teenage bride, he was impotent or nearly so and sexually uninterested
in women. His name was linked, rather unconvincingly, with those of

several well-known actresses of the day; but this only reflected his (and their) genius for self-publicity. Few indeed were the women (apart from the ultra-sophisticated Lady Blessington) who would have been prepared to play pea-hen to such a resplendent peacock. A sexually-vigorous d'Orsay could have sealed his own fortune by making his young heiress bride pregnant, but she had eventually run away from him, apparently inviolate and probably more in disappointment than in disgust.

D'Orsay's overspending eventually led himself and Lady Blessington into financial trouble. He was a prodigious gambler, and would play throughout the night at Crockford's. Edwin seems to have tried to emulate him, though with little success. According to the painter John Martin, Landseer had at one time a serious gambling problem and was only saved from ruin by his friend and business manager Jacob Bell. The animal painter was often heavily depressed by his losses, and Martin recalled finding him so low on one occasion that he insisted on taking him off for a walk during which Landseer, who may have been over-dramatising, seems to have cheered up fairly rapidly. Some of d'Orsay's cavalier attitude to money probably rubbed off on Edwin. Far from paying tradesmen, the dandy looked on the adoption of their goods as a form of advertisement worth far more than the goods themselves. It is said that at the height of his popularity he only patronised tailors who slipped banknotes into the pockets of his new clothes before they were delivered, and that he returned more than one garment complaining that the lining of the pockets was unsatisfactory. Yet his personal extravagences led him deeper into debt. At first d'Orsay did not mind over much: he was amiably disposed towards finding new suppliers when the old ones were niggling enough to consider him non-creditworthy. But he seemed genuinely hurt that his creditors, those dull but reliable creatures from whom he had so generously accepted largesse, should turn suddenly into people who actually wanted their money *back*. For a time he tried to set up as a society portraiturist in a basement studio in Gore House. To protect their reputations, lady-clients would clandestinely call by way of the garden—just the kind of piquant touch that assured a portrait-painter's reputation. However, not even the thrill of forbidden fruit could atone indefinitely for the almost spectacular banality of the likenesses, and d'Orsay's tendency to exaggerate rather than ameliorate prominent facial features.

Eventually the Count became a *shy-cock*, unable to leave Gore House between the hours of dawn and dusk, except on a Sunday, for fear of arrest. This did not of itself affect d'Orsay's gambling; but it did sometimes interfere with his work. One of his best-known portraits was of the Queen on horseback, but the picture urgently required retouching by the artist himself during normal business hours. It was Landseer who insisted that the Count must disguise himself while they called together on the engraver. Accordingly, in the drabbest of clothes and with his face half-wrapped in a necker-chief, the Count and his companion sallied forth into what, for d'Orsay, were shark-infested seas. They completed their business without incident, Landseer, an expert retoucher, no doubt doing his share. Emboldened by his success in travelling sartorially *incognito*, d'Orsay then suggested visiting *Madame Tussaud's*, the only place open at that hour. While they walked from room to room in the famous waxworks, they found themselves being followed by two mysterious men. When one of them approached him, d'Orsay was convinced that the game was finally up. 'Madame Tussaud has sent me to ask if you would do her the honour to let her model you in wax?' The count almost fainted with relief. 'In wax!' he said, 'in marble, bronze, iron, my good fellow. Tell her, with my love, she may model me in anything!'

It was perhaps a reflection on Lady Blessington's status as a bought wife that her husband left her very inadequately provided for. To offset d'Orsay's extravagence and uphold her own standard of living, she had to find other sources of income. She had already written both fiction and memoirs, and in the early 'Thirties deter-mined to become a full-time literary figure. The increasingly popular *Annuals* gave her that opportunity. These had started in 1828 when Harrison Ainsworth with Charles Heath the engraver first produced *The Keepsake*, a compendium of prose, poems and pictures of lovely women which sold at a guinea. It was followed in 1833 by the *Book of Beauty*. Whatever their content, the Annuals could not be faulted on production. They were beautifully printed on the finest paper, illustrated with high-quality steel engravings and sumptuously bound in watered silk. They were soon very much in the fashion. 'That epidemic,' Lady Wilde later wrote of them, 'that raged with considerable flimsiness and platitude.' They had begun promisingly enough, with semi-serious literary content and engravings from the work of Turner, Martin, Stanfield and others. However, snob-appeal soon began to replace art; and it became apparent that they would fare better with a titled lady rather than a literary gent at the helm. So Lady Blessington became one of what the painter Uwins scath-ingly described as 'the Annual-mongers', editing the *Book of Beauty* and later *The Keepsake*; and Edwin was quickly roped-in as one of the artist-contributors.

His first offering was his portrait of *Georgiana, Duchess of Bedford*, which appeared in *The Keepsake* in 1829 characteristically accompanied in the following vein by some adulatory verses, ostensibly addressed to Georgiana by an admiring gallant:

> Lady, thy face is very beautiful,
> A calm and stately beauty; thy dark hair
> Hangs as the passing winds paid homage there;
> And gems, such gems as only princes cull
> From earth's rich veins are round they neck and arm;
> Ivory, with just one touch of colour warm,
> And thy white robe floats queenlike, suiting well
> A shape such as in ancient pictures dwell . . .

The poet goes on to amplify 'his dream' that Georgiana should have lived in olden times, with knights in their thousands dying for her hand. Alas, the admiring poet was no gallant, but L.E.L. (Letitia Elizabeth Landon), poetess and novelist, and one of the few women emancipated enough to move in the Blessington-d'Orsay circle. Born in the same year as Edwin, she later married George MacLean, Governor of the Gold Coast, where she died aged thirty-six after accidentally swallowing a dose of prussic acid—though it was whispered that she had been poisoned by her husband's African mistress.

The *Book of Beauty* would produce several other Landseer portraits —including engravings of *Lady Georgiana Russell* and *The Marchioness of Abercorn with Child and Dog* in 1834, *The Countess of Chesterfield* in 1835 and *Lady Fitzharris* in 1838. It was yet another example of Landseer wasting his time and trivialising his art. The beautiful Lady Blessington herself became something of an Annual-bore. Where her gatherings had previously been purely social, they now often turned into occasions for cadging contributions from her distinguished guests. Some of her literary and artistic friends tended to stay away during the height of the Annual boom. However, Landseer already saw his art partly as a means to a social end anyway—and was apparently quite prepared to ransack his portfolio, as well as to talk and sing, for his supper.

The Countess's esteem for Edwin was apparent in her letters. 'Remember you *promised unconditionally* to come' ran a typical note, 'so no excuses of a previous engagement'. Landseer produced at least one very fine drawing of Lady Blessington, taking account of her beauty without being overawed by it, which showed that had he embarked on a full portrait it might well have stood comparison with the famous one by Lawrence. In 1832 he was commissioned by Margaret to paint a portrait of her handsome hound, a present from

the King of Naples. *Waiting for the Countess* was one of twenty-eight
works by Landseer sold at the auction of Lady Blessington's effects:
also included was a rare proof of *Laying Down the Law before* the
introduction of the Duke of Devonshire's obtrusive dog. The sale had
been precipitated by the pressure of d'Orsay's creditors, who began
using every possible ruse to bring him to book. One day, it is said,
a delivery-man purporting to be from the pastry-cook's with
delicacies for the evening's dinner thus gained access to Gore House.
He was, in fact, a sheriff's officer with a warrant for d'Orsay's arrest.
Laying down his tray of goodies, he quickly proceeded upstairs.
D'Orsay greeted him with customary aplomb and invited the intruder
to sit while he got himself dressed. By taking elaborate care over
every item of his dress and toilet, he managed to spin out the
procedure for an hour and a half. The fascinated bailiff scarcely
noticed the sun sinking slowly in the west, until it was too late.
D'Orsay then calmly reminded him that, as it was now after sunset,
the writ no longer ran; and the chagrined sheriff's officer was conducted to the outer gates. But the dandy's coolness had been very
much assumed. On the following day he fled to France, where Lady
Blessington would shortly join him. Meantime she was left behind to
arrange the sale of what was announced as the 'costly and elegant
effects of the Rt. Honble the Countess of Blessington, retiring to the
continent'. The event was gleefully patronised by several of the
titled hostesses who had been Margaret's most jealous and bitter
rivals. Thackeray was also there, later bemoaning in a letter to a
friend 'a dismal sight—Gore House full of snobs looking at the
furniture. Foul Jews; odious bombazine women; brutes keeping their
hats on in the kind old drawing-room . . .'. 'It was,' he concluded, 'a
strange sad picture of Vanity Fair!'

Yet Landseer had, under d'Orsay's undoubted influence, established himself as a young swell long before the collapse of Gore
House. In 1829 Haydon recorded seeing him 'lounging through Bond
Street on a blood horse, with a white hat, & all the airs of a Man of
Fashion'. Even in art Edwin tended to gravitate towards other
swells. Gilbert Stuart Newton, with whom he had travelled in
Scotland in 1824, was also no stranger to affectation. 'He overflowed
with self-esteem,' in Redgrave's opinion. Landseer and he became
close if rather snobby friends who sometimes considered themselves
too grand to abide by their commitments to other artist-companions.
Constable wrote to Leslie in 1830: 'I missed you by going to see the
Gallery, where I had invited Newton and Landseer to meet you—
neither of whom came—or left any message—and as I class them
with the *nobility* (they have adopted their habits) I sat up till twelve

to receive them'. The Nova Scotian-born Newton, eight years older than Edwin, was a painter of limited power but a fine colourist, who specialised in scenes from Shakespeare, The Vicar of Wakefield and Gil Blas. Among many stories of his vanity was the one quoted by a fellow-artist who was presumptuous enough to point out an odd mistake in one of his pictures. 'Yes,' Newton airily acknowledged, 'it is purposely left so. Every picture should have a fault; this is the one fault in mine.'

Influences like d'Orsay and Newton were heady fare for a young painter as socially impressionable as Edwin. Constable watched his mannered progress with laconic dismay. Though he had two years earlier written of his 'love' for the animal painter, he could not resist a mischievous aside in a letter to Leslie in 1835:

Landseer was at dinner (perfect)—his shirt frills reaching from his *chin* to below his *navel*—his head was decorated with 1000 curls. He has great self-knowledge.

CHAPTER SEVEN

THE NEW PATRONAGE

*I hear that Chalon has £700 from the publisher of a print of his
drawing, what then ought you to have?*
—William Wells in a letter to Edwin Landseer

TWO FACTS were beginning to emerge about Edwin—he was
an artist of exceptional skill and a businessman of almost un-
believable ineptitude. 'You must have given away hundreds
of pounds, Landseer,' was the comment of his fellow-artist Goodall,
referring to the animal painter's bestowal of sketches everywhere,
which in itself threatened to lower the currency of his art. 'He was
always very delicate and shy,' said Lord Tankerville, 'as to the
question of money for his pictures, and got very, very insufficient
prices for his earlier works.' The prices he asked for his paintings
were ludicrously low, and completely at odds with his established
reputation. Occasionally an honest patron would take him to task,
but most were only too pleased to believe in their own good fortune
when Edwin named his price, hastily making out the cheque before
he could change his mind. The whole subject of money embarrassed
him. He therefore relied almost entirely on the generosity and good-
will of his more enlightened patrons. In 1836 he produced for Sir
Francis Chantrey a portrait of the latter's favourite dog Mustard
which was subsequently styled in *Blackwood's Magazine* 'an immortal
picture'. While it was hardly that, it inspired the kind of correspondence all too familiar at the time, with Chantrey adding a characteristic footnote:

> Now, on the score of Money—a delicate question to a high-
> spirited young Dandy who can live on *Air*—I have to request that
> you will do yourself and your profession *justice* without one word
> about friendship—delicacy—or Stuff. *This I insist upon and with
> this you must comply or I no longer remain*
> Your sincerely
F. Chantrey

Mark this, Mister Landseer!

Edwin having named his price, Chantrey was replying in the following week:

> I am more than satisfied that you have produced a picture of my favourite dog Mustard that stands without a *rival*. I always expected that the proper recompensory price would have been at least two hundred guineas—you say one hundred and fifty. The question between us now stands thus—either I must feel obligated to you for 50 Gs or you will feel under obligation to me for the same sum. I remain your Debtor . . .

And a creditor Edwin all too often remained, apparently reluctant to admit that he was a professional painter rather than a gentleman.

Landseer's move to St. John's Wood had effectively removed the artist from his father's control, and for many years he was without a regular mentor in business matters. Besides, John Landseer's deafness, and the increasing eccentricities of behaviour into which it led him, unsuited him for business dealings. He had to carry an ear trumpet, into which acquaintances had to bawl at the tops of their voices. Like so many people immersed in a silent world, he developed the unfortunate habit of thinking aloud. One day, it is said, he called at his son Charles's house in Southampton Street, but found he wasn't in. Since it was raining heavily, the painter Corbould, who lived across the street, invited him into his house. He took Landseer Senior into his studio to show him his work, and there was one picture on the easel which the old man praised highly and continued to stare at. Presently Corbould was treated to an odd soliloquy—'I never saw such damned rubbish in my life. How on earth can he make a living at it? Such a nice, pleasant fellow, too; but can't paint and knows nothing of it . . .!', and so on in the same vein. Corbould, obviously a man of some humour, related the story with great glee to Charles; but others were not so amused. John Landseer's long-standing reputation for speaking his mind was brutally reinforced by his deafness, and he obviously had no place as a negotiator in the world of discretion, diplomacy and fine manners that Edwin imagined he now inhabited.

In the late 'Twenties Landseer was fortunate enough to meet Jacob Bell, who began gradually to act as his business manager, though it was several years later before he was able to exert any real influence on the sale of Edwin's works. Both men were bachelors and became firm friends. They had much in common: even more important, Bell had strengths that were complementary to Edwin's failings. He loved socialising and sport and dogs and horses and art: he was also a small, wiry and combative man who relished a business challenge. His London home at the corner of Cavendish Place and Langham Place was the haunt of writers and artists and pretty women. W. P. Frith (whose *Derby Day* Bell bought) found him 'very useful to me in procuring models. Few people had a more extensive acquaintance, especially among the female sex . . .'. Landseer and Bell both carried the keys to each other's houses. When the portraiturist Lucas and Landseer were returning one day from a meeting of the Artists' General Benevolent Fund, of which they were both committee-members, Edwin suggested they call on Bell, who was not at home. Landseer, however, selected a key from a bunch in his pocket and let them in, helping himself and Lucas to a brandy-and-soda. 'Now I must leave my card,' he then told the portrait-painter, turning one of his own cabinet-sized paintings face to the wall to let his friend know that he had called.

Few businessmen art patrons could have had more unlikely beginnings than Bell, who had been an art-school drop-out; a contemporary of W. P. Frith and Edward (*'Book of Nonsense'*) Lear at Sass's Academy in Bloomsbury, one of the first of the private art schools. Sass was a vain and punctilious man whose habit it was to send pictures of himself to the Royal Academy inscribed *Portrait of a Gentleman*, and whose eventual mental breakdown was announced by a tendency to sit on hats, his own and other people's. His attempts to provide his pupils with a thorough grounding in shapes and forms often resulted in mind-boggling tedium. His most prominent instrument of torture was a large plaster ball over which Frith himself had to labour for six weeks, struggling with the problems of conveying light, shade and rotundity in Italian chalk on white paper. Bell was already well advanced in his documentation of the shape, and had almost earned his reprieve, when his patience finally broke. On one Monday morning, having just watched a public hanging at Newgate, he drew the criminal and his scaffold in the centre of the sacred ball. Unexpectedly Sass appeared in the doorway. There was a pin-dropping silence, after which the professor of art delivered himself of a long peroration, the substance of which was his refusal to harbour Bell any longer—'I should be robbing your father *if I did it*'—and ending on the words, 'You may *leave, sir*!'.

Bell had been raised in a strict Quaker household. At first he had worn the Quaker coat to Sass's, but the other pupils had poked so much cruel fun at him, writing *Quaker* in chalk across his back, that he had abandoned it (much against his father's will) for a more democratic garb. Rebellion was a feature of his early life. He was later expelled from the Quaker community because of his strong objection to segregating the sexes by seating men on one side of the chapel and women on the other. To emphasise the point he dressed himself up as a woman and seated himself one Sunday in the forbidden pews. Being eyed suspiciously, he took fright, finally leaving the chapel with all eyes upon him and a walk which, with each lengthening panic-stricken stride, further belied his femininity.

The indignant Mr. Sass had hardly cast Bell into the outer darkness. Bell senior had a well-doing chemist's shop in Oxford Street, which Jacob proceeded to expand into a large and prosperous business. Later on he became the founder of the Pharmaceutical Society. His interest in art remained strong, but his most valuable contribution to it was as companion, adviser, ministering angel and patron to Landseer. 'His friend Bell took him in hand' said the Earl of Tankerville, 'and got him better prices for his work—thousands instead of fifties and hundreds'. This is generally true, though Bell himself was not entirely unaware of being in a position of privilege where Edwin was concerned. *Dignity and Impudence* became one of the three paintings by which the name of Landseer is today best known, yet Bell paid only £50 for it. To a friend who remonstrated with him, Bell said, 'Do you mean to say that *you* wouldn't have taken the picture for fifty pounds?'. The logic was not immaculate, nor entirely excusable by the fact that Jacob Bell left it to the nation anyway, as he did eighteen other Landseers.

Bell's rigid Quaker father did not at first approve of his son's picture-buying activities, but his subsequent attitude showed that he was perhaps forty-nine per cent Quaker and fifty-one per cent businessman:

> 'What business hast thou to buy those things, my son, wasting thy substance?'
> 'I can sell any of *those things* for more than I gave for them—some for twice as much.'
> 'Is that verily so?' said Bell senior, impressed. 'Then I see no sin in thy buying more.'

Certainly Landseer, so unworldly in money matters, needed someone of Bell's business acumen. The pharmacist worked hard for more than twenty years to secure better prices both for Landseer's pictures and for the engraving rights. However, when Edwin was in the homes of the gentry—eating their food, drinking their wine, shooting their game and feeling unprofessionally obligated to them—there was little Bell could do to help him. Bell also lacked the ability to manage and discipline his client (as John Landseer once had done) and was often too anxious to subscribe to the almost universal practice of flattering Edwin's ego. On one occasion, while the two

men were going through some early pictures of Landseer's, they came
on an unusual portrait, *A Cross of a Dog and a Fox*—the artist had
recorded the result of this freak piece of breeding in 1824 and it had
been published in *Annals of Sporting* in the same year. Landseer
looked at the picture for a moment then threw it with all his strength
through the open window into the garden. He looked at Bell: 'You
may have it if you will take the trouble to fetch it,' he said. Bell
immediately hurried outside to claim the rejected prize. One feels it
might have been better for Edwin's character if the pharmacist had
left the rather mediocre picture where it had lodged in the branches
of a tree.

The balance of patronage was already beginning to shift from the
aristocracy to the *nouveau riche* merchant and business class; and
Edwin was soon painting on a regular basis for the three most powerful of these—William Wells, John Sheepshanks and Robert Vernon.

Sir Walter Scott had secured Edwin the introduction to William
Wells who (Jacob Bell apart) was the non-aristocratic patron with
whom the painter became most closely involved. He was a tough old
bird, having been at one time the skipper of an East India clipper,
before settling down to life as a country squire. He played host to
numerous artists at his fine country home Redleaf, near Tunbridge
Wells, which subsequently became a hotel. His regular guests
included the R.A.s Goodall, Cooke, Lee, Grant and Frith; but Landseer, who had a standing invitation, was the most popular of them all.
Although described by Redgrave as 'a great lover of art and artists',
there was a fiery side to his nature. He was sometimes known as
'Tiger' Wells, partly for the lack of ceremony with which he turned
away parties of people who arrived unexpectedly at his home with
the intention of viewing his collection of paintings. Constable was one
artist who would not have quarrelled with the sobriquet. Wells disliked the great man, finding his own favourite F. R. Lee immeasur-
ably superior as a landscape painter. When Constable once showed
him some of his sketches, his only comment was to note patronisingly
that some of the studies 'might be of service to Lee'. If Constable's
name came up at table it was usually as a pretext for Wellsian wit.
When Jacob Bell told his host that he had 'laid hold of a Constable',
Wells' retort was, 'Much better than a constable laying hold of you!'.
But very little better in Wells' true estimation. After unsuccessfully
wooing the powerful patron (partly through Landseer), Constable
was finally forced bitterly to conclude that 'this most kind and
benevolent Mr. Wells would gladly put the last shovel of earth on my
coffin with his own hands'.

Landseer, however, basked in the old autocrat's favour from the late 1820s onward. Not that he always behaved himself. Wells had the kind of stiffly dignified feathers that Edwin loved to ruffle. He would make a point of requesting beer with his dinner, knowing of Wells' almost obsessive objection to the habit; and his refusal to attend church on Sundays, as every guest was expected to do, annoyed his host even more. But he was always able to provide a panacea to Wells' petulance in the form of a new sketch or painting.

Wells kept at Redleaf a compendium known as The Scribblers' Book, requiring all his artist-guests to contribute at least one sketch to this album, which subsequently ran to two volumes. Although the Book included contributions from Goodall, Frith, Lee, Cooke and Grant, the prime scribbler, both in quality and quantity, was Landseer. One of his most interesting entries was a back view of Turner captured by Edwin one varnishing day on his palette. It showed the great painter in a head-dress he often affected in cold weather, with his head tied up like a pudding in a silk handkerchief and his hat on top of that. So good a likeness was it that his fellow-artists begged Landseer not to clean his palette off. However, someone had the bright idea of pressing a piece of white blotting-paper onto the still moist paint, from which a presentable copy was obtained and sent to Mr. Wells for his Book. There was also a lightning sketch of a man admiring the wares outside a poulterer's shop, which illustrated Landseer's ability to convey a great deal by the simplest means, 'the rows of strung-up geese,' as Manson observed, 'being indicated by a few cunning pen strokes'. Cartoons and caricatures by Landseer proliferated throughout the Scribblers' Book . . . of the poet Samuel Rogers at the opera; of the eccentric-looking violinist Paganini; of fellow-artists like Etty, Abraham Cooper, Chantrey and Jones, who prided himself on being constantly mistaken for the Duke of Wellington. ('That's funny,' was the Duke's acid comment, 'no one ever mistakes me for Mr. Jones!)'.

The hall at Redleaf was also lined with Landseer sketches of game of every description from red deer to snipe. When a particularly fine specimen of a bird fell to the gun, its posture would be carefully preserved by moss and pebbles in order to make a composition for the painter. Frederick Goodall, who often painted in the same room with Edwin at Redleaf, thought that the best sketch Landseer ever made there was of a sheepdog hanging by its neck from a tree, having been found guilty and convicted as a sheep-killer: the ghosts of the sheep the dog has savaged to death surround the dangling corpse 'holding up their feet to him as much as to say, "The day of retribution has come!"'. The morbidity and the sentimentality were by this time equally familiar ingredients in Landseer's work.

Everything Landseer did at Redleaf was virtually consecrated, and the walls of Wells' bedroom were covered only in the artist's pictures. But the works he actually commissioned were the most prized—all the more so in the long run by reason of the anxieties and delays that usually intervened between germination and birth.

Landseer had promised to paint for Mr. Wells a picture of his favourite spaniel, Trim. Wells accordingly appointed a place for the portrait on the door of his bedroom, but the months went by and the place remained unfilled. To Wells' growing annoyance, Landseer seemed to have forgotten his promise. He continued to visit his patron, amusing the other guests with his jokes and anecdotes and perhaps wondering at times why his host looked so piqued and petulent. At length Wells vented his annoyance. Edwin charmingly admitted his remissness but promised, 'I'll come down next Thursday and stay till Monday, and the picture will be done before I leave'. On the Thursday he duly arrived, just in time to dress for dinner. 'It seems I've arrived at the right moment,' he cheerfully announced to his hopeful host. 'Your man tells me you're going to drag the big pond tomorrow. It's something I've always wanted to paint, and I'll be able to get lots of sketches done!' Wells looked baleful but made no comment. On the Friday Landseer, as he had promised, spent the entire day watching and sketching the pond being dragged. On the following morning when he came down to breakfast, Wells looked up hopefully, but his first words were, 'I hear you're shooting the far wood today. It must be packed with game. I'm really looking forward to it!' So off he sent shooting with his frowning host, spending the evening discussing the successes of the day whilst the unpainted Trim snoozed in the firelight at his master's feet.

By the Sunday morning Wells' temper was on the testy side. Landseer had done little except relax and enjoy himself since he came; and now it was time for all the guests to accompany their host to morning service. But Edwin, in his usual flippant way, pleaded 'a terrible headache'. Almost beside himself, Wells tightly absolved Landseer from his religious obligation. 'Do as you think best. You know well enough by this time that this is Liberty Hall—for you at all events!' And he stamped off to church, the remainder of his guests sheepishly following.

When they had gone Landseer went to the room where he already set up his easel and empty canvas. With the gamekeeper holding Trim, the artist set to work. When the house-party returned from church less than three hours later, the picture was painted, finished and hanging in the place of honour long reserved for it on Mr. Wells' bedroom door. It showed Trim life-size with a rabbit in his mouth, and written on the trunk of a tree in the background of the picture were the words, 'To W. Wells, Esq., with the author's respects. Painted by E. Landseer in two hours and a half, Redleaf, August 1831'. Later a servant who saw it shook his head admiringly and remarked, 'The old dog looks like a picture'; and an engraving of the *tour de force* appeared over that title in the *New Sporting Magazine*.

Landseer's tendency to procrastinate was later to be associated with deep nervous strain and unhappiness; but in his early days it was often, as in Trim's case, something to be gloried in; an almost ostentatious display of his rapidity and his adroitness with the brush. Not the least of his pleasure was in the outspoken admiration of his fellow-artists. 'His rapidity of execution was extraordinary' declared Frith; whilst Goodall went even further: 'I suppose no other artist— certainly not in my time—ever painted with such facility or rapidity . . .'.

The mid-Thirties were, in fact, to be the last carefree years of Edwin's life. Even his letters—like this one to his sister Jessy from Redleaf in December of 1836—reflected a gaiety that was later to be in ominously short supply:

> Mr. Wells pudding is so small that I am resolved to quit his home immediately—it is too disgustin that a man of his benevolent character and good property should presume to make a diminutive Xmas Pudding—and another thing has made me very unhappy, he has been guilty of coughing in church. This, and spitting in the Porch, can never be received in Heaven as the Compliments of Season. 'To err is human to forgive divine' . . . These are heavy charges for a man his age who ought to set a good example to the poor. The All Powerful Being to whom we all acknowledge our sins will I trust be to his faults a little blind—as Redleaf is so pretty and we have had several bottles of *mulled* Wine. However, till he clears up his Pudding crime, I think it is prudent to leave him and shall be home tomorrow evening.

John Sheepshanks was a rather different kind of patron from Mr. Wells. He was the son of Joseph Sheepshanks, a Leeds clothier, who had left him a fortune. As a prosperous sleeping partner in the firm, he moved to Bond Street, and thence (about 1833) to a mansion in Blackheath, where he cultivated roses and collected antiquarian books. He had begun by collecting the Italian masters but, perhaps put off by the fact that the production of old Italian masterpieces had remained a thriving cottage industry, he turned to modern British painters like Turner, Constable, Wilkie, Leslie, Mulready, Callcott and Landseer. He always retained his strong Yorkshire accent and never married—'Is there a lady in the world who would care to be called Mrs. Sheepshanks?', he would ask, either with undue faintheartedness or excessive guile. Although parsimonious towards himself, boasting that his personal expenses including bus fares amounted to only £2. 0. 6d. per annum, he was, according to Redgrave, 'liberal to excess to others'. The others included his servants who dined regularly on turkey, of which their master was sometimes grateful to have the leavings. Nonetheless he kept a fine cellar and it was a familiar sight at the close of a Wednesday evening to see the diminutive Sheepshanks arm-in-arm with one or more of his departing guests reeling across the heath until brought down by a sudden dip in the ground. Picking each other up, the guests would then solicitiously make it their business to see Mr. Sheepshanks safely home again. Sheepshanks, in turn, would once again insist on seeing his guests on their way . . . until, once again, they would all roll down some unexpected hollow. Then the guests must see their convivial host back to his doorway . . . and so on, in a kind of inebriated attempt at perpetual motion.

Landseer was one of the select body of artists and engravers who had a standing invitation to those Wednesday gatherings, and no doubt took part in the Blackheath Stumble. Several less favoured painters purported to find Sheepshanks something of a cultural snob. C. W. Cope, invited to view his collection of rare etchings, was of the opinion that 'he seemed to me to value them more for their rarity than for their merit'. Calling on him one day for his money, the landscape painter Linnell was hurriedly ushered into an ante-room from which he could hear the convivial clatter of knives and forks. 'I can't take you in there,' Sheepshanks explained, 'because I have got some R.A.s at dinner.' Being so small, he was equally in awe of physical strength; and his patronage of Mulready dated from the time when the burly Irish painter used his fists to disperse a band of 'rough fellows' who had set on Sheepshanks in the street.

The Yorkshireman, however, can hardly have been said to be 'liberal in excess' to Landseer. He was a supreme opportunist where paintings were concerned. One of his most successful purchases underlined the manner in which the businessman patron was taking over from the aristocracy. This was Landseer's famous painting of *The Highland Drovers' Departure* which the Duke of Bedford had commissioned for £500. Since the good Duke was in 1837 undergoing one of his occasional remorses of conscience about his over-spending, he expressed his willingness to forgo 'so beautiful a work' if Landseer could find an alternative purchaser. Sheepshanks stepped eagerly into the breach. Other fine Landseer paintings like *Jack in Office*,

The Old Shepherd's Chief Mourner and *The Tethered Rams* were bought by the Leeds clothier for prices described by the (admittedly affluent) W. P. Frith as 'ludicrously small'. Clearly Sheepshanks was one of those who took full advantage of Edwin's embarrassment over money, and his tendency to price his work too low. 'Well,' declared Sheepshanks defensively, 'I always pay what is asked for a picture or I don't buy it at all—never beat a man down and never will.' On the other hand, he was a genuine collector; not a speculator. 'Never sold a picture and I never will!' He was as good as his dour word, leaving 233 pictures and 289 drawings to the nation in 1857, six years before his death. But the nation's gain had been partly Landseer's loss.

Robert Vernon, unlike Wells and Sheepshanks, was born poor. He was, in fact, a horse dealer who had made a well-timed fortune from contracting to supply equine cannon fodder to the Napoleonic wars. He was as shrewd an assessor of a painting as he was of a horse, relying on no one's judgement but his own and rationing himself as much as possible to only one picture a year from each of his 'stable' of favourite artists. He weeded out and sold pictures, not for profit (which he did not need) but in order to replace an artist's existing works with better ones, his intention being to leave his collection to the nation. Vernon was not always a popular man. The painter J. C. Horsley found him 'the complete jobber by nature as well as by trade'. Having once paid the modest sum of £50 for a Horsley painting, he insisted on deducting £5, the cost of the frame, because he didn't like the one Horsley had suppled. Horsley also alleged that Vernon habitually tried to reduce guineas to pounds—perhaps only another way of saying that artists always tried to raise pounds to guineas. Many artists, including Maclise, found him a boring host whose interest in art was merely snobbish and assumed; but Landseer was a frequent guest at Ardington House near Wantage in Berkshire and at his large townhouse in Pall Mall where he had his gallery. Like Wells, Vernon preserved even Landseer's trifles with reverence. On one occasion, while watching a game of billiards in the hall at Ardington, Edwin decided to amuse himself by drawing in chalk the life-size head of a stag on the black scoring-board that screened the fireplace. Vernon not only refused to allow the board to return to its former place, but had a sheet of glass sent for with which to protect it. Sometimes the old horse-dealer's enthusiasm for Landseer's work had less fortunate consequences. When a rare heron was shot at Ardington, he at once ordered the bird parcelled-up and sent to St. John's Wood as the basis of a picture commission. But Landseer was in Scotland at the time, and sharing himself out among his numerous

Highland hosts. For more than a fortnight the package followed the painter from place to place. When it finally reached him it was in a state of total decomposed unapproachability. Vernon donated his collection of paintings to the nation in 1847, two years before he died.

One can imagine with what feelings of patriotic pride, Vernon, Bell and Sheepshanks left their precious Landseers to be freely enjoyed by all the people. After all, the painter then was, as someone later said, 'the one great artistic fact of his time'. His patrons could hardly have foreseen the swing in artistic and critical taste that would consign most of their treasures to the storage vaults of the main London galleries.

CHAPTER EIGHT

THE DOG YEARS

Not a dog in London but knows him.

—The Mask

FOR CONVENIENCE sake some commentators have divided Landseer's artistic life subjectively into three sections—his dog phase, followed by his stag phase and culminating in his lion period. It is a woeful over-simplification, though with a certain truth. By the age of forty most of the best-known dog paintings were behind him, and most of the famous deer studies lay ahead. Yet dogs always occupied pride of place both in his art and in his life.

Throughout his life, in fact, Edwin became a kind of unofficial Minister without Portfolio of dogs. He was consulted on every aspect of their upbringing, training and feeding: he was sometimes assumed to have veterinary knowledge of them. Humane societies requested his help as an expert witness in cases of dog cruelty. He campaigned (though hardly to the point of self-sacrifice) against the ugly practice of cropping dogs' ears, as James Ward had against the docking of horses' tails: 'Animals who dig in the earth should have their ears protected as nature has provided' he sensibly declared. He spoke equally hotly against the practice of chaining up dogs for long periods. He even had a reputation as a dog-psychiatrist—though Millais later instanced one of his less successful cures when Edwin approached on all fours a notoriously savage dog tied up in a yard and snarled so convincingly that the terrified animal snapped his chain, jumped the wall, ran off howling and was never seen again. Often, however, when a pet dog went missing he was the first to be consulted as to its possible recovery. Certainly he knew many of the dog-thieves and shady dealers who operated in London at the time when dog-stealing was a prosperous minor industry.

On one occasion, according to C. S. Mann, Landseer had procrastinated for several months in characteristic fashion over painting a dog belonging to his patron, William Wells. 'Too late,' said Wells when Landseer finally declared his readiness to paint the animal, 'I've lost him.'

'Probably stolen,' was the painter's expert diagnosis. 'Will you give me the commission if I recover him for you?'

'Gladly,' said Wells.

Landseer then paid a call on a well-known 'dog fancier' of his acquaintance, carefully described his patron's pet and told the man he would be well rewarded if he managed to make the missing animal materialise.

'Black and tan, sir; wi' very long ears, large eyes,' mused the dog fancier. 'I've seed that dog somewhere, I swear! I daresay I could have him for you in a fortnight.'

'But I must have him in forty-eight hours' protested Landseer.

The dog fancier shook his head. 'Can't be done in that time, sir.'

'All right,' said the painter, 'bring him as soon as you can.'

At the end of a fortnight the dog fancier duly appeared complete with the missing dog. Landseer was delighted, but puzzled. 'Why couldn't you have brought him before?' he asked.

The dog fancier shuffled his feet. 'Well, sir, you're an old friend and won't peach; but the fact were, *I* stole the dog. But I sold it to a trump of an old lady in Portland Place for such a howdacious good sum, I felt it wouldn't be right not to let her enjoy it for at least a fortnight.'

'Not a dog in London but knows him,' declared the *Mask* in a potted biography which had Landseer's birthplace as 'most probably near the *Isle of Dogs*', going on to record the youthful artist's '*dogged* determination to outstrip all competitors in the *canine* race' and much else in the same varicose vein. Another publication, the *Amulet*, put the same thoughts into rhyme:

> I've known full many a painter in my time
> Of many an age and many a school and clime;
>> But, Sir, I never knew
>> Such a dog-fancier as you.
> What Rubens was to lions, Cuyp to cows
>> Morland to sows and hogs
>>> You are to dogs.
>
> There's not a dog but owes you more, I trow
>> Than e'er he owed his pa
>> Or his dog-ma
>> And not a cur that meets
>> You in the streets
> But ought to make you a profound bow-
>>> Wow!

Ending on the apology, no less excruciating for being inevitable:

Excuse these doggerel rhymes, my dear
Landseer.

To Lady Richmond Ritchie Landseer's power over dogs was 'mes-
meric'. She recalled on one visit to St. John's Wood a servant opening a door and three or four dogs bounding in, 'one a very fierce-
looking mastiff. We ladies recoiled, but there was no fear; the creature bounded up to Landseer, treated him like an old friend, with
most expansive demonstrations of delight. Some one remarking
"how fond the dog seemed of him," he said, "I never saw it before in
my life".' Goodall remembered on a visit to Redleaf Landseer
bringing a fine retriever 'which used to go out, through the woods
with us in the afternoon and evening. I saw Landseer take off his
glove and put it in the fork of a tree whilst the retriever was running
about. But after we had gone a few hundred yards he showed the
dog that he had only one glove; and without the slightest hesitation
the creature ran back, and in a few minutes brought the glove in his
mouth'. It is also related that when a lady asked him how he had
gained such knowledge of dogs and such power over them, he replied,
'By peeping into their hearts, Ma'am'.

The heart-specialist was always surrounded by a covey of dogs. He
is said to have been so shattered by the death of his rough white
terrier Brutus that he thereafter sought safety from heartbreak in
numbers. Brutus had been the ideal boy's dog—adventurous and
aggressive, yet loyal and affectionate. Edwin's response to this
loyalty was obvious in the number of early compositions of which
Brutus was the hero. Whatever his sagacity, Brutus had few claims
either to breeding or beauty. Some commentators have remarked on
the rather undistinguished nature of Edwin's later troop of dogs which
were, of course, sometimes creatures of illustrious lineage and great
refinement with the brain-pans bred out of them (a feature not without its parallels among his human companions). His Scottish sheepdog Lassie was a favourite model of later years; and Mrs. Adams-
Acton talked of a valuable dog called Brechin who met with a sad
end when a thoughtless hanger-about at the seaside threw an old tin
can into the choppy waters: Brechin went after it and seized it in his
mouth, but with his nose inside it could not see where he was going,
swam out to sea instead of in to shore and was lost in the turbulent
waves. 'Sir Edwin,' it was said, 'went home in a state of distress he
said had never been equalled all his life.' While sympathising with
Landseer's distress, one cannot help speculating that the rough-bred
Brutus could never have done anything quite so stupid.

Of other people's dogs Landseer sketched and painted hundreds.

So many titled and wealthy ladies and gentlemen clamoured to have their pets immortalised by him that the waiting-time for a sitting, a standing or a begging was usually between two and three years. Knowing his love of dogs, the ladies especially would try to tempt and cajole him with their paragons of canine virtue. One letter from the Duchess of Beaufort, writing from Badminton, was typical of many:

> I think if you knew what a beautiful little dog I have got you would come any distance to see it—She throws Dash quite in the shade. Such paws were never seen before, and she is the most amiable of her sex besides.

Edwin's misplaced gallantry, his obliging nature and the pressure of too many commissions all combined to produce canine portraits that owed more to the owner's adoring eye than to Landseer's own. Hair was sometimes improbably trim or impossibly silky: worse still, he began to capitalise heavily on the knowing or the mistily adoring look, the quaintly angled head, the cute begging pose, the excessively highlit eye. His larger dogs especially could suggest such an infinity of sagacity, tolerance, understanding, common sense, loyalty and sheer decency as to put mere humans to shame.

In fairness to Landseer, it must be remembered that dogs actually *are* quasi-human. They live with humans and are expected and encouraged to fill human roles—the staunch protector, the playmate, the helpless child, the faithful friend and many more. They are taught to respect human codes of conduct and hygiene: there are human taboos on where and when they may relieve themselves, clean their private parts, make love and so on. If they had hands they would undoubtedly be required to use knife, fork, spoon and napkin. They themselves quickly learn the value of the knowing look, the forlorn expression, the paw on the knee, the begging posture. Landseer, in many instances, only had to draw and paint what he saw. *Dignity and Impudence*, often quoted against him, is no other than the popular Sunday newspaper doggie photograph of our own day—so were the absurdly dressed-up tykes of *Comical Dogs*. Though they deliberately exploited quaintness, they did not falsify expression: they were, however, the forerunners of the insufferably cute newspaper photographs showing a litter of puppies or kittens suspended inside a row of socks on a washing-line. The dogs of *Laying Down the Law*, *Jack in Office* and *Hector and Diogenes* certainly went beyond the bounds of credibility in their portrayal of canine expression; but these were attempts at satire, a genre in which Landseer remained conspicuously unsuccessful, being always more concerned with form than with content. Nevertheless, the painter was far from guiltless. *Uncle Tom and His Wife for Sale,* like his earlier dead drake study *The Widow,* exalted animals to the state of marriage partners, with tearful expressions to match. *'Good Doggie',* a picture of a dog at prayer, showed the extremes to which Landseer was at times prepared to take his quasi-humanising: this pious pomeranian was owned by Lady Murchison and coyly described in Frank Buckland's *Memoir* of her as 'the well-known inhabitant of Belgrave Square'. It was shown at the Royal Academy, which seemed to indicate that the painter himself took it seriously. Few of his dog portraits were, however, as excessive as *'Good Doggie';* and the 'Thirties saw a succession of canine studies many of which redound to his credit today.

His *Jack in Office* of 1833 attracted great popularity as an engraving, and is probably vaguely familiar from attics and junk shops to most people over fifty. It showed a smug and plump white terrier guarding the viands on its master's cat's and dog's meat barrow, whilst four other miserable tykes cringe, skulk and sniff hopelessly around it: one is a wretched starveling bitch, another automatically begs. In fact, the canine vulgarian on the barrow bore a complete resemblance to the butcher's dog of *Low Life;* and it is plain, as Ruskin testified, that the hungry tykes can expect no sympathy from their overfed brother. If the picture's intention is satirical, it could only convey the juxtaposition of *nouveau riche* and poor; the inference perhaps that the last people the poor can expect largesse from are those recently risen from the ranks themselves. But that may be taking it too far. It is a satisfactory, if rather obviously composed picture, with the meat-peddler's dog as king-of-the-castle; yet even today there is more to admire in it than to deplore.

It the same year Edwin showed his last (and posthumous) portrait of Sir Walter Scott, who had died the year before. The novelist's dogs were prominently featured, among them the giant deerhound Maida and his terriers Ginger and Spice, both said to be Dandie Dinmonts. Called *Sir Walter Scott in the Rhymer's Glen,* it was a full-length portrait, nostalgically commissioned by Scott's admiring friend, Mr. Wells of Redleaf.

In 1834 Landseer produced another much praised dog portrait in *Suspense,* shown at the British Gallery. In effect, it was the portrait of a seated bloodhound, but invested with an air of drama. The dog's attention is fixed on a closed door; a gout of blood on the floor and a plume fallen from a cavalier's hat, indicate that his badly wounded master has been carried into the next room. Unlike so many of Landseer's works, it achieved its effect by simplicity. The single figure of the dog dominates the canvas, yet with a few subtle touches the painter has added a period and a story, Even so, he obviously left too much to certain imaginations. In Richard Redgrave's interpretation of the picture the discarded plume became 'torn locks of hair, and the gouts of blood upon the floor make us sure that the murderer is within, and that the waiting bloodhound has tracked the villain and his victim to the hiding place'. Even allowing for the vagaries of imaginative interpretation, the picture remained a minor triumph in animal art.

The Sleeping Bloodhound of the following year was another that attracted much interest. The bloodhound Countess had belonged to Jacob Bell and was in fact not sleeping, but either dead or dying. It was the bloodhound's custom to wait for Bell on a balcony at his Putney home if he was late in returning. One evening, hearing the wheels of her master's carriage on the driveway, she leapt up in excitement, missed her footing and fell twenty-three feet to the ground below. When Bell reached the hound, its tail feebly wagging in recognition, the animal was apparently near to death. The druggist, determined to preserve the memory of his favourite, allegedly placed Countess forthwith in his dog-cart and drove straight back across the river, abruptly waking Landseer from his slumbers. Edwin, who had at first been annoyed by this gross interruption, had almost immediately warmed to the challenge, making a rapid sketch of the dying animal (which he had already been promising to paint for almost three years anyway). Algernon Graves' version of the story, however, differs slightly from that of F. G. Stephens. Countess, he avers, died in the course of the night and Bell waited until morning before taking her to St. John's Wood—a rather more likely account. The interruption of Landseer at his labours was still, technically, an offence; but Landseer had apparently abandoned the canvas on which he was working. 'This is an opportunity not to be lost,' he told Bell. 'Go away, and come back at two o'clock on Thursday.' It was then Monday midday and in fact the fine 3′ 3″ by 4′ 1″ canvas *was* completed in less than three days.

Another accomplished bloodhound portrait, the head of *Odin*, was also widely quoted in testimony of Landseer's rapidity of execution. It was finished in two hours, standing comparison as a record-breaker with the famous picture of William Wells' favourite spaniel and with another life-size portrait head and shoulders of a fallow deer, also completed during a Sunday morning visit to Penshurst church by the more pious of Wells' weekend guests. *The* record oil, however, was apparently one of *Rabbits*, on the back of which was Landseer's proud inscription, 'Painted in three quarters of an hour'.

To 1836 also belonged a picture of Sir Francis Chantrey's dog, *Mustard, Son of Pepper*, which collected great praise at the time; but whose main interest seems to have been as the celebration of a unique event—the two dead woodcocks in the picture had been bagged by Chantrey with a single shot (ballistically, no doubt, the equivalent of a hole-in-one).

The Old Shepherd's Chief Mourner, shown at the Royal Academy in the following year and now in the Victoria and Albert Museum, was in some ways Landseer's crowning achievement in canine subject-pictures. The chief mourner was, of course, the dead shepherd's dog. For once Ruskin's praise was loud and lavish. It struck the great critic as being 'one of the most perfect poems or pictures . . . that modern times have seen'. He then went on to detail its good points in tones of rhapsodic inaccuracy:

> Here the exquisite execution of the glossy and crisp hair of the dog, the bright, sharp touching of the green bough beside it, the clear painting of the wood of the coffin and the folds of the blanket, are language—language clear and expressive in the highest degree. But the close pressure of the dog's breast against the wood (*its breast is against the blanket*); the convulsive clinging of the paws, which has dragged the blanket off the trestle (*the blanket is on the coffin, not the trestle*); the total powerlessness of the head, laid close and motionless upon its folds; the fixed and tearful fall of the eye in its utter hopelessness; the rigidity of repose, which marks that there has been no motion nor change in the trance of agony since the last blow was struck upon the coffin-lid (*if the dog had not moved, how could he have 'dragged the blanket off'?*); the quietness and gloom of the chamber; the spectacles marking the place where the Bible was last closed (*the dead man's glasses are on top of the Bible*), indicating how lonely has been the life, how unwatched the departure, of him who is now laid solitary in his sleep: these are all thoughts—thoughts by which the picture is separated at once from hundreds of equal merit, as far as the mere painting goes—by which it ranks as a work of high merit, and stamps its author, not as the neat imitator of the texture of a skin or the fold of a drapery, but as a Man of Mind.

Despite the fact that Ruskin had apparently left his notebook at home while viewing the picture, the praise was richly deserved. It is no surprise that the drawing of the dog was masterly; but the composition, too, is excellent, the other ingredients of the picture (the few pieces of furniture and knick-knacks) exactly complementary, truthful, never intrusive. Its companion, *The Shepherd's Grave*, painted in the same year, was predictably less successful: Ruskin's 'perfect poem or picture' had perhaps been too complete and satisfactory to allow of more than one bite at that particular cherry. Faithful even *beyond* death had long been an obsessive theme with Landseer. In 1830 he had shown his *Attachment* at the Royal Academy, based on the true incident of a young man who had fallen from a precipice of the Helvellyn Mountain in Wales. His remains had not been found for three months—still guarded by his faithful terrier bitch. The fact that the incident had occurred in 1803 showed how deeply it had become imprinted in Edwin's mind. It was a theme that would find a strongly responsive chord in the Victorian consciousness, as witness Edinburgh's statue to the memory of Greyfriars Bobby, a true-life legend for which Landseer's pictures had sentimentally paved the way.

In the following year one of Landseer's Academy exhibits showed something of the human reciprocation of this dogged loyalty in '*The Life's in the Old Dog Yet!*'. A hunted deer has cast itself over a cliff onto a narrow ledge below: two deerhounds have, in the heat of the chase, followed it, one of them paying for its boldness with its life. A gillie has been lowered by rope to the ledge, where he cradles the other dog's head in his lap and shouts to the unseen stalkers above the advice that gave the picture its title. It was a strong, vigorous, beautifully-drawn and boldly-coloured composition. A favourite story surrounding the picture was that, when shown some twenty years later at the Art Treasures Exhibition in Manchester, an elderly viewer confused the number and title in his catalogue of an adjacent picture of *Lear Disinheriting Cordelia* with those of '*The Life's in the Old Dog Yet!*'. 'So there is, *to be sure!*' the old man was heard to mutter, peering in fascination at the Shakespearian picture. On the occasion of the same exhibition, according to some, a strange nemesis seemed to be stalking the picture. Its owner, Mr. Henry McConnell, for whom it had been originally commissioned, had a curious prejudice against railways and would only consent to lend the picture on condition that it was transported to Manchester by road. However, on its return journey, the horse-van containing it was struck by a train on a level-crossing: it was believed at the time that the painting was irreparably damaged, a portion of the canvas having allegedly been caught by and wound around one of the wheels of the engine. Algernon Graves, however, threw a characteristic dash of cold-water over the colourful story, insisting that he had afterwards examined the painting and could not 'believe that it was ever smashed'. 'As an art expert,' he added with due modesty, ' . . . I should have discovered some damages when looking for them.' Although Landseer went to some trouble to emphasise his title, '*The Life's in the Old Dog Yet!*', a reasonably colloquial line of speech, the picture was almost invariably dubbed, '*There's Life in the Old Dog Yet!*', and the painter accused of coy titling. Although in that particular instance his critics were marginally more guilty than he was, another exhibit of the same year proved that he still clung to his belief in the sentimental title. His impressive painting of hinds in a craggy Highland landscape gathered about the rutting stags as the two clash on a cliff-edge for supremacy was dimplingly named, '*None but the Brave deserve the Fair*'.

A Distinguished Member of the Humane Society of the same year was another offering much less undistinguished than its inflated title suggests. The *Distinguished Member* was a large Newfoundland dog called Paul Pry. Landseer had been much impressed by its beauty when he first saw it at home carrying a basket of gaily-coloured flowers in its mouth. Its owner readily gave the artist permission to paint the dog. Landseer received a mere £80 for the picture, a beggarly return for a canine portrait into which the painter was said to have breathed 'Promethean fire'. The engraving, which was dedicated to the Royal Humane Society, became immensely popular. The stately Paul Pry lounged for his portrait on a table in Edwin's St. John's Wood studio. In the painting the table-top became a quayside, against which the green water ominously laps. There was a subtly-painted mooring-ring set in the stones which caused Landseer temporarily to fall-out with his friend, the banker-poet Samuel Rogers. Rogers had brought some ladies to see the newly-completed picture and Edwin, in the room adjoining the studio, overheard him say, 'The same old story! But the ring's good; yes, the ring's good!'. The next morning Landseer was invited to one of the poet's famous eleven o'clock breakfasts, where Rogers was fulsome in his praise of the picture. 'You didn't say so yesterday,' Landseer rapped. 'Why don't you stick to the rusty ring?'

Edwin was able to take his revenge on Rogers, a man of remarkable ugliness, in caricatures like the one of the poet confronting a monkey with every sign of brotherly recognition, and another of him in his bath scrubbing his back. The unfortunate Rogers was seldom allowed to forget his lack of beauty. Sydney Smith gravely offended him by suggesting that the only way he could possibly sit for his projected portrait was with both hands covering his face in an attitude of prayer. It was alleged that Landseer had wanted to paint a portrait of Smith, to which the witty cleric had replied (paraphrasing the words of King Hazael) 'Is thy servant a dog that he should do this thing?'. In fact, the *bon mot* had been fathered by the press; and Smith, meeting Landseer in the park, greeted him with, 'Have you seen our little joke in the papers?'. 'Are you disposed to acknowledge it?' Landseer asked. 'I see no objection,' said the preacher, whose nose for harmless publicity was as keen as the painter's. Edwin's speculative portrait of the Smith of Smith's might well have been a good one, judging from his pen-and-wash caricatures which captured all the famous clergyman's twinkling humour and forthright independence of mind. Among the other cognoscenti who gathered at Rogers' breakfasts were Lady Caroline Norton, Thomas Moore and the somewhat pedantic Macauley, described by the banker-poet as 'a book in breeches'. No doubt Landseer found a wit and literary interest there that was missing from some of his more aristocratic stopping-places.

Dignity and Impudence, first shown at the British Institution under the title of *Dogs*, became one of the pictures by which Landseer's name is best remembered. Its market value, which would have been considerable, has never been tested, since it was bought by Jacob Bell for a mere £50 and left by him to the nation. (It is now in the Tate Gallery.) The two familiar dogs are the terrier Scratch and the bloodhound Grafton. The story goes that the owner of an extremely pretty poodle bet Scratch's male owner an embroidered waistcoat against a dozen pairs of gloves that her dog was the more attractive of the two, the wager to be decided by Landseer's spontaneous reaction on the following day when he saw both dogs. Next day the poodle struck all its most quaint attitudes and performed all its most engaging tricks virtually unnoticed by the great animal painter; but when he went to the stables and clapped eyes on Scratch his first words were, 'Oh, what a beauty!'. 'Fairly won,' declared the sporting owner of the rejected poodle, and on the following day the owner of *Impudence* was to be seen in a fine new embroidered waistcoat.

The bloodhound Grafton which often posed for painters and sculptors, and which belonged to Jacob Bell, subsequently suffered a serious *loss* of dignity. He and another dog, Hafed, had been locked together in a stable overnight. 'On the following morning' wrote Bell to Landseer, 'they were found at opposite corners of the stable crouching on the ground looking very foolish—blood was spattered on the straw and on the walls to a height of 5 feet 2 inches.' Hafed was 'much injured': Grafton, considered the aggressor, was also in a bad way; and for his sins left to die on the straw. However, he recovered, having earned himself only a conditional reprieve. 'In future Grafton shall wear a muzzle & unless he is very careful how he behaves I will shoot him.'

In common with several other Landseer paintings, *Dignity and Impudence* became the basis of various political cartoons, the best-known of which was featured in *Punch* about fifty years after the picture first appeared. It showed the Prime Minister Disraeli as *Dignity* and the Irish-American playwright Dion Boucicault, who had been presumptuous enough to write Disraeli requesting free pardon for some Fenian prisoners, as *Impudence*. Political caricature is perhaps the final accolade—the acknowledgement that a painting has passed into the visual equivalent of the language. On this basis *Dignity and Impudence*, *The Monarch of the Glen* and *The Stag at Bay* are Landseer's three best-known paintings—their groupings instantly recognisable. Among many cartoons based on *The Monarch of the Glen* was one in 1880 showing Gladstone as Landseer's slightly narcissistic-looking stag, his antlers being represented as the Bills the great man had forced through Parliament. *The Stag at Bay* was the frequent choice of political cartoonists, even as recently as 1974 in *The Daily Telegraph* with the beleagured stag representing British Industry, Harold Wilson the hound who has perished in the struggle and Mr. Wedgwood Benn, tail-waggingly confident of triumphing over every problem. Another obvious candidate was the dramatic stag picture, *The Challenge*, in one representation showing the proud but ageing Disraeli being challenged by up-start back-bencher stags, full of the vigour and insolence of youth. The lesser-known pictures, of course, belonged more closely to their own era. *The Tethered Rams* was a painting much admired at the time (1839) for its fine handling of the texture of the sheeps' coats. Seven years later it, too, inspired a famous *Punch* cartoon, *The Tethered Minister*, with the Premier Sir Robert Peel as the tied-up ram and Wellington and Lord John Russell as his sheepdogs. Lord John was fated to appear in other Landseer-inspired cartoons, including *A Jack in Office*, in which Georgiana's youngest stepson (Prime Minister between 1846 and 1852 and again in 1865–66) appeared as the smug and uncaring dog on the barrow. Wellington also figured prominently in such pastiches, particularly by virtue of the resemblance of his proboscis to the beak of Victoria's favourite parrot.

By the late 'Thirties Landseer had virtually achieved canonisation as a painter of dogs. Even a usually measured critic like P. G. Hamerton would later suggest that the dog pictures were above and beyond normal criticism and somehow dependent more on a canine than a human yardstick: 'The best commentators on Landseer, the best defenders of his genius, are the dogs themselves; and so long as there exist terriers, deerhounds, bloodhounds, his fame will need little assistance from writers upon art'. The *Athenaeum* was no less prone to critical exaggeration: 'He could draw a hair on a blank sheet of paper and one would know from what sort of dog it was taken—it would be a story in itself'.

As a young man, therefore, Edwin feared few critics who walked
on two legs. The age was proud to have fathered such an animal
artist; not just a masterly painter but (unlike so many of those scrofu-
lous daubers) an attractive, well-mannered, witty and engaging
human being. He had also proved himself accomplished both in portraiture and landscape, and there seemed few limits to his talent. The
only considerable businessmen-collectors of the time, Wells, Sheepshanks and Vernon, were all three his admiring friends and patrons.
The weekend-invitations rolled-in from the great houses: the Highlands claimed him once, sometimes twice, a year. To the nobility, for
whom every occupation was a part-time one, he presented the right
image of an amusing companion and an occasional painter—an
impression he did his best to perpetuate by his offhand attitude to
fees and his eagerness to be in on every social and sporting occasion.
Occasionally some one like his old patron William Wells, who knew
from his days on the clipper-ships what hard graft was, would en-
deavour to take him to task:

> In one of your letters to him (Lee) you confess that you had not
> done much more (at the Doune) than amuse yourself, therefore
> turn to and work hard, and to do that you must rise early for the
> days are now nothing in duration for an artist, at 3 o'clock the
> light is inadequate and gone by 4.

One can imagine Landseer smiling wryly at the advice: it was already his custom not to rise before noon—unless, of course, for a bird-
shoot or a deer-stalk. But a later reference in Wells' letter was no
doubt more thoughtfully received:

> I long to hear of your commencing with our Sovereign Lady the
> Queen.

CHAPTER NINE

'GENTLEMEN, THE QUEEN!'

He is an unassuming, pleasing and very good-looking man, with fair hair.
—Queen Victoria's opinion of the 35-year-old Landseer

BY HIS mid-thirties Edwin had acquired a clientele to make him the envy of any British artist. His patrons and sitters had already included the Russell, Abercorn and Gordon families, the Dukes of Aberdeen, Argyll, Atholl and Devonshire, the Earl of Tankerville, the Countess of Blessington, Lady Fitzharris and Lady Constance Grosvenor; not forgetting a number of rather more self-made luminaries such as Wellington, Sir Walter Scott and Lord Melbourne. Cynics might have been excused for thinking that he seemed to be graduating purposefully towards the future Queen herself.

In 1835 the portals of royal privilege finally edged open when he painted *Prince George's Favourites*, the white pony Selim, the Newfoundland dog Nelson and the spaniel Flora. The Duchess of Kent looked on with evident interest. Her own favourite dog was little Dash, a King Charles Spaniel, that had been the companion of her daughter, Princess Victoria, since 1833. In 1836, when the Princess was 17, her mother gave her an oil on panel portrait of the dog, partly no doubt as a reward for diligence. 'After my lesson,' she wrote in her diary, 'Mamma gave me a portrait of Dear Dash's head, the size of life, most beautifully painted by Edwin Landseer. It is extremely like'. The girl, in fact, seemed to be almost besotted by her *Dear little Dasby*, even on that day which was ostensibly one of the two most important in her life, her Coronation. As C. R. Leslie wrote in a letter to his sister on the 24th of July, 1837:

She (Victoria) is very fond of dogs and has one very favourite little spaniel, who is always on the look-out for her return when she has been from home. She had of course been separated from him on that day longer than usual, and when the state coach drove up to the steps of the palace, she heard him barking with joy in the hall, and exclaimed 'There's Dash!', and was in a hurry to lay aside the sceptre and ball she carried in her hands, and take off her crown and robes *to go and wash little Dash.*

Such a four-footed paragon clearly demanded further artistic attention, and four months later the new Queen was writing in her diary:

> Saw Lord Conyngham and Edwin Landseer, who brought a beautiful little sketch which he has done this morning, of a picture he is to paint for me of Hector and Dash. He is an unassuming, pleasing and very good-looking man, with fair hair.

Edwin's lack of assumption was not something that had impressed everyone he met; but a queen was a queen, and his relationship with her remained on the whole that of a humble and extremely loyal subject. When she became engaged to Albert, Victoria insisted that Landseer paint her portrait as an engagement present for her German fiancé. The oil sketch Edwin produced in 1839 was slight enough: it played extremely safe and was pleasing (*pleasing* and *not pleasing* would become the new Queen's main expressions of artistic criticism). Victoria, however, was neither very beautiful nor very vain, and she at first paid court to Landseer mainly as the immortaliser of her favourite pets.

Dogs, of course, were to occupy a significant place in Victorian society, providing a much-needed outlet for sentimentality. It became the age of astringent morality—supporting hundreds of thousands of prostitutes; the age of prosperity—a prosperity based largely on sweated labour and the exploitation of faceless coloured peoples. The facade of cosy sentiment was a dire necessity.

Children, pictorially and otherwise, might have answered the cloying need; but the Victorian attitude to children was ambiguous. True, a certain amount of popular painting was based on the angelic —conversely, on the excessively naughty—child. Most parents, however, subscribed to the theory that sparing rods meant spoiling children, who should also be seen and not heard. Victoria and Albert if they did not altogether set the pattern certainly were very effective in sustaining it. Albert's severity towards his eldest son was to produce a classic psychological reaction—but that was still in the future. Though she later became a doting child-lover, the younger Victoria could be notoriously short of patience where babies and infants were concerned. Pregnancy she described as 'the darker side of marriage'; when she found herself with child for the second time she celebrated the discovery by dashing a cup of tea in Albert's face. She talked with disgust of 'that terrible froglike action' of babies, nor was she above describing another woman's darling as 'a very nasty object'. Her attitude had at least a certain amount of consistency in a society where many of her subjects of five and six years old were employed 600 feet below the surface opening and closing shaft doors and pushing trucks along mine tunnels three feet high—where, in the year before she came to the throne, 38 children under thirteen and 62 under eighteen had been killed in colliery accidents.

To make children objects of sentiment might then have seemed excessively hypocritical. Animals were the more obvious outlet. Horses were not the answer: they were largely regarded as beasts of transport and burden. The economic lifetime of a horse would be calculated in Victorian times much as the economic lifetime of a motor vehicle is calculated today. A London omnibus horse (always a mare) would be bought at the age of five for £25, worked for five years and sold for £5. However, two-thirds of them would die in service, the carcases sometimes exceeding 1,300 in a year. The dynamic effort required of a tram-horse would be found to be even greater: its economic destiny, too, could be conveniently calculated in fractions—it would cost a shilling a week more to feed and would be worked-out in four-fifths of the time. Cab-horses, merely hired-out to their temporary masters, lasted three years before being sold to a tradesman for a third of their buying-price. A coach-horse had an economic life of four years. In the big jobbing-stables these animals were only calculations on a balance-sheet. Privately-owned horses might fare a little better, and the favourite family hack was an occasional subject for portraiture. A few were even pensioned-off: Landseer would later portray two sway-backed equine *Pensioners*, their ears reminiscently pricked as the hunt goes by. Even the best of them, like cars today, had to conform to certain inconvenient dictates of fashion. The practice of ear-cropping (so evident in the paintings of Stubbs) had died out; but the fashion of pruning at the other end was in full vogue, a docked tail being popularly supposed to set-off a horse's rump. Objects of sentiment these unfortunate creatures hardly were. They were dropping dead in the street every day, the passers-by scarcely sparing them a glance as the contractor or the coster haggled over the price of the carcase with the cat's-meat man.

Dogs, however, were a different matter, creatures of leisure and pleasure, uninvolved with work and worry. Victoria loved them in plenty round her feet, and she had discovered in Landseer possibly the finest captive dog-painter of all time. Dog portraiture had, of course, a dul function—to capture the subject in life and perpetuate its memory in death. And the death of one of Victoria's pets always plunged the royal household into deepest gloom. Little Dash was one

of the first to go. On Christmas Eve 1840 Albert broke the news to
the Queen 'which grieved me so much. I was so fond of the poor little
fellow, & he was so attached to me'. He was buried in the grounds of
Adelaide Cottage, his tombstone enjoining the passer-by to profit
by the example of the little spaniel whose attachment was without
selfishness, his playfulness without malice and his fidelity without
deceit. Thanks to Landseer Victoria had more than one memento of
her first canine love.

April 1844 was a bad month for Victoria. First Cairnach, a Skye
terrier, died ('It is so sad . . . He was such a beautiful dog, & had
such dear engaging ways') then Islay, another favourite terrier.
Albert once again was the bearer of 'the sad news that my faithful
little companion of more than 5 years, was no more. I was much
shocked & distressed'. In both cases there was again some consolation
for the Queen in the exact likenesses previously produced by Landseer.

Eos, Albert's Italian greyhound, was the next among the favoured
to depart. She had already been granted a second lease of life after
being badly wounded during a Windsor shooting expedition by the
Queen's trigger-happy Uncle Ferdinand of Saxe-Coburg Gotha.
Landseer sketched and painted her many times. The most famous
portrait, a body-profile, showed Eos with her master's gloves and hat,
a painting that had occasioned one of the little domestic subterfuges
so dear to both Victoria and Albert. The portrait was to be a surprise
present from the Queen but Albert asked one afternoon for his gloves
and his hat; so a servant arrived at Landseer's studio on a lathered
horse to fetch the missing articles before the Prince's suspicions were
aroused.

The death of Eos in July 1844 rivalled that of Dash himself in
dramatic intensity. It was Albert yet again who, grim-faced, broke
the news to his wife. 'I could see by his look that there was bad news,'
the Queen once more confided to her Journal. 'She had been his constant & faithful companion for 10 & $\frac{1}{2}$ years and she was only 6 month
old, when he first had her. She was connected with the happiest years
of his life, & I cannot somehow imagine him without her . . . As for
poor dear Albert, he feels it too terribly, & I grieve so for him.' The
Prince himself worked on the monument raised at Windsor to the
departed favourite, described by him in a mournful letter to his
Coburg grandmother as 'a symbol of the best and fairest section of
my life'.

Punch, feeling that there were perhaps more important things to
worry about and grieve over than the expiry of royal dogs, promptly
reported a spoof court-case, arising from the suspicious circumstances

surrounding the famous greyhound's death. There was, *Punch* in-
ferred, ample motive for a crime. It is well-known, said the mock-
deposition, that 'Yeos' was 'allowed to go anywhere by the Queen's
command, and must not be thwarted in anything'. A scullery-maid,
Sarah Scrub, whose duties no doubt included sweeping up 'Yeos's'
leavings, is accused of having poisoned the dog; but strenuously
denies having tampered with its *pâté de foie gras*. 'Did you make him
too rishe by too mush of de nastie salt buttare?' harshly enquires the
Prince, whose Teutonic origins apparently made him talk that way.
But the tearful scullery-maid insists that she fed 'Yeos' nothing but
the best *fresh* butter. She is eventually set at liberty on the coroner's
discovery that the dog's tail appeared to have been recently wagged
and that the pulse, had it not stopped, would have been normal. The
pastiche owed something to fact. The royal dogs did tend to be a law
unto themselves. They had the run of the Palace, and their dietary
habits were not entirely secret. A later acquisition, Lootie, a
Pekingese said to have belonged to the Empress of China, enjoyed
a carefully-prepared menu of boiled rice with a little chicken and
gravy, although she later condescended to eat cooked meats with
breadcrumbs or powdered biscuits. Such details were not always
relished in a society where many went hungry.

Irreplaceable though such favourites were, they were constantly
replaced; and their successors, like Waldmann and Däckel, the
dachshunds, kept Landseer in steady employment. Other subjects
included the Skye terrier Dandy, 'who is such a beauty'; and whom
Landseer sketched in pen and wash as *Dandy listening for the Queen*
whilst he himself was awaiting the appearance of her Majesty. In
pastel he immortalised the Duchess of Kent's favourite Maltese dog,
Lambkin, of whom the Queen eventually wrote in the inevitable
letter of condolence: 'I hope you have had him buried in a nice spot
& have got a little bit of his beautiful *silky-white* hair'.

Nor did what *Punch* chose to call 'the Queen's menagerie' end
there. Victoria's two Brazilian marmosets, uneasily seated on a pine-
apple watching a wasp, became a famous Landseer subject when
shown at the Royal Academy in 1842. Their tiny wizened faces are
almost too human, which no doubt partly accounted for the popularity of the engraving. There were also various pet birds to be
painted. The numerous royal parrots, macaws and love-birds presented a relatively unfamiliar challenge to Landseer, but one to which
he responded with great skill. Victoria's special favourite was Lory,
a present from her uncle Prince Ernest in 1836 and 'so tame that
. . . you may put your finger into its beak, or do anything with it,
without its ever attempting to bite'. Landseer's portraits of the royal

pets had struck a new high (or low) in realism and exactitude. When the Queen visited the Royal Academy in 1840 to see the new group which included her red macaw and love-birds, Thackeray appointed himself her imaginary guide:

> Yonder is Mr. Landseer's portrait of your majesty's own cockatoo, with a brace of Havadavats. Please your royal highness to look at the bit of biscuit; no baker could have done it more natural. Fair maid of honour, look at that lump of sugar; couldn't one take an affidavit, now, that it cost elevenpence a pound? I know only one thing sweeter, and that's your ladyship's lovely face!

Thackeray, a friend of Landseer's made little secret of his contempt both for Prince Albert and for Edwin's new-found status as royalty's favourite artist. In 1844 his mock-review of the Royal Academy exhibition in *Punch* dwelt on the work of a Mr. Sandseer (at other times it was the Earl of Landseer) and guyed the current obsession with princely detail:

> Among the portraits we remarked—691. Portrait of the hat of His Royal Highness Prince Albert; with his Royal Highness's favourite boot-jack. His Royal Highness's Persian wolf-dog Mirza in lying on the latter, while the former is in the possession of His Royal Highness's diminutive spaniel, Miss Kidlumy . . . This magnificent piece of art has all that Mastery of execution, that chiaroscurity of handling—above all, that thrilling, dramatic interest which distinguishes the most popular of our painters.

Such unkind barbs, unerringly directed by a friend, must have pained Landseer considerably. He knew, of course, that there was an element of sour grapes in the criticisms—jealousy of Edwin's intimate acceptance by the royal couple. But he was also aware of his new order of priorities, which put his old literary and artist friends a long way behind the Queen, Prince Albert and various members of the nobility. There was now no lack of critics to question his artistic integrity, some of whom even blossomed into rhyme, like one alleged painter-poet in the scurrilous pages of *Punch*:

> I would I were the great Landseer
> To paint the best of dogs and deer;
> I would not care for glory, since
> I pleased my Queen and charmed my Prince.
> And yet I must not wish for that.
> To paint my gracious Prince's hat,
> To paint his cane, his gloves, his shoes,
> To paint his dogs and cockatoos,

And naught besides, would weary me;
And so I would not *Landseer* be.

Although he was clearly the hot favourite, even Landseer had his limitations. There were, in fact, unofficial lines of demarcation in Victorian animal portraiture. Edwin tended to concentrate on the royal dogs and the more exotic small fauna introduced from time to time in the household. Horse portraits were normally apportioned to James Ward, J. F. Herring, R. B. Davis and George Morley; and beef and mutton on the hoof to T. S. Cooper and F. W. Keyl, whose ponderous fat-stock heifers rejoiced in such dainty names as *Princess Helena*.

There was yet another aspect of the Queen's animal-love to which Edwin was able to pander—she was an unrepentant circus-fanatic. Ever since as a young princess she had jumped her white cob in and out of the ring at Ducrow's Brighton show, circuses had never lost their fascination for her. She would summon artists to appear before her (often at great inconvenience and expense) and present them with jewelled tie-pins and necklaces (the long-term value of which was perhaps mainly sentimental). Lion-queens who put their heads inside the gaping mouths of wild cats had especial appeal—a practice in which the hallitosis can hardly have been less formidable than the risk of decapitation. Naturally, her Majesty would afterwards ask the girl was she not nervous when she put her head inside the lion's mouth; and the Lion-queen would reply, on cue: 'Not as nervous as now, Ma'am'.

Throughout the Queen's reign the circus was losing status. At one time it had regarded itself as the theatre's direct rival, and a young lady who left Lord George Sanger in favour of the music-hall was sadly dismissed as having 'gone over to the enemy'. The great Edmund Kean himself had been a circus-acrobat when a fall from a horse at Bartholomew Fair broke both his legs. Since the accident rendered him unfit for the higher calling, circus-folk in their magnanimity tended to forgive him for devoting himself thereafter to the inferior profession of stage tragedian. Of course, the circus, too, staged high dramas and tragedies in which, however, the horsemanship was usually stronger than the elocution. Thus, Charles Dickens in a letter to his biographer John Forster recalled a dramatic performance at a Ramsgate circus 'where *Mazeppa* was played in three long acts without an H in it: as if for a wager. Evven, and edds, and orrors and ands, were as plentiful as blackberries; but the letter **H** was neither whispered in Evven, nor muttered in Ell, nor permitted to dwell in any form on the confines of the sawdust'.

In January 1839 there appeared at Drury Lane a Dutch-American wild beast tamer called Isaac van Amburgh. He was, allegedly, the first tamer to mix several species of wild cat in the same cage; and the first 'gentler' of wild animals. Previously wild animal acts had consisted of a chaotic scramble in which the beasts were prodded with red-hot irons, blinded by the smoke of pitch torches and deafened by gunfire and Chinese gongs. In the general confusion the bold tamer would make his entrance and exit. Van Amburgh, on the other hand, ostensibly ruled by love, reclining in his mobile cage amidst a mixed groups of lions, tigers, leopards (or cheetahs) and a lamb. A handsome figure, he affected the dress of a Roman gladiator, and took London by storm. Lions and tigers at that time had a truly fearsome reputation for savagery. That a man should lie down among them was regarded as an act almost of biblical self-assurance.

Her Majesty's first visit to see van Amburgh incited little comment. But when she went another four times in January and February, many representatives of the legitimate theatre, including actors and dramatists, were distinctly piqued. Nor did Victoria make any effort to hide her delight. 'One can never see it too often,' she wrote in her Journal, 'for it is different each time. Van Amburgh, it seemed, 'remained about $\frac{1}{4}$ of an hour, showing them off & making them perform tricks. He has great power over animals, & they seem to love him, though I think they are in great fear of him. He took them by their paws, throwing them down & making them roar, & he lay upon them after enraging them.'

The most outspoken of Victoria's critics was Landseer's friend, the actor Macready. In his Journal he disparagingly kept a tally of the Queen's visits to the wild beasts, noting her habit of 'going upon the stage after the pantomime to see them fed'. In the following month he complained about the *Times* Court Journal 'which contains a wretched piece of trash justifying the Queen's patronage of Mr. van Amburgh'. Perhaps a more deep-seated reason for his petulant annoyance with Victoria emerges in a later entry, listing some of the guests at the Queen's ball to which Macready had not been invited: 'It is not a pleasing reflection, without caring for the thing itself, that my pariah profession should entitle me to the lavish expression of public praise, and exclude me from distinctions which all my compeers enjoy'.

Landseer doubtless had the Queen in mind when he set about recapturing the delights of van Amburgh's performance on, as *Punch* tartly recorded later, 'about half an acre of canvas'. It was exhibited at the Royal Academy in 1839 and at once acquired by Victoria, ultimately adorning the Horn Room at Osborne. 'Most beautiful . . .

a wonderful piece of painting . . . just exactly as I saw him,' sighed the Queen. Many of the wider-eyed critics agreed with her, though Thackeray professed himself delighted at 'finding Mr. Edwin Landseer out in a bad picture'. Its main value today would be to circus-historians. The two spotted cats which the Queen referred to in her Journal as '2 Chetas, or Kind of leopards' seem to be neither quite one thing nor the other. And a snarling lioness illustrates the mistake often made by the younger Landseer (and by many another eighteenth and nineteenth century artist, including on occasion Stubbs himself) of painting the awesome reputation of the wild beast rather than the animal itself.

Victoria's espousal of van Amburgh so soon after the notorious Lady Flora Hastings affair was perhaps unfortunate: many people were still anxious to discern in their tiny young Queen an outsize streak of cruelty. It was some ten years later that the death of a Lion-queen, 17-year-old Helen Bright, gave *Punch* the long-awaited opportunity to vent its full disgust:

> One minute the girl was alive, in all her pride of domination, ruling the beast for tuppences—the next the tiger had fixed his teeth in her neck, the jugular poured out the life; and, in brief course, a Coroner's Jury sat upon the body. 'Accidental death.'
>
> What has become of the tiger? Has it been killed? Or will the human blood that in its ferocious instinct it has shed, make the brute a more valuable beast—a greater attraction to the show? . . . Will it . . . become the only quadruped tenant of MADAME TUSSAUD's Chamber of Horrors?

The unfortunate tiger, according to circus-historians, had been provoked beyond endurance by this slip of a girl, who had kept flicking her whip in its face. But there was no *Save the Tiger* movement in those days. Nor did *Punch* spare the feelings of Victoria and Landseer, journalistically resurrecting the van Amburgh painting, and roundly condemning the pair for conspiring to 'immortalise his Majesty and four-footed subjects':

> We hear that, since the death of the Lion Queen, and purely to exert the influence of high example, the picture has been taken down, packed up and is about to be shipped as a present to the EMPEROR OF MOROCCO. In the dominion of his Majesty, Lion Tamers may certainly find a more congenial atmosphere than in the highly civilised and Christianised Great Britain.

The painting, needless to say, remains in the royal collection!

Nor, with the Queen's picture, had Landseer exhausted van

Amburgh. The Duke of Wellington had been another of the latter-day Daniel's countless admirers. Together they had discussed the anatomy of fear and courage; a subject in which both in their different ways had a professional interest. The Duke determined that he, too, must have a picture of the dashing wild beast tamer at work. Landseer obliged with a painting even more pantomimic than the Queen's, though the Duke himself was mightily pleased with it. On requiring the artist to name his price, Landseer asked 600 guineas, whereupon Wellington wrote him a cheque for 1,200; a story Edwin constantly related in rebuttal of rumours of the Duke's parsimony. For the Duke to have written a cheque was in itself a compliment to the artist. Another painter who fulfilled a commission for Wellington found his fee being counted out in notes. On his polite suggestion that a cheque would be perfectly acceptable, the good Duke looked aghast: 'What, and let Coutts know what a bloody fool I've been!'.

The life-size picture of the pomaded trainer subduing his beasts with nothing more than a riding-whip was shown at the Royal Academy in 1847. The public seemed to like it, despite the fact that the entire foreground was barred like a jeweller's window. Thereafter it hung in the library at Apsley House surmounted by the text from Genesis concerning the Creator's dominion through mankind over everything that moved on the earth—which, in that instance, seemed to reduce God to the status of a menagerie-keeper. Thus did Landseer profit from van Amburgh's visit, which also provided him with the inspiration for works of art to come. The King of Beasts in Victoria's picture lolling on a plinth behind his trainer with an expression of inveterate kindness and decency on his large face was obviously gazing straight towards Trafalgar Square. The lion lying down with the lamb was another concept that would haunt Edwin for the rest of his life, and which was to surface pathetically in his last years. It was a phenomenon he had first witnessed in the unlikely and smelly confines of van Amburgh's travelling cage.

FOREIGN PARTS

I N THE autumn of 1839 there died at his Highland retreat
Haydon's 'good kind friend to me, & all Artists', John, 6th Duke
of Bedford. On November 7th Landseer wrote to his Aunt from
Haddo House: 'I can think of nothing correctly, but the melancholy
time I passed at Doune, and the sad termination of our anxious
watching'. In the previous year Edwin had made the Duke's portrait, a stiff and formal affair, uncertainly drawn, with the jacketed
arm like a length of drainpipe. Watching his patron's demise had
obviously been a thoughtful as well as a sad time for the artist. However, he allowed a decent time to elapse before proposing to the
widowed Georgiana. The proposal seems to have put her in a dilemma:
she began to seek the advice of close friends. It was uncharacteristic
of her thus to place her fate in the hands of others: the desire to do the
right thing had played little part in her life so far. She confided her
problem to the old family friend Lord Holland, who firmly advised
her against marrying the painter. It seems odd that she should have
expected any other counsel from the bastion of a country in which,
as Thackeray believed, even a grocer would hesitate to let his daughter marry a mere artist. Perhaps Landseer was being pressing, and
she was buying a little extra time. However, her final answer was a
refusal.

The effect on Edwin was shattering. Later, recording the rejection
in his diary, Haydon wrote:

> Jerdan dined with me yesterday. He said he had seen a note of
> Lord Holland's of the advice he gave to the Dutchess of Bedford
> relating to the *marrying of Edwin Landseer*. Landseer has been
> nearly driven mad by her declinsion . . .

It certainly seems to have been the traumatic event of his life. He
was not used to rebuffs or refusals of any kind, and the rejection of

his hand in marriage by a woman in her fifty-ninth year was doubt-less a severe blow to his pride. 'The remains' of Georgiana's beauty, having given birth to ten children, were by now inconsiderable. Frank Davis, in the *Illustrated London News* of March 25, 1961, commented tartly on the theory that the Duchess's refusal had been the cause of Edwin's later mental breakdown: 'I should have thought the proposal itself could as easily have been a symptom'. Had the two lovers, of differing generations, been the only elements involved, the assump-tion is certainly a fair one. But Landseer's whole attitude bespoke his anxiety over Georgiana's youngest children of whom he was the alleged father—Alexander, now eighteen, and Rachel, thirteen.

Edwin's proposal was only rational in the light of his attempts to make an honest woman of Georgiana. The fact that his proposal was largely a selfless one no doubt rendered the blow of her refusal even more severe.

The formidable Lady Holland had, of course, a much more logical explanation for Landseer's subsequent illness—'the fatigue and mental anxiety of having been on the *hanging* Council of the Royal Academy where there are so many jealousies and bickerings . . . has overset his nerves'. It was an unlikely explanation indeed—Landseer's attitude to councils and committee business and to other people's pictures was never an unduly dedicated one. The caste-conscious Lady Holland doubtless appreciated Georgiana's refusal; if it hadn't been her idea, rather than Lord Holland's in the first place. In fact, her attitude to Georgiana appeared to execute a complete *volte face*. It had for many years been hostile in the extreme, greatly to the disappointment of the 6th Duke. Landseer had been a regular guest at Holland House since 1834 and on one occasion, as he pushed her through the garden of her London home in a wheelchair, Edwin had been innocent enough to pause and point out how much Georgiana enjoyed the view of Harrow across the Holland's garden from her house on the hill above. Immediately Lady Holland ordered her fence to be raised to shut out the Duchess's view. It was that sort of obsessive bitchiness that was suddenly transformed, as she dwelt on Georgiana's widowhood: 'She bears up with great moral courage the sad change in her condition, besides very many vexations and even mortifications. Her looks and whole *maintien* are strikingly handsome. The melancholy badge of widowhood on her head so frightful in general, does not disfigure her'. There is relief as well as admiration in the tone, as though she applauded Georgiana's deter-mination not to let the side down by marrying a mere professional artist, albeit one to whose charm Lady Holland was herself sus-ceptible.

A few months later, on the 21st of January 1840, Landseer suffered another blow by the death of his mother. She had always been a vague, unmentioned, possibly unmentionable figure; perhaps an invalid, perhaps a recluse, perhaps a tippler, whose fourteen confinements and eight bereavements may have reduced her to a passive acceptance of life. She was sixty-six years old and the cause of her death was given as abscess of the liver. The exact nature of Edwin's relationship with his mother is not on record; though his need to relate to an older woman who could mother, correct and sometimes scold him was much in evidence throughout his life.

Georgiana's clergyman son Wriothesley, two years younger than Edwin, at once picked up his pen to comfort the family's favourite painter on his 'afflicting loss'—a letter which became a long sermon on how much more philosophically the Christian is able to bear such bereavements and ending: 'I should be most thankful if you would allow me to alleviate your sorrow by books, by letters, by visits or anything that I can do . . .'. Lord Wriothesley had long considered Landseer a suitable candidate for conversion. Ten years before he had, unsolicited, sent the painter some 'good books', and later wrote enquiring how he was getting on with them:

I trust that the two read together may put you in possession of the spiritual gifts I so earnestly desire for you, but there is *one book only* that is needful. Study its divine contents and pray to be enlightened.

His reputation as a kind of silly-ass cleric was further sustained in letters to Landseer earnestly soliciting his advice on colours for the drawing room: 'Buff and Apricot have been in agitation. Mr. Westmacott strongly recommends a *deep* peach blossom—in short we are in a complete state of perplexity . . .'. Georgiana's eldest issue was at one stage accused of rising to eminence on the shoulders of his half-brother, Lord John Russell, then Secretary of State, and *The Times* weighed-in with charges of nepotism: 'When we see the stalls of cathedrals . . . only affording a trellis-work to support the exuberant branches of overloaded aristocratical families, we are disgusted at the perversion'.

A figure of such professional piety must have been heavily offputting to Landseer, who strenuously avoided church-visits except on state or social occasions. His rather diffident small portrait of Wriothesley (now at Chatsworth) seems to reflect something of this caution—although painting the dog-collared son of his lover may of itself have been something of an ordeal.

However, not all of Wriothesley's pious sentiments and his offers of good books could prevent the physical and nervous ill-health into which Landseer rapidly declined. His doctors advised both a change and a rest, and Jacob Bell volunteered to travel with him to the Continent.

Georgiana seemed to be well aware of her own part in Edwin's breakdown in health. On the eve of his departure the painter had a letter from Sir Stephen Hammick, medical adviser to the top people including the Bedfords and the Hollands:

> The Duchess is so very unhappy and anxious about you that she cannot be reconciled at your intended trip *till* I have seen you and has wished me to visit you at Dover and have some conversation with you.

The continental trip was neither a success nor a failure. Edwin and Bell travelled in leisurely almost lethargic fashion through Belgium and up the Rhine to Switzerland, via France and Germany. Distracted as he was, Landseer sketched sporadically, and seemed only moderately fascinated by what he saw. The cart-pulling dogs were only of passing interest to his pencil: most of his drawings were of horses and mules and draught oxen, creatures that had never particularly fired his imagination and which seemed to mirror his listless frame of mind. He was heavily conscious of being under doctors' orders; and if he ever got carried away Bell was there to remind him that he was on a supposed rest-cure. He therefore attempted no sustained work, confining himself to quick and spontaneous sketches (many of them none the worse for that) and virtually nothing of what he did was afterwards worked out on canvas.

Edwin's letters home were a mixture of travel news and analyses of his health, like the one to his Aunt on August 28th 1840:

> We arrived at Bruges yesterday, the place is quite charming, people, buildings, dresses, in short everything picturesque and paintable. I am as well as can be expected after so much travelling. My head soon gets out of order, when I am obliged to give up doing anything and go to the open air. Altogether I am better.

There was plenty to occupy his pencil. He sketched figures praying in a Belgian church; draught horses at Bruges; sketches that humorously contrasted the lean horse of England with the round-rumped Belgian vanner and the aquiline Englishman and his whippet with the Belgian tavern-keeper whose dog is as portly as himself. Many of them were the sketches of a man with too much leisure on his hands—he even found time to sketch a pump at Frankfort, a rather pointless and inexpert exercise.

The two men encountered several unexpected hazards. To his friend Henry Collen, Landseer complained of having been bitten by bedbugs—'odious odoriferous enemies' and 'hearty bloodsuckers' Collen described them in his reply. Later his old friends, the Simpsons, of Maldon, Essex, wrote him an affectionate letter: 'When I heard,' said Mrs Simpson, 'of you intention of leaving England, I was thoroughly tempted to offer my services as a nurse, because I flatter myself that I am rather *good* at that'. Her husband, Wooley Simpson, added his customary addendum to his wife's screed, assuring his 'dear Sir Heartie (that) I have the greatest affection for you—Keep your bowels open, say your prayers and Eschew naughty women, and you will be alright'.

One or two finished pictures did emerge from the tour. The fine pen-and-ink study *Oxen at the Tank: Geneva* was perhaps the most notable; a nicely-composed picture though possibly a little too resolutely bovine to be popular. *The Stable*, another effective drawing, showed two old workhorses in a stable and the carter mending a horse-collar while a boy looks on; it was inscribed *on the road between Liege and Aix-la-Chapelle*. A pretty sketch of *Shepherds at Strasbourg* obviously gave the artist some inkling for a later allegorical painting, *The Shepherd's Prayer*. One of the two paintings of note to emerge directly from the continental experience was *Refreshment: a Scene in Belgium* (1846), a group including a white pony in pannier harness, two Belgian draught-dogs, a woman and a boy, The other, *Geneva*, a mixed group of horses, mule, ox and dog eating was not exhibited until 1851, and was one of the handful of subjects for which Landseer sought assistance—his Scottish friend David Roberts R.A. added an arch and a church tower to the background.

Those who had hoped to see the kind of transformation in his art that Spain and North Africa had wrought in the style of Phillip and Lewis were disappointed. The Scottish Highlands remained Landseer's only magic place. He returned with a portfolio of useful sketches (some of which Queen Victoria and Prince Albert later etched): they were mostly of worthy Belgian citizens and their draught animals, of the detailed peculiarities of continental dress, of the picturesque bell-hung harness and, of course, of a rather one-dimensional-looking Frankfort drinking pump. Yet he had no apparent desire to turn them into pictures; and, if he had, the need was hardly a pressing one, the first continent-inspired painting not appearing until six years later.

Italy might have been a more likely country to travel to; though Edwin had probably been warned against excessive heat. He certainly later regretted that he had never visited that country. The route he and Bell chose had been picturesque rather than inspirational: the scenery failed to move him as the Scottish lochs and mountains had done. Twenty years earlier, when he had been looking for backgrounds to his Alpine mastiffs, he would doubtless have given his eye-teeth for a visit to Switzerland: now there was no sense of purpose or urgency. They were merely two young men on a continental jaunt, one of them for the sake of his health. Ironically, though, it was Bell's ill-health that cut short their visit: he developed quinsy, and after almost two months of travelling the two men came home via Paris.

On his return Landseer continued to see Georgiana, but their relationship was never quite the same again. There may even have been twinges of remorse. Despite Grenville's imputations of sybaritism and self-indulgence, the 6th Duke had assuredly been a good friend to all artists; from James Ward, on whose behalf he had circularised all the great nobles and landowners, to Landseer, for whom he had doubtless (though in a different way) performed the same service. With the Duke dead and with his most exalted patroness firmly ensconced on the throne, Edwin had to tread the path of discretion. His ill-judged proposal of marriage was, of course, a talking point both in aristocratic and artistic circles. If he had not made it, he could perhaps more easily have sustained an intimate relationship with Georgiana. She was, after all, nearly sixty; and many, even in those censorious days, might have been prepared to tolerate a now apparently harmless relationship between an elderly Dowager Duchess and her favourite artist. However, the proposal had suggested that love, if not lust, was still strong; and there would have been plenty of raised eyebrows and knowing smirks if Edwin had continued to frequent Georgiana's households on the old easy terms of familiarity.

Jealousy may have been another factor. Georgiana's eye for a likely man had still not entirely dimmed. When the royal couple visited Woburn Abbey in 1841 she was captivated even by Albert, writing to Landseer: 'Prince Albert has the most bewitching countenance I ever saw'. Edwin, who was certainly capable of petulance, may have felt that his own countenance better deserved that compliment. It may therefore have been a general tit-for-tat motive that induced the artist's alleged interest in Anna Maria, the wife of Francis, who succeeded his father as the 7th Duke of Bedford. In his autobiography, *A Silver Plated Spoon*, the present Duke cites 'a well-founded family rumour that Anna Maria was the mistress of Landseer'. Whatever the basis of the rumour, one factor at least is not inconsistent: Anna Maria was nineteen years older than the painter, the kind of figure on whom Landseer's affections might conceivably fall in his bizarre search for a lover who was also a mother.

Historically, the 7th Duchess is a little difficult to take seriously. She is credited in some quarters with introducing the custom of afternoon tea—certainly a much less harmful diversion than her other claim to posterity; her part in the lamentable Flora Hastings affair in which Lady Flora, a virginal lady-in-waiting with an enlarged liver of which she subsequently died, was cruelly and humiliatingly suspected of being pregnant. Lady Portland was perhaps the main villainess in this sorry affair and even Lady Flora's outraged brother ascribed the then Marchioness of Tavistock's courtly tale-bearing more to stupidity than to malice—'She is a weak woman, though not at heart a bad one'—whilst her brother-in-law William wondered 'how Lady Tavistock could have dabbled in such nastiness'. Victoria herself had behaved with callous indifference and woeful lack of judgement, and it had been a sad start to the young Queen's reign.

The 7th Duchess, a daughter of the Earl of Harrington, had been Lady Anna Maria Stanhope before her marriage: subsequently she became first Lady-in-Waiting to the Queen. She had been an attractive young woman. When she married Francis in 1808, she had also been greatly admired by his youngest full brother, Lord John Russell. The future Prime Minister, however, had made something of a practice of mooning after his brothers' women—nine years later he had proposed to Bessy, only two hours after his brother William's successful proposal. Lord John later attracted dark rumours as a possible begetter of bastards from affairs with servants, those born on the wrong side of the monogrammed sheets being promptly shipped off to America. (A suspiciously arithmetical rumour even credited him with having left 103 bastards extant at his death.) The money-conscious 7th Duke was somewhat reluctant to meet the bills necessary to promote John's public career, and it was left to Lady Holland to supplement his political aspirations. The former Marquis of Tavistock, in fact, though a man of honour, seems to have been rather staid, self-righteous, intolerant of frivolities and over-dedicated to stately chores; and Anna Maria's faithfulness to her paragon may occasionally have wavered. However, she had only one child, the subsequent 8th Duke, born in 1809, so Landseer cannot be accused in that instance of swelling the ranks of the aristocracy. It is clear at least that stately sexual licence, like stately wife-neglect, was hardly confined to Georgiana alone; and that Anna Maria may in fact have crushed the young painter to her sometimes bereft bosom. On the other hand, the linking of her name and reputation with

Landseer's may simply have been a case of archival confusion with
Georgiana's

If Landseer at that time felt rejected as a man, he was certainly
much sought after as a painter. At times there was a note almost of
hysteria in the desire of new patrons to own one of his pictures. Thus
Lord Monson to Edwin's friend, the painter David Roberts,* in June
of 1841:

> There is one, however, with whom I am anxious to lose no time,
> and that is Edwin Landseer. Would you be my ambassador, and
> ask him what would be the cost of his painting me a picture? I
> should like him to come here and paint my portrait, with some
> remarkable dogs, with which, I think, he would be pleased. The
> picture, however, must be of the very best, for I want to point to
> my walls with a national pride, and ask—'Who dares to say that
> we have no first-rate artists in England?' . . .

> * *The Life of David Roberts*, James Ballantine, 1866.

CHAPTER ELEVEN

A RIGHT ROYAL REPUTATION

Ah! my dear friend, you have only to come to England now to lose all relish for art.
—B. R. Haydon to his friend Kirkup in Italy

I F EDWIN had been able to confine himself to recording animal life for the royal pair, all might have been well. In that branch of art his reputation, even before his fortieth year, was unassailable. It was a domain of which he was king, in which he carried himself with enormous self-confidence. If he had a partial blind spot it was the domestic cat which he had seldom attempted since his early twenties, and never with total success. Even in that department his royal patrons seemed anxious to accommodate him—they were never great cat lovers. But, of course, they did want to see themselves as well as their menagerie of animals; and that was where the seams gradually began to show in Edwin's omnipotence. Had he been a conventional animal-specialist, content to set up his easel for an agreed fee in the royal stables or byres, life would have been considerably simplified. But he was obviously much more than that. He had allowed himself to become not only a favoured friend to the royal couple, but in effect, *the* Court painter. The challenge and the implication were clear. Edwin could often paint excellent portraits, but sometimes he painted very bad ones. The bad ones were never so bad as in their finished state. These were the likenesses he had failed in the first instance to capture completely: in his anxiety to please he worked and reworked them until there was nothing on the canvas except a lifeless replica of a total stranger. His erratic treatment of the human face and figure doubtless had early origins. John Landseer had encouraged his desire to draw animals, but had given him little groundwork in the human form. The prevailing bias against nude models had not helped. Even in pre-Victorian times, there had been no lack of suggestions that a woman who posed in the nude could only be a prostitute, the artists who sketched her only lascivious voyeurs and the places which countenanced such on-goings only dens of iniquity. The edict prohibiting students under the age of twenty to draw from the female nude was later amended to allow them to do so if they were married; resulting predictably in a crop of premature, penurious and disastrous marriages. But Edwin's attitude to the nude, whether male or female, was never a happy one, causing some strange lapses into disproportion. There were, of course, no such restrictions on the human face, and many Landseer portraits testify to the soundness of his early training. However, the 'disaster' portraits almost invariably had one thing in common—they were of people of high station whom he was desperately anxious to please: it was usually the anxiety that inhibited the style. Worse, the nagging despair and worry caused him actual illness. As many of his artist-friends agreed, it contributed towards the physical and nervous breakdowns that bedevilled him for the last thirty years of his life.

Yet even in portraiture Edwin managed to remain the royal favourite for a time—if at some cost to himself. At the height of his favour he was commissioned to paint *Windsor Castle in Modern Times*, a family picture set in the Green Drawing Room with Victoria standing and Albert seated (an unusual piece of pictorial deference, especially since the original sketch had shown the couple standing together). Albert is in floppy Robin Hood hunting-boots which make him look, apart from the face-hair, like a pantomime principal boy. The infant Princess Royal is also present, intrigued by the dead game birds littering the place and proclaiming Albert's skill as a hunter-provider. The royal dogs are much in evidence, including Eos, whom the Prince fondles, a cairn terrier which is licking his hand and another which begs for his attention. In the far distance in the sculpturesque garden can just be spotted the Duchess of Kent being pulled by a servant in her bath-chair. If Albert (for once) dominated the picture, he had also dictated its style. The slick enamel-like surface exactly reflected his Germanic taste. Give or take an animal or two, it could almost be by Franz Xaver Winterhalter himself; a name that would soon become painfully familiar to Landseer. It was one of Edwin's 'nervous' pictures, which occasioned him great difficulties and delays; one of those to which he was afraid to write *finis* and which stood on his easel for five years. In 1845 Victoria wrote with evident relief in her diary: 'Landseer's Game Picture (begun in 1840!) with us 2, Vicky . . . is at last hung up in our sitting room here'. Many critics rightly detected artistic toadying in its overcareful execution and lacquered finish, but Landseer's reward was her Majesty's commendation—'a very beautiful picture . . . altogether very cheerful and pleasing'.

An even more desperate production was *Queen Victoria and Prince Albert in Costume*, dressed as Queen Philippa and King Edward III for the *bal costumé* of 1842, which Frank Davis rightly described as 'preposterous'. Unable to breathe any life, warmth or spontaneity into the painting, Landseer resorted to over-elaboration, minutely recording every spangled detail of Victoria's costume and the hilt of Albert's sword. Haydon recorded the opinion of the portraiturist John Lucas, painting in Buckingham Palace at the same time as Edwin: 'The Queen called him in to see Landseer's picture. Landseer did not like it, & said awkwardly it was in its Infancy'. Edwin ought to have seen his own embarrassment as the gypsy's warning. However, he seems merely to have whistled in relief at the Queen's expression of approval, and congratulated himself on surviving to struggle with a further such hopeless commission on another day. His feelings about some royal set-pieces were expressed in his horrified reaction to Frith's commission to picture the Prince of Wales' marriage: 'For all the money in the world, and all in the next, I wouldn't undertake such a thing!'. The statement had a ring of artistic bravado. It seems more likely that if Victoria had offered him the commission to paint the inside of her shoe, Landseer's reaction would have been eager and loyal acceptance.

In 1842 Prince Albert had the inspired idea to invite eight leading painters to decorate in fresco the octagonal room of the Summer House in Buckingham Palace Gardens. There already were several frescoes in the four-roomed pavilion, some of them subjects from Sir Walter Scott. The common theme of the eight new works was to be Milton's *Comus*, which Prince Albert had seen staged in March 1842 at Covent Garden, and which later earned the pavilion the subtitle of Milton Villa. Naturally, Landseer was one of the eight Academicians chosen to paint a theme that would be 'both moral and beautiful': the others were Eastlake, Leslie, Stanfield, Uwins, Ross, Maclise and Etty. Etty subsequently fell by the wayside. 'Poor man,' the royal couple are said to have remarked with somewhat chilling sympathy, 'he doesn't know what we want.' He was replaced by the Scottish painter William Dyce. The whole scene is perhaps reminiscent of a play by Anouilh; the pretty Summer House ('a little Chinesey box', as Lady Eastlake described it); the eminent artists working there two or three at a time, conversing on topics of the day and admiring each other's efforts with urbanely-disguised jealousy; interrupted from time to time by the appearance of Victoria and Albert at their most informal. But the play was not without its farcical elements. 'The artists' as T. S. R. Boase* noted, 'ran almost comically true to form.' Of the eight frescoes, three repeated the same subject and two another. The whole thing became a polite and

* *English Art 1800–1870*, 1959.

patriotic chore for which the painters lacked both enthusiasm and imagination; and the *Quarterly Review*'s high-flown hope of seeing work which would define 'the true starting-point of an English school of fresco-painting' remained cruelly unfulfilled. Landseer himself chose to depict the *Rout of Comus*, an orgiastic scene showing Milton's enchanter with a bevy of writhing animal-headed monsters, as well as glimpses of female pulchritude. He worked on it mainly in his studio, as always hating to paint with others looking over his shoulder.

The most unwelcome of all the visitors while the pavilion was being thus transformed was undoubtedly Haydon. He applied for permission to watch the work in progress which Eastlake, the controlling artist, refused him. Unabashed he turned up anyway— in his own words, 'to the astonishment of all'. He had, predictably, little taste for the 'miserable arabesques' he saw. As he recorded in a letter to his friend S. S. Kirkup in November 1844:

> Ah! my dear friend, you have only to come to England now to lose all relish for art. Etty's, so help me Heaven! Etty's second attempt is unworthy a café chantant at Paris. Uwin's is a poultice; Leslie's dark; Stanfield's, a diminished scene from the Lyceum; Ross is not so bad as Etty's . . . Landseer is doing his at home . . .

Eastlake's, however, he found to be' worthy of the best school to be named'—though he later handed the palm to the substitute Dyce. When he saw Landseer's he did not like it, adding that he found the practice of painting fresco at home 'not manly'. He went on to anticipate the royal pair's disappointment with the 'wretched patch-work', which would lead them to blame the artists 'instead of their own folly in employing so many instead of placing the whole decoration in the hands of one competent man!' But this entry in his diary, though waspish, was percipient:

> All the flesh of their Frescoes looks as if dipped in the stain of a tan-pit, so utterly are they without cool tones. If they can put blue into the Sky, surely they can put a due mixture of it into the flesh. There are also no reflections, and the effect is hot & offensive & dirty; black, sooty—as if painted with boiled fish eyes.

Dyce had a different complaint, bemoaning the fact that for all his efforts—days lost, preliminary sketches, designs and a full-size cartoon before embarking on the picture—he received only £100, the fee Eastlake had negotiated with Prince Albert. *Punch* had accused the royal couple of taking advantage of their status to undercut artists' prices. Certainly Albert expressed great initial surprise at the cost of paintings in Britain, but he subsequently became resigned to paying something like the going rate. The Prince was, of course, a shrewd buyer; many important pictures, including purchases of the early Italian schools, passed to the National Gallery after his death. Nor was his taste embedded in the past. He tried to free water-colours from their gilt complex, advocating white mounts instead; although he frequently made artists nervous by suggesting improvements in their work with a hard pointed instrument. His artistic tact suffered other lapses, too. On one occasion, visiting Landseer's studio, he picked up and examined a canvas that stood face to the wall. The painter let the Prince know that he had committed a serious breach of studio etiquette, and Albert apologised.

The Summer House decorations, however, were hardly among Albert's greatest triumphs as a patron. The unloved and unlovely frescoes mouldered along with the pavilion itself which was removed in 1928. It had been left neglected due to shortage of manpower throughout the 1914–18 War (some censure was passed on Queen Mary for this lack of after-care in royal patronage) and was later found to be damp and decayed beyond restitution. Landseer never repeated such an experiment, preferring to confine his fresco-painting to the spontaneous efforts in Highland bothies and shooting-boxes, however, with similar long-term results.

The painter had continued to act as the confidant both of Victoria and Albert in the clandestine production of their 'surprise' anniversary pictures. Since these usually involved short notice and a deadline, they were freer in execution, less overworked, than the larger portrait commissions. A favourite dog was almost always introduced; to please Albert his Italian greyhound was much featured. The Queen had been particularly anxious that the surprise portrait of the baby Princess Royal with Eos and a dove should be finished in time for Albert's birthday, the 26th August 1841. But Landseer was in procrastinatory mood. At eleven on the evening of the 25th the picture had still not arrived at Windsor, so a servant was sent post haste to the painter's studio to fetch the masterpiece 'done or not done'. He woke the artist at two in the morning and was back at six with the painting wrapped in a tablecloth. Two years later it was Albert's turn to astonish the Queen by pictorial sleight of hand on her birthday. Taking advantage of Victoria's absence, he smuggled Landseer into the nursery to paint the recently arrived Princess Alice, jokingly known as 'Fatima' because of her chubbiness. The ruse went undiscovered. When the Queen appeared in the breakfast-room on her birthday she found herself confronted to her delighted surprise by the flower-bedecked finished portrait of 'Fatima', with the terrier Dandy keeping her company.

Landseer several times painted the Queen on horseback. His *Queen Victoria and the Duke of Wellington reviewing the Life Guards* showed her on her favourite grey Arab Comus. The picture is almost a sketch. Landseer could never be bothered with crowd scenes and the serried lines of the mounted troopers are suggested with almost cartoon-like economy, as well as being so far out of perspective as to argue chronic inattention during his lessons in the subject at the Academy schools. Individual portraits of the Queen on horseback became one of his recurrent themes, a labour of loyalty and love, but also one which reflected his diminishing vitality. His study made in 1839, freely and spontaneously, with oil colours and a camel-hair pencil, was a vigorous and colourful portrait, and obviously the study for a larger work that remained unfinished at his death. Age, artistic infirmity and over-familiarity gave a somewhat laboured look to later attempts at the same theme, which always showed the horse in three-quarter profile with the off foreleg raised. It was not the kind of fixation to which Landseer was normally prone, and seemed to argue slight creative atrophy in the presence of her Majesty. Certainly one of the proudest moments of the painter's life occurred when Victoria arrived unexpectedly at his St. John's Wood home one day mounted on horseback. It was a spontaneous gesture on the part of the Queen, to help him with one of the equestrian portraits. She waited patiently while Landseer went to change, before mounting a groom's horse to ride with her. A sketch he kept prominently displayed in his studio reminded both himself and his visitors of the incident, which he would later recall, sometimes with tear-blurred eyes. For a painter, there can have been few greater evidences of royal favour, few more refined pieces of social one-upmanship, than having your neighbours see the reigning monarch wait outside your gate while you changed your coat.

In his heyday Landseer was to the royal couple, as the Cunningham *Lives* described him, 'a privileged friend'. He was a frequent guest at Windsor, Osborne and Balmoral. He would accompany the Queen on her walks, gallantly helping her over stiles and with her nature sketching. His penchant for the demure and harmless quip was always very much in evidence. Once, as he walked with Victoria on the terrace at Windsor Castle, a large bee persisted in giving the Queen its undivided attention, despite all her attempts to flick it away. 'What can make it follow me like this?' she finally remarked in exasperation. 'I know not, your Majesty,' retorted Landseer, 'unless it be a queen bee!' Even Albert, whose dislike of jokes was well known, seems to have at least tolerated Edwin's sallies. Sitting up late at Balmoral, his boredom with Landseer's fund of anecdotes would sometimes show in scarcely-stifled yawns, while the Queen would beg for 'Just one more story!'. Most of those stories are today's chestnuts—like the one about the Highlander who had trained his collie to search out money and who one day on the moors made a wager that his remarkable dog would retrieve a hidden five pound note. 'And did he?' Victoria asked eagerly. 'Well, your Majesty, not the note,' replied Landseer, 'but he brought back the five sovereigns in change.' Later, as the painter was retiring for the night, Prince Albert delivered through a servant, in his vein of heavy-handed humour, the message that the Queen had *not* believed his story about the five pound note.

Another story that Landseer often repeated, and probably told the Queen upon whom it touched, was the true one about the famous model Bishop, who was also a pig-dealer. Sitting to the painter one day and complaining of the difficulty in getting sufficient 'wash' for his pigs, he engaged Landseer in conversation, thus:

'They tell me, sir, as you knows the Queen?'

'Know the Queen? Of course, I do. Everybody knows the Queen,' said Landseer.

'Ah, but to speak to, you know, sir—*comfortable.*'

'Yes, I have had the honour of speaking to her Majesty many times. Why do you ask?'

'Well, sir, you see, there must be lots of pigwash from Buckingham Palace and them sort of places most likely thrown away; and my missus and me think that if you was just to tip a word or two to the Queen—which is a real kind lady, one and all says—she would give her orders, and I could fetch the wash away every week with my barrer.'

Landseer's fund of Cockney stories made little appeal to the Prince who, even if he had relished jokes, was largely insulated against British dialects anyway. Besides art, on which he loved to discourse, the two main interests he shared with Edwin were shooting and billiards (at which Landseer was an adept). Albert was a frequent and sometimes unexpected visitor to Landseer's St. John's Wood house. On one occasion he fell foul of Edwin's manservant, probably the long-serving William Butler, who became both overprotective and rather too big for his boots. The master having neglected to tell his man of Albert's impending visit, Butler refused him entry, on the grounds that the painter wasn't at home. 'He's gone into the country,' blandly insisted the servant, whose opinion of Albert may have been that of many of his fellow-countrymen, high and low. Sweeping past him with the remark that, 'You must be worth a hundred pounds a year to your master!', the angry Prince

strode into the painter's studio, where Landseer disarmingly took
the heat out of the situation. 'Well, your Royal Highness, you can
scarcely call this place a town!'

An engaging and loyal innocence was the keynote of Landseer's
relationship with the royal couple and their young family. There
were occasional notes of acerbity. 'Her Majesty is all *whim* and
fancy—the Prince *and* the Queen' he complained in an unfinished
letter to Georgiana's daughter, Lady Abercorn; though adding 'but
then I am rewarded by *romping* with the Princess Royal who is a
sweet child as ever was seen—good-humoured, fresh-looking, healthy
and (really) very pretty'. Yet echoes of a slightly harsher attitude to
royal patronage on the part of both the painter and his business
manager sounded in a laconic note from Jacob Bell to Landseer in
1842: 'Boys has just been here and consented to give our price for the
copyright of the Royal Mother and brats'.

Nonetheless the intimacy with the royal couple was strong.
Landseer taught the Queen and her Prince both to draw and etch.
One day in 1842 Edwin's genial brother Tom dressed in his un-
comfortable best to accompany Landseer to the Palace. The object
of their visit was to display the complete process of engraving to the
Queen. Edwin etched a portrait of the little dog Islay in thirty
minutes, which Tom then 'bit in' in ten; a Mr. Holdgate then printed
the plate on a press that had been previously erected in the Palace
under the supervision of Henry Graves, who was also present. The
lesson reinforced the knowledge that Victoria and Albert already
possessed. Between 1840 and 1844 the royal pair frequently amused
themselves by etching designs from Landseer. They were a mixed
bag, mainly from the painter's continental sketches, but also including a dead stag and, of course, some royal dogs, and displayed a
remarkable degree of sensitivity and skill, considering the limited
time the Queen and the Prince had at their disposal to perfect such
diversions. Of course, they also bespoke Landseer's knack and
patience as an instructor. Edwin also found time to make the drawings, which Tom etched, for Victoria's private notepaper. By the
mid-1840s the royal couple were surrounded by Landseer paintings
and drawings, and Landseer-inspired etchings, in most of their places
of residence. They included an unusual venture into pictorial humour
in the portrait of *Princess Victoire of Sax-Coburg and Gotha*, the
Queen's cousin, shown from the back so as to juxtapose the Princess's
characteristic hair-style and the drooping ears of her pet spaniel.
Though a slight enough portrait, it greatly took the fancy of Victoria,
who hung it in her dressing-room at Buckingham Palace.

It was obvious that some official recognition of Edwin's industrious loyalty must soon be forthcoming, and in May 1842 the Prime Minister wrote to Victoria:

> Sir Robert Peel humbly submits his opinion to your Majesty that Mr. Landseer's eminence as an artist would fully justify his having the honour of a Knighthood, and would not give any legitimate ground of complaint to any other artist on account of a similar distinction not being conferred on him.

The Queen seemed to regard Landseer's reluctance to accept the honour as a position of shyness from which he could be coaxed, a natural desire to back rather than stride into the limelight; but four days later the Prime Minister wrote to her again from Whitehall:

> Sir Robert Peel . . . begs leave to acquaint your Majesty, that he has just seen Mr. Landseer.
>
> Mr. Landseer repeated his expressions of deep and sincere gratitude for the favour and kindness with which your Majesty had contemplated his claims for professional distinction, but appeared to retain the impression that he had yet scarcely done enough to entitle him to the honour which it was contemplated to bestow on him.
>
> In the course of the conversation he observed that he was now occupied upon works of a more important character than any that he had yet completed, and mentioned particularly an equestrian portrait of your Majesty. He said that when these works were finished, and should they prove successful and meet with your Majesty's approbation, he might feel himself better entitled to receive a mark of your Majesty's favour.
>
> As these were evidently his sincere impressions and wishes, Sir Robert Peel forbore from pressing upon him the immediate acceptance of the honour of Knighthood.

As always, Landseer was keeping his options open.

CHAPTER TWELVE

PRINCE CHARMING, R.A.

Now pray do come.
—Lady Cumming in a letter to Landseer

LANDSEER'S REASONS for refusing the honour of knighthood in 1842 do not ring completely true. Although the great composite royal family portraits were yet to come, he had certainly produced a large enough body of highly praised work to merit the comparatively modest honour. Indeed, many critics would shortly be saying that his best work was behind him. He still, of course, felt uncertain in his health and in his apparent rejection by Georgiana; but his love of social distinction should perhaps have been sufficient to make him a snapper-up of this carefully-considered trifle. Part of the reason for his refusal of the title lay in his deep uneasiness about his social position. He had, after all, been nurtured by such iconoclasts and non-conformists as John Landseer, Haydon and Fuseli: the umbilical cords, though attentuated and frayed, were not entirely severed. Yet it was probably the influence of the intellectual bohemians like Dickens and Thackeray that weighed most heavily with him.

There were always artists and illustrators in the Dickens Circle—Stanfield, Maclise, Wilkie, C. R. Leslie, Cattermole, Cruikshank and Leech among them. Although Landseer had never been personally as close to the great novelist as some of the others—notably 'noble old Stanny'—he had been regarded at one stage very much as 'one of the boys': the convivial set of writers and artists, known at one time as the Portwiners, who entertained one another (sometimes more well than wisely) in their homes, in the clubs, on the town. Landseer's ever-increasing preference for high society rather than theirs was doubtless a sore disappointment to them.

Dickens and Landseer shared the same capacity to work hard and play hard, their best work sometimes going hand in hand with their most frivolous behaviour. At the time of the young Queen's engagement, Dickens had acted the lovesick fool. His friend Maclise, then painting her portrait, had impressed the novelist with his enthusiastic descriptions of the young Queen; and Dickens went about spouting lovelorn parodies—half-serious, half-frivolous—much to the annoyance of his wife. Rumours got about that he was mentally unbalanced and Landseer unwittingly fanned the flames. Dickens had a pet raven called Grip on which he doted. His twin-preoccupation with Grip and Victoria prompted Edwin to remark that he considered his friend 'raven-mad'—an innocent aside which was interpreted in some quarters as a serious comment on the novelist's mental state.

The two men had met when Dickens was engaged on *Nicholas Nickleby*. Landseer, with his social resourcefulness, his fair wit and his powers of mimicry, was an obvious candidate for the circle. Edwin was no Oscar Wilde; but his comments like the one on an Athenaeum Club offering—'They say there's nothing like leather; this steak is!' —no doubt raised the right kind of raucous booze-aided laughter. 'All the world's favourite' was the verdict on Landseer of John Forster, Dickens' friend and biographer, and the painter was a leading light in the gatherings at the novelist's Devonshire Terrace home. In contrast to the more rarefied social stratum in which he was already moving, the tone of the writer-artist set was very much one of elbow-nudging banter and badinage; the exuberance was fifth-form; they recognised one another's strengths, but their shortcomings were socially much more fun. When Dickens began to affect a full set of whiskers, much to the dismay of Forster who had commissioned Frith to paint a (hopefully beardless) portrait, he was conscious enough of his newly-acquired face-hair to ask Landseer what he thought. 'Oh, I like it very much,' was Edwin's comment. 'It means I shall see less of you than ever.' Progressively less is what Landseer did see of Dickens after 1844. Late in that year he caused the novelist offence by failing to attend a private reading of *The Chimes* at Forster's home in Lincoln's Inn Fields: it was an event on which Dickens placed great significance and from which no loyally-invited friend was expected to be absent. The rupture, though temporary, was perhaps never entirely healed. Two years later Landseer did his sole illustration for Dickens, a spirited drawing of the dog Boxer for *The Cricket on the Hearth*. The intimacy of the friendship perhaps did not so much fade as fail to fulfil its opening promise, a circumstance for which Landseer must take the major share of the blame. As Manson said of the painter at the time: 'His stiff behaviour and distant air were so painful that many of his old comrades preferred to stand aloof rather than behold the deterioration of his nature and character. This vexed him in turn, for in his innermost heart he felt that his friends were justified and that he was to blame'.

Thackeray shared Dickens' regret at the painter's increasing preoccupation with high society. He was a forthright and pungent art critic whom several painters, Charles Landseer among them, were reportedly searching for at various times with physical violence in mind. In Charles's case it was probably bravado—Thackeray was much larger and stronger than he was. Anyway, the writer was an adept at dealing with painters in private as well as in print. On their first meeting, the young Frith, who had perhaps presumed too much on short acquaintance was disconcerted to have the famous novelist's face thrust into his: 'I tell you what it is, Frith, you had better go home: your aunt is sitting up for you with a big muffin!'. Edwin's sensitivity over critics was to grow with the years; but he did seem to recognise the partial justice in Thackeray's thinly-veiled accusations of 'selling out'. The good-natured Mulready was another who, watching his fellow-artist's high-flown social performance, was genuinely worried that 'all this incense' might spoil him for future work. Since it was Landseer's way to seek to avoid the cruel pin-pricks rather than to voluntarily let a little of the air out of himself, he began seeing less of the intellectual bohemians in whose company he had spent so many happy hours. Yet pure social shamefacedness no doubt played a large part in his refusal of the knighthood offered him at a rational juncture in his career. Even during the worst of his posturing he never seemed entirely to believe in the part he was playing. Old friends who had found themselves repelled by his vanity, his airy mannerisms, his horrendous name-dropping, the terrible throwaway accent which he could adopt or drop at will, would often be astonished on the following day to discover a man apparently recovering from a hangover—shrewd, self-mocking, slightly shamefaced with an almost perilously self-effacing notion of his own worth and his own work. 'If,' he once told Frith, 'people only knew as much about painting as I do, they would never buy my pictures.'

Lady Richmond Ritchie, Thackeray's younger daughter, first saw Edwin in 1845 when she was a young girl. The occasion was another *bal costume* of Queen Victoria's; and Thackeray took both of his young daughters along to glimpse the splendour of the occasion. The impressions are those of a wide-eyed young girl, and are no doubt slightly garbled (for one thing she has prematurely knighted the painter). But they are also a vivid reflection not only of how she saw Landseer and his society friends, but of how the artist saw himself. He was probably as much aware as was the overawed young girl of the fact that 'his company was a wonder of charming gaiety':

One wonderful—never to be forgotten—night my father took us to see some great ladies going in their dresses to the Queen's fancy ball. We drove to ------- House (it is all very vague and dazzlingly indistinct in my mind). We were shown into a great empty room, and almost immediately some doors were flung open, there came a blaze of light, a burst of laughing voices, and from a many-twinkling dinner-table rose a company that seemed, to our un-accustomed eyes, as if all the pictures in Hampton Court had come to life. The chairs scraped back, the ladies and gentleman advanced together over the shining floors. I can remember their high heels clicking on the floor: they were in the dress of King Charles II; the ladies beautiful, dignified and excited. There was one, lovely and animated, in yellow; I remember her pearls shining. Another seemed to us even more beautiful, as she crossed the room all dressed in black . . . and then somebody began to say 'Sir Edwin has promised to rouge them,' and then everybody to call out for him, and there was also an outcry about his moustaches that '*really* must be shaved off', for they were not in keeping with his dress. Then, as in a dream, we went off to some other great house, Bath House perhaps, where one lady, more magnificently dressed than all the others, was sitting in a wax-lighted dressing-room, in a sumptuous sort of conscious splendour, and just behind her chair stood a smiling gentleman, also in court dress, whom my father knew, and he held up something in one hand and laughed, and said he must go back to the house from whence we came, and the lady thanked him and called him Sir Edwin. We could not understand who this Sir Edwin was, who seemed to be wherever we went. Nor why he should put on the rouge. Then the majestic lady showed us her beautiful jewelled shoe, and one person, who it was I cannot remember, suddenly fell on her knees exclaiming, 'Oh, let me kiss it'. Then a fairy thundering chariot carried off this splendid lady, and the nosegays of the hanging footmen seemed to scent the air as the equipage drove off under the covered way.

Edwin emerges as a kind of middle-aged Prince Charming; but somewhat at the expense of his obligations as a painter. His frenetic social life certainly militated against any return to the 'niggling' touch in painting, but it also deprived him of the ability to look at the body and the direction of his work in any true perspective. Lady Ritchie quotes a later letter of his which no doubt seemed to Land-seer at the time 'a wonder of charming gaiety'. Today it has a rather pathetic sound:

I shall like to be scolded by you. This eve I dine with Lord Hardinge, and have to go to Lord Londesborough's after the banquet, and then to come back here to R. A. Leslie, who has a family hop—which I am afraid will entirely fill up my time, otherwise I should have been delighted to say yes. Pray give me another opportunity.

Written with my palette in the other hand, in honest hurry.

The plethora of invitations that so often pushed his work into second place seemed to be a matter of genuine pride with Landseer. Word had got around that the famous painter was not only a 'lion'; but one who would always lend a sympathetic ear to any seductively-worded invitation. From the 'Thirties through to the mid-Sixties the invitations—often from mere acquaintances and sometimes from total strangers—were a constant theme in his life. All begged, wheedled and cajoled: all promised an infinity of good things, reading at times like travel brochures. Lady Cumming in 1835 had invited the artist to her home in the north of Scotland, holding out the promise of 'the exquisite beauty around us . . . the name of Landseer resounds when we come upon anything splendid . . . you will not regret having given us the pleasure of your company . . . Now pray do come . . . I shall only insist upon a week and you shall have as many (months if you will) as you choose . . . I pledge my word that you will go to your charming works with renewed vigour and do finer things than you have yet produced . . .'.

Thirty years later, the invitations continued unabated, the brochure-like tone and the promises depressingly familiar. Thus as Evelyn Denison writing from Newark. 'How much pleasure it would give us, if now, or at any future time during this autumn or winter, you should feel disposed to some rides on fine turf, on well-bred quiet horses, among the old oaks of Sherwood Forest.' This holiday paradise was only '4 hours from London, you might leave King's Cross at 12 and get here at 4 . . . I doubt if you ever seen such a primeval oak forest as I could show you . . .'.

Doubtless Landseer's hosts received more in return for their hospitality than the temporary lease of a famous name. Edwin's social accomplishments were many. In W. P. Frith's recollection 'he sang delightfully, and was one of the best storytellers I ever knew'. As William Bewick noted admiringly he could 'do almost anything but dance upon the slack wire. He is a fine billiard-player, plays at chess, sings when with his intimate friends and has considerable humour'. His gift for storytelling and mimicry equalled (some said surpassed) that of London's finest light comedian—'Even Charles Mathews . . . was sometimes in the background' recalled Lord Tankerville. And, of course, the sophisticated Mathews could not even begin to compete with Edwin in animal and bird noises. Landseer could even teach mimicry by proxy: his brother Charles told Richard Redgrave that Edwin had taught Herring, the surgeon, to do a fine imitation of Haydon, whom the medical man had never seen. On one occasion, at a dinner at Sir Francis Chantrey's, Landseer had (according to Redgrave) taken advantage of his host's temporary absence to ensconce himself in Chantrey's high-backed chair at the head of the table, behind which was the door. The servant was rung for and duly appeared, whereupon Landseer proceeded to order more port in perfect imitation of Chantrey's voice. While he was discussing just which particular bottle he required the host re-entered, to his servant's pop-eyed astonishment. The bottle itself was 'enjoyed the more for the wit that won it'.

It is perhaps not without its significance that Landseer could often caricature best those whom he mimicked most effectively. He produced some amusing cartoons of Chantrey's struggles to land a monster fish, thereafter sitting miserably in his shirt-tail as his clothes dry out over a tree.

The repertoire of impersonations was large, many of which Lord Tankerville was privileged to hear: 'In the description of his day's stalking, or at another time of some debate in Parliament, you would see the wild Highlander or the Duke of Wellington before you in face and language'. Some of Edwin's reincarnations of the Duke were based on his visits to the great man's gallery. On one occasion, Landseer had asked Wellington, who prided himself on his knowledge of all the paintings in Apsley House, about the identity of a portrait of a lady in Elizabethan dress. The Duke, to his obvious annoyance, was stumped: he stalked off muttering and returned much later, when Landseer had completely forgotten about his enquiry, to hiss in the painter's ear, '*Bloody Mary!*'. Another time Landseer noticed that behind one of the Duke's pictures, a portrait hung high up, there was a nail in the wall pressing against the canvas. 'Where?' said Wellington. 'I don't see it.' Landseer carefully pointed it out again. 'I don't see it all,' obstinately insisted the Duke, who hated to be proved wrong. 'I don't see anything of the kind.' 'I assure you, there is one,' said Landseer. 'No, no,' said the old soldier, 'I don't see it'; and dragged Landseer off on the remainder of the tour. In the next room, however, Edwin turned from admiring a painting to discover that the Duke had disappeared from his side. Surreptitiously, through the opening of the door, he noticed that the old man had returned to the portrait, eyeing it from various directions. He then pulled up a chair, with which he mounted a table, and by placing a stool on top of that, managed at great hazard to himself to reach the place where the nail made its protusion. 'God, there *is* a nail, there *is* a nail!' Landseer heard him mutter.

Edwin's reputation as a wit has sometimes been exaggerated. Most verbal wits also have some mastery of the written word, and Landseer Senior had ensured that Edwin would never excel in that department. Mimicry was obviously his great social talent, and included the much-admired ability to take-off lower-class accents. One of his true stories, though attributed at different times to *The Old Shepherd's Chief Mourner* and the later *Dialogue at Waterloo*, was of the burly constable at the Royal Academy Exhibition who caught the artist touching the canvas as he explained its points to some ladies, and warned him not to repeat the offence. 'My good fellow,' Landseer confessed, 'I have touched it over and over again.' 'Well, if I'd seed you I'd have run you in,' said the constable, laying a heavy hand on the painter's shoulder and conducting him round the corner to his superior officer, where, of course, the matter was quickly explained. *Collapse* (presumably) *of uniformed party*!

The artist's long-serving manservant William was another hero of many a Landseer story. A friend had asked Landseer to look after his valuable small dog, about which the pedantic William was one day the bearer of sad news. 'Touching that there dog, sir . . . that there dog they sent us here . . . he've scratched hisself h'out!' The tiny animal had apparently burrowed its way under the old carriage gates and run off. Landseer, so sensitively fond of his own dogs, was in a terrible state of anxiety, ordering bills to be printed and distributed with the dog's description. All to no avail, however; until five days later, bringing up his master's hot-water bottle, William blandly announced: 'About that there dog . . . that there dog they sent us here . . . he've scratched hisself h'in again!'.

The dropped (or assumed) aspirate was another of Landseer's favourite anecdotal gimmicks, with his manservant once again a fruitful source. Thus the officious William to a railway-porter:

William: 'Now then! Now then! Down with them there luggage and look for hours.'
Porter: 'What's yours marked?'
William: 'Hell!'
Porter (after a prolonged search): 'Well, there aint no luggage here marked "Hell"!'
William: 'Well, where the 'ell 'as it got to then?'

Landseer's ghost stories were also in great demand—and he liked to make his listeners' flesh creep in other ways, too. At dinner once he told the lady next to him about the French sculptor he had met in

Paris who showed him how to polish marble with leather: when Edwin remarked on the extreme whiteness of the leather the sculptor had replied, 'This is my poor wife's skin. She was a very fair woman'. The lady, whose peeling of a prawn had inspired the story, hurriedly moved on to the next course.

The artist could often be relied upon to execute some rapid throw-away sketches as well. One of his accomplishments was the ability to sketch simultaneously two different subjects—on one occasion a fully-antlered stag's head with one hand and a horse's head with the other. We are told that the stag's and horse's head were both 'perfect'; though the simultaneous drawings of a staghound and a deer reproduced by Monkhouse stop some way short of perfection. As an exercise in ambidextrousness it must be admired, even though it ranked no higher than a party trick.

The wonder is that Landseer had any time left for the normal practice of his art. Nevertheless, his critical reputation steadily grew throughout the late 'Thirties and the 'Forties. In 1838 in the *Quarterly Review*, Lord Francis Egerton (after roundly denouncing Turner) had written: 'If there be one painter of our own time who deserves praise for the example of labour united with genius, it is Mr. Landseer'. Lesser critics seldom attempted to remove the seal of approval that Ruskin had set on Edwin's reputation with his rapturous review of *The Old Shepherd's Chief Mourner*. The performance of that office would be left to Ruskin himself.

Otters and Salmon was one of Landseers Royal Academy pictures of 1842. One can appreciate the excellent public relations job done on the otter's behalf by Gavin Maxwell's books when one reads Victorian critics like F. G. Stephens who pictures the animal 'cringing stealthily at the side of the fish . . . snarling in the fashion of his kind'; or of James Manson's 'snarling, snapping, suspicious otter (which) glances viciously at a mate, as if in fear of disturbance—all poachers seem alike—before falling to'. Such commentators must have felt the wicked animal had his come-uppance two years later in a picture called *The Otter Speared*. Others felt a sense of outrage; and some that Landseer was once again wearing his more reprehensible instincts on his sleeve. The painting, a mixture of sadism and (some would say) phallic symbolism, shows an otter transfixed and writhing on the end of a spear held aloft by a huntsman, with the baying hounds to which it will presently be flung clamouring down below. Ruskin was predictably incensed:*

I would have Mr. Landseer, before he gives us any more writhing

* *Modern Painters* Part III, Sec. 1 Ch. xii.

otters, or yelping packs, reflect whether that which is best worthy of contemplation in a hound be its ferocity, or in an otter its agony, or in a human being its victory, hardly achieved even with the aid of its more sagacious brutal allies, over a poor little fish-catching creature, a foot long.

It was, of course, a clear clash of ideologies. To the hunting class, to which Landseer belonged, an otter was the enemy; a thief, a skulking salmon-poacher. To Ruskin, literary gent, the animal was something else again—a tiny creature swamped by ludicrous odds. Manson waxed indignant over Ruskin's attempt to make Landseer 'a scapegoat'; but the painter had brought the rebukes upon himself. If the intention had been to show the barbarities of otter-hunting, Ruskin would no doubt have been appeased; but *The Otter Speared* foretold no such break with the hunting set. Landseer's morbid obsession with death was by this time no secret; but his portrayal of the otter's death-throes revived old accusations, as well as giving alert pre-Freudians pause for thought.

In the same year that saw *The Otter Speared* visitors to the Royal Academy clustered round another, and much less controversial, canvas that was obviously destined for great popular success. *Shoeing* had been a further illustration of Landseer's chronic tendency to procrastinate—or, put another way, of the slow but sure germination of an artistic idea. The painting, of a bright bay mare called Betty belonging to Jacob Bell, was originally intended as a study of a mare and foal. Betty was accordingly covered by a stallion. In time the foal arrived. Passing through the wet and tottering stage, it was soon in ideal condition for painting. Frequent bulletins were relayed to St. John's Wood reporting on the youngster's progress and anxiously requesting an appointment for a sitting (or a standing). But Edwin, apparently, had other fish to fry. Meanwhile, the foal was passing from the cute to the coltish stage. Further calls to Landseer . . . all in vain. Eventually Bell was forced to recognise that the stripling had outgrown its mother. Though forced to abandon this attempt, he was still determined to have his mare and foal portrait. After a heartfelt apology and other encouraging noises from the painter, Bell put Betty once more to a stallion. In due course there arrived another sturdy foal. A resumption of the fevered communications to St. John's Wood: more excuses from the great artist. The second foal ate and grew. Still no action from Landseer. Bell finally confessed defeat, selling the sadly-overgrown 'foal' as a four-year-old. Such was the Master's contrariness, however, that a year later on a visit to Bell he admired the fine condition of the mare and expressed an urgent wish to paint her. Rather than submit the aging Betty to the rigours of motherhood again, the scene in the smithy was quickly arranged.

Ruskin did not like the painting. 'All lovers of art must regret to find Mr. Landseer wasting his energies on such inanities as *Shoeing*, and sacrificing colour, expression and action to an imitation of a glossy hide.' Other knowledgeable critics detected flaws that were not even there. The mare was standing unhaltered—but in fact the animal in question would not tolerate a halter while being shod. The toe of the off forefoot was strangely pointed, apparently not taking its share of the mare's weight—but this, too, was a peculiarity of this particular animal which was posed repeatedly and adopted the same stance each time. Even the donkey was dismissed as a mere piece of window-dressing—though the idiosyncratic mare could not be induced to stand still without her long-eared companion. It was a little hard on Landseer to find himself castigated not only for subject and treatment, but for literal accuracy as well.

Not content with accusing Landseer of over-grooming his mare, in the same essay* Ruskin attacked his dogs as well, comparing the English painter to his detriment with Paul Veronese:

> In the first the outward texture is wrought out with exquisite dexterity of handling, and minute attention to all the accidents of curl and gloss which can give appearance of reality . . . This is realism at the expense of Ideality . . . With Veronese there is no curling or crisping, no glossiness nor sparkle, not even a hair; a mere type of hide, laid on with a few scene-painter's touches. But the essence of dog is there, the entire magnificent generic animal type, muscular and living . . . This is ideal treatment.

It was hardly ideal treatment for Landseer who was growing increasingly sensitive to critical attack. Ruskin's praise of *The Old Shepherd's Chief Mourner*—that 'perfect poem or picture'—had perhaps led the painter into a feeling of false security where the waspish Oxford graduate was concerned; but Ruskin, having lodged such a large account to Landseer's credit, plainly felt that thereafter he could afford to make regular and hefty withdrawals.

Whatever the faults of *Shoeing*, it is certainly no inanity. It is an attractively presented horse portrait, skilfully avoiding the dry profile approach so beloved of other artists, in which the weakest element is probably the crabbed figure of the stooping 'blacksmith' (said to have been posed by Jacob Bell). Ruskin's non-recognition of Stubbs perhaps illustrated his inability to appreciate painters who had studied the consistency of muscle and hair. There were, of course,

* *Modern Painters* Part III sec. 2, chapt. iv.

some artists who succeeded in making their racehorses look like anatomical charts with only the numbers and the index missing; but on
the whole Ruskin's contempt for 'curl and gloss' seemed a more
suitable formula for soft-toy makers than for animal painters. Perhaps his penchant for hairless animals was an extension of the
phobia which reduced him to such shuddering impotence on his
wedding night.

Relations between Landseer and his ex-horse-coper patron Robert
Vernon had meantime become slightly strained. To his customary
dilatoriness, the painter now added the sin of treating private commissions as personal property. In 1838 Vernon had commissioned
Edwin to paint a picture including three of his favourite breed of
dog, King Charles Spaniels. It was agreed that Landseer should
feature a friend of his in the painting, the lovely Ellen Power, Lady
Blessington's niece, for whom the artist cherished more than a passing fancy. The price was also agreed and the cheque written, after
which there followed the long wait by now so familiar to Landseer's
patrons. Four years went by without any picture. Then one day,
walking in the Haymarket, Vernon espied in the print publisher
Thomas Maclean's window an engraving quite obviously derived
from the painting he had commissioned but had not yet seen. Inside
the shop the astonished patron was informed that the painting,
though unfinished, had been considered in a forward enough state
for Thomas Landseer to engrave it.

Vernon was naturally far from satisfied. Not only had Landseer
omitted the elementary courtesy of informing his patron of his
intention to engrave, it was clear that for an engraving to have been
made at all Vernon's precious commission must have been completely
out of commission for some considerable time. He wrote indignantly
to the artist who replied with a characteristically vague undertaking
to deliver the picture as soon as it was finished. In the meantime,
however, the engraving had been so unfavourably criticised that
Landseer swore, his commission notwithstanding, that he would
never touch the picture again. Vernon Heath, the patron's nephew
and assistant, tried to intervene; but Landseer was adamant—the
painting would never be completed nor shown in any exhibition in
Britain.

The reasons advanced for Landseer's rejection of *The Lady with
the Spaniels* were perhaps more closely involved with the lady herself
than with the engraving. Not all his engravings had met with
favourable criticism, but he had not for that reason become obsessive
about the originals. Over the previous few years Edwin had produced
an unusual set of three pictures of heads, one called *My Horse* (the

head of an Arab derived from the canvas *Return from Hawking*) and another entitled *My Dog* (the head of the giant Newfoundland from *A Distinguished Member of the Humane Society*). The last of the three was *My Wife*—the head of the attractive Miss Power, whom Edwin had sketched several times. To Landseer's annoyance Maclean published a print of the female head, which the painter claimed was unauthorised by him. Such complaints were a regular feature of Landseer's relations with his publishers—Maclean was not the first, nor would he be the last, to misinterpret (deliberately or otherwise) the artist's often vague instructions. The provocatively-titled print became the subject of much comment. Algernon Graves dismissed *My Wife* as a mere artistic witticism; but it was obviously much more than that. It seems probable that, with his rejection by Georgiana behind him, Edwin had set his cap at Ellen Power. The would-be jocular tone of *My Wife* was fairly typical of the painter and could have meant one of three things—either it was a private joke, or it was part of an attempt to coerce a slightly reluctant woman into a permanent relationship, or it was a straightforward out-of-the-blue proposal of marriage. The first explanation can be discarded, because of the extreme, almost paranoiac irritation surrounding his rejection of one of Ellen's two portraits and both of their engravings. Landseer's behaviour, in fact, displayed all the classic symptoms of a lover with a flea in his ear, whose gallant and even slightly patronising attempt to compromise his bachelorhood had fallen flat. The publicity engendered by the print cannot have helped to smooth his path; nor presumably did the long-standing involvement with Georgiana. Possibly the couple had even had an affair. Gore House was considered advanced in sexual matters. Male–female relationships there, according to T. S. Cooper, tended to be 'fast'; and Landseer's 'description of the amusements and general "goings on" there, which he stated openly and with no reservations, was, to say the least of it, questionable . . .'. That Ellen Power was extremely pretty, with the same softly-rounded beauty as her famous aunt, is apparent both from *The Lady with the Spaniels* and from the chalk drawing of her with a pet bird, engraved for the *Book of Beauty* and now in the Wallace Collection.

Naturally Robert Vernon intensified his demands for a picture in fulfilment of his commission. By that time Landseer was almost incapable of working without the deadlines provided by the annual exhibitions. He therefore promised Vernon that he would have his picture ready for the British Institution Exhibition of 1845. The project then became a classical example of Landseerian brinkmanship. When the time for sending in pictures arrived, the painter delivered an empty frame, promising that the painting itself would follow in good time. Days passed and still no picture arrived. It was now time for the Hanging Committee to complete the arrangement of the exhibits. Somewhat nonplussed, and after close discussion, they took the empty frame and solemnly hung it in a prime place 'on the line'. Varnishing day was now approaching, with nothing showing in Landseer's frame except a section of the gallery wall; so the Keeper anxiously wrote to Robert Vernon at Ardington House. Accordingly, the patron's nephew, Vernon Heath, was despatched to find out what the painter was thinking about. He arrived at Landseer's St. John's Wood home at about eleven in the morning, sending in his card. The servant returned saying it was impossible for his master to see Heath. Heath's response was to send in the letter from the Keeper, which brought an anxious-looking Landseer out, palette in hand. Heath followed Edwin into his studio where the artist pointed to an empty canvas on an easel. 'I shall send that to the Institution tonight,' he vowed, 'a finished picture.'

Robert Vernon did not believe that Landseer could fulfil his promise—but, sure enough, on the following day the finished canvas stood in its appointed place. *The Cavalier's Pets* measured $27\frac{1}{2}''$ by $35\frac{1}{2}''$. It showed two of Vernon's favourite miniature spaniels, one a King Charles and one a Blenheim, lying on a table beside a large befeathered cavalier's hat and a spur, which served both to emphasise the diminutiveness of the dogs and to place them cleverly in a period context. Naturally, the picture helped to enhance the painter's by now almost legendary reputation for rapidity of finished execution—'The ostrich feather in the gallant's hat', as Manson rightly observed, could not 'have been more exquisitely rendered had he taken two months'. The tiny pop-eyed spaniels themselves were endearingly calculated to pierce the hearts of every Victorian lapdog lover. Alas, shortly after the picture's completion, both suffered sad (and similar) ends: the white Blenheim fell to its death from a table, and the King Charles through the railings of a staircase in Vernon's home. So the painting quickly gained additional *in memoriam* value. Its execution had been a typical Landseer triumph, not only artistically but emotionally—transforming the painter overnight from a patron's nightmare to a patron's best friend.

Landseer, in fact, did complete *The Lady with the Spaniels*, though reiterating his apparently love-lorn vow that it would never be exhibited in Britain. One day Victoria and the Prince Consort called at his studio on a picture-shopping expedition. The Prince was anxious to make a present to King Leopold, and wanted to know if Edwin had anything available. He pressed Edwin to complete the almost finished *Lady with the Spaniels* on the understanding that it would leave the country forever. Landseer agreed and the canvas was sent to the King of the Belgians. However, it *was* shown (doubtless to the chagrin of Landseer's shade) at an exhibition in London in the year after the painter's death. After the enforced retreat to France with her aunt a few years later, the beautiful Nellie herself somewhat faded from the scene. In 1901, while appearing in the highly successful play based on the character of d'Orsay, *The Last of the Dandies*, Beerbohm Tree was approached by a shabbily-genteel old lady then living in a charitable institution in Fulham who, as an eyewitness, questioned the authenticity of the playwright Clyde Fitch's version of the Count's death. She was apparently Nellie Power.

In 1846 Landseer consolidated himself in the good graces of Robert Vernon with the two companion-pictures, *Peace* and *War*. Though Vernon paid £1,500 for the pair, he did not have long for selfish enjoyment of them, giving them to the nation in the following year along with the rest of his collection. Both pictures were irreparably damaged in the disastrous flooding of the Tate Gallery in 1928; as indeed were the sentimental canine cameo *Uncle Tom and His Wife for Sale* and a later work, *The Maid and the Magpie*. *Peace* represented an idyllic scene set on the white cliffs of Dover, with a shepherd, his wife and child and a mixed flock of sheep and goats. It was engraved three times and became a firm Victorian drawing-room wall favourite, enjoining benignity and calm upon the entire household: it is noticeable in the original engraving that the remains of a rusty old cannon lying in the grass have been shined-up by the tidy-minded engravers, Cousen and Stocks, to look as though they had come straight from the foundry. Though much less of a family sedative than its companion-piece, *War* was one of the finest of Landseer's pictures; a skilful portrayal in microcosm of an entire battle. Two guardsmen and their horses lie in the ruins of a burning cottage: one of the horses is still alive; its sleek black body, straining head and fear-distended nostrils dominate the canvas. The irony implicit in the splendidly turned-out corpses, the finely-bred horses, the black sheepskin-covered saddle with the dead warrior's elegantly-booted leg still thrown across it, all lying either lifeless or condemned to die, yet scarcely sullied, in the rubble of an innocent country cottage, is marvellously conveyed. Even the single delicate pink flower that has survived the holocaust is not overdone. It was a perfect little picture, with nothing to add, nothing to take away. There are other Landseer works that might less regretfully have been lost to the nation.

If 1846 was a popularly triumphant year for Landseer with his

Peace and *War*, *The Stag at Bay* and the Belgium-inspired *Refreshment*, it was considerably less so for his erstwhile mentor Haydon. On the morning of Monday June 22nd of that year, the High Artist placed on his easel a small portrait of his wife, committed to his diary 'The last thoughts of B. R. Haydon' (mainly in praise of his heroes Wellington and Napoleon), raised a gun to his temple and pulled the trigger. The bullet, from a pistol purchased that same morning at the gunsmith's Rivière's in Oxford Street, was, however, of too small a calibre to properly penetrate the brain. Still conscious, Haydon seized one of his razors and inflicted a deep seven-inch gash in his throat. He fell dead before his cartoon of *King Alfred*, spattering the picture with his blood. At noon his daughter found his body.

'He stabbed his mother,' intoned Turner darkly when he heard the news, referring to Haydon's bitter relationship with the Royal Academy, which had trained the historical painter but had never vouchsafed him honours. The Duke of Wellington's reaction was more down to earth: his only thought was to recover the hat that he had lent Haydon for the detail in a picture and he sent a servant round to reclaim it. Haydon died, it was more ironically suggested, 'for jealousy of Tom Thumb'. He had exhibited two of his cartoons in the Egyptian Hall to a total of 133½ paying visitors whilst Barnum's famous midget, General Tom Thumb, in the next room, had drawn 12,000. But that had only been the final blow to his artistic pride: the greatest had occurred in 1843 when his proposed designs for the decoration of the new Houses of Parliament had been rejected in favour of others probably inferior to his own. 'A Day of great misery,' he had recorded in his diary. 'I said to my dear love, "I am not included". Her expression was a study. She said, "We shall be ruined" '
. . . Ever-defiant, Haydon had gone on to produce the two cartoons from his rejected designs which competed so unsuccessfully with Barnum's midget—and a third, his *Alfred*, that was found embellished with his life's blood. Yet the immediate reason for his suicide had been financial—the apparent failure of an unknown party to lend Haydon the £1,000 he had promised him. The would-be lender was designated by the painter's son Frederic only as *L*-------.

The rift with Landseer was never healed. One reason for its perpetuation had been recorded in Haydon's diary: 'When I was in prison I saw nothing of him'. It was an oversight that not even Edwin's youthful snobbism had made excusable: debtors' prison was, after all, a resolutely middle-class institution.

The arch-priest of High Art was dead. He had been a lesser painter and a better writer than he knew, though always a deeply dedicated artist. His example, however, had not been in the practice of his art, but in his tortured and uncompromising life. And his Victorian fellow-artists were only too willing to interpret that example as a dire and timely warning to themselves. Symbolically at least, the way was now clear for even steeper descents into domestic tableaux and popular sentiment, and the art that was merely the first process in the production of a thousand homely engravings. It is not on record whether Edwin recalled with any sense of irony his one-time mentor's encapsulated advice, 'Study animals, and be the Snyders of England!'. Nor can it ever be recorded what the shades of Snyders (or Stubbs or Géricault) would have said when confronted with the prayerful pomeranian of '*Good Doggie*'.

CHAPTER THIRTEEN

DEATH AND GLORY

Who does not glory in the death of a fine stag?
—Landseer, in a letter to Lord Ellesmere

IF LANDSEER'S artistic love of dogs had endeared him both to the Queen and her husband (in that order), his ability to portray deer reinforced his reputation with Albert and Victoria (in *that* order). Dogs and deer became his most frequent, and most accomplished, subjects; and while it would be unfair to suggest that he cultivated them expressly to please the couple, it is also undeniable that he could not have chosen two animal species closer, in their different ways, to the royal hearts. Albert had early on displayed his ability as a keen if erratic shot. On his first visit to Balmoral, he was writing to his stepmother:

> We have withdrawn for a short time into a complete mountain solitude, where one rarely sees a human face, where the snow already covers the mountain tops, and the wild deer are creeping stealthily round the house. I, naughty man, have also been creeping stealthily after the harmless stags, and to-day I shot two red deer—at least, I hope so, for they are not yet found . . .

Two stags in the bush were hardly satisfactory to one of Albert's thorough teutonic nature, which demanded palpable results. Thus the batches of birds and animals released in Windsor Park were sometimes said to be almost tame—many a sitting pheasant had its come-uppance, many a hare was sent to kingdom come whilst sniffing in friendly fashion at the muzzle of its hunter's gun. To seasoned British sportsmen this was blasphemy; and the larger the game the bigger the blasphemy. Albert's practice of having a trench dug two miles long (with various offshoots) in order to creep up unobserved on his prey also fed popular suspicion of his unsporting 'German ways'. Deer-drives, with beaters frightening the herd towards the guns, were likewise frowned on by the purists. Of such a drive at which the Prince was guest of honour, one British sporting journalist tartly wrote of hundreds of deer crowding into a little pass 'within twenty-five yards of the guest of no importance'. An 'open-ended' deer-drive was one thing, but the drives the Prince sometimes joined in Germany were the subject of even more astringent comment. Herds of deer were driven by beaters into enclosed stockades where the sportsmen, their seated ladies watching, proceeded to pick off the panic-stricken beasts from a raised platform. The one touch of refinement was the waltz-playing orchestra in the background which helped to drown the squeals of badly wounded deer as the gamekeepers went around slitting their throats. The practice of deliberately setting deerhounds on a stag in order to watch it being done to death also did little to enhance Albert's sporting reputation. Later, as his shooting improved, the Prince began to appreciate the importance of the clean shot, preferring to stalk quietly with a couple of gillies and a dog. But by that time his reputation had set.

Victoria herself was susceptible to the thrill of deer-stalking; though, unlike the present Queen, she never personally shot any stags. In the beginning it was her pleasure to wait at home in wifely fashion for her husband to come off the hill. 'At length—a little before three—Albert returned, dreadfully sunburned and a good deal tired: he had shot a stag. He said the exertion and difficulty were very great.' In 1842 she still thought deer-stalking 'a curious sport'. Two years later, however, she was a convert, perhaps because 'Albert enjoys it so much; he is in ecstasies here'. She began to accompany her husband on his expeditions, recording the events in her Highland Journal, including the exasperating day when, a great herd having appeared on the brow of the hill, 'most provokingly two men who were walking on the road—which they had no business to have done—suddenly came in sight, and then the whole herd all ran back again and the sport was spoilt'. She was charmed by the Highlanders' assurances, when her Prince unexpectedly bagged a fine royal stag one day, that she had a lucky foot; and there was certainly nothing squeamish about her view of the sport at close quarters:*

> Albert aimed, and shot twice, and he fell . . . The noble animal never rose, but struggled and groaned, so that Albert went and gave him another shot, which killed him at once. It was a most exciting sight . . .

At 18 st. 6 lbs. this was the heaviest stag Albert ever shot, and Victoria transcribed the details to the Deer Book, which Landseer found admirably kept, with its exact drawings showing all the points

* *Leaves from the Journal of Our Life in the Highlands*, 1868.

of the well-antlered heads. The Queen also enjoyed the wild torch-lit stag dances, with their 'hooching' jigs and reels, that followed a successful day on the hill.

Far from criticising such activities, Landseer was at pains to portray them in as epic a style as possible. Inevitably the paintings often aroused sympathy for the beleagured, wounded and dead stags, though this was rarely part of Landseer's intention. He had expounded his philosophy of deer-stalking in a letter to the Earl of Ellesmere in 1837:

> There is something in the toil and trouble, the wild weather and the savage scenery, that makes butchers of us all. Who does not glory in the death of a fine stag? on the spot—when in truth he ought to be ashamed of the assassination. I quite agree with your Lordship, there are many people one could shoot with greater pleasure and greater justice. Still, with all my respect for the animal's inoffensive character—my love of him *as a subject for the pencil* gets the better of such tenderness—a creature always picturesque and *never* ungraceful is too great a property to sacrifice to common feelings of humanity.

Landseer did not always stress the stag's 'inoffensive character'. Indeed, he liked to enthral every kind of audience—from T. S. Cooper's young daughters to a tableful of Academicians—with his tales of deer-stalking's dangers; though it has never been a sport noted for its human fatalities, unless as occasionally happened some stalker (like Lord Dalkeith later in the century) accidentally fell on his own gun or an estate servant was gored by a 'tame' park-stag, of notoriously uncertain temper when confined in a paddock. It was always the dogs that bore the brunt of the danger, as many of Landseer's more elegiac canvases showed. Nor was the element of water in such as *The Stag at Bay* and *The Hunted Stag* a mere artistic embellishment: a wounded stag when pursued will usually make for the nearest water to make his final stand. The painter was often accused of over-dramatisation in his stag pictures—too many dead and dying hounds in particular. But he was only recollecting in paint what he had himself seen several times. A well-trained deerhound would take the stag by the throat and never let go until it had brought the animal down; and many a tenacious dog disappeared forever into some raging Highland torrent clinging to the throat of a desperate stag bent on drowning its tormentor. Some of the best dogs would pursue a wounded deer for up to three days, a brand of fidelity that clearly impressed the artist almost as much as the collies that pressed themselves against their dead masters' coffins and graves. Naturally,

Landseer's best Highland pictures blended the elements of stags and dogs, with the two subjects he painted most expertly wrapped together in an often gory destiny.

Landseer, it has been said, was himself not the best of shots. He sometimes disgusted the gillies by thrusting his gun into their hands just when he had a fine stag at his mercy and pulling out his sketchbook instead. They would grumble freely in the *gaelic* about being expected to act as nursemaids to a mere London scribbler. 'However,' as the forest-keeper Ewan Cameron later recalled of one such occasion, 'Sir Edwin must have had some of the *gaelic* in him, for he was *that angry* for the rest of the day it made them very careful of speaking the *gaelic* in his hearing after.' Nonetheless, the gillies often tricked him: sometimes as they lay low on the top of a hill one of them, slightly behind him, would surreptitiously stick up his head to frighten-off a stag to which the artist had laboriously crawled close in his protective coloration of grey tweed. At times, however, the laugh was apparently on Landseer. Cameron remembered one occasion when the painter, as the poorest shot in the party, was stationed where the herd was considered least likely to run. But, perhaps through sighting or scenting the others, most of the herd came his way after all. Being in sportive rather than sketching mood, Landseer laid about himself 'famously' with his rifle, Cameron adding reminiscently that 'we found him surrounded with dead stags lying all about'.

One head-keeper called Fraser was slightly more laconic about Landseer's prowess with a gun. He remembered being out one day with the painter, who had missed a great number of good chances. With the sun just beginning to set in a golden haze, the two men spied a herd of deer, some stags among them. There was one small 'staggie' standing separate from the others, a few yards off the herd. Landseer asked for his rifle, announced his intention of bagging one of the stags, took elaborately careful aim and fired. The experienced Fraser swore that the artist had fired into the brown of the herd; but, to Landseer's great glee, the small staggie standing apart from the others fell dead. 'Ah, there' crowed the great painter, 'that's what I call a real good shot, Fraser, and such a long one, too! I aimed at his heart, and you will see when we get up there he is shot clean through it!' When they reached the dead animal, however, they discovered it had been shot through the eye.

Landseer could doubtless have quoted the great stag pictures in justification of his slaughter of the innocents. From 1842 they began to enthral a public more used to the rather moth-eaten deer of the parks and heaths that the Sunday-trippers fed with bits of stale bread. *The Sanctuary* had been a commission from William Wells, but the Queen so admired it that the squire of Redleaf loyally stepped down. It showed a hunted stag finding refuge on one of the islets in Loch Maree. It also illustrated Landseer's ability to run with the deer and hunt with the hounds, since the painting was widely interpreted as an anti-blood sports tract, an impression the artist did little to discourage. His friend William Russell contributed a long descriptive poem, *The Stricken Deer*, which certainly captured the essence of a picture much better than the usual gallery footnote and ended with the lines:

> See, where the startled wild-fowl screaming rise,
> And seek in marshall'd flight those golden skies;
> Yon wearied swimmer scarce can win the land,
> His limbs yet falter on the watery strand.
> Poor hunted hart! the painful struggle o'er,
> How blest the shelter of that island shore!
> There, whilst he sobs, his panting heart to rest,
> Nor hound nor hunter shall his lair molest.

Two years later came *The Challenge*, exhibited at the Royal Academy as *Coming Events cast their Shadows before them*, a powerful painting of a stag on the shore beneath a star-studded sky bellowing its defiance at the challenger that swims towards it. It is a masterly canvas, full both of a romantic beauty and of a menacing calm shortly to be broken by the clash of antlers in the sharp night air.

In another two years Landseer produced his famous *The Stag at Bay*—the hunted animal has taken to reedy water to make its final stand: having vanquished one dog it awaits the attack of the other. It became one of the pictures that has perpetuated Landseer's name, even among those who have never seen a reproduction of it. It was much coveted by Victorian collectors. The owner, Lady Pringle, was repeatedly offered for it what in those days amounted almost to a blank cheque: one gentleman offered £10,000. Though by no means rich, she turned down all the would-be purchasers, declaring that no sum of money would induce her to part with Landseer's *chef d'oeuvre*.

In 1847 the painter exhibited his *Deer Drive: Glen Orchy*, showing a drive through one of the high passes in Blackmount in Argyll, the home of the Marquis of Breadalbane, where Landseer was a frequent guest. The picture, one of his largest works, was bought by the Queen. With *The Random Shot* in the following year, Edwin returned to his almost obsessional preoccupation with the individual animal tragedy. A doe has been fatally wounded, the victim of a stray shot casually let-off by a stalker to empty his gun. The bloody tracks in the crisp snow show that she has managed to make some distance before dropping dead. Her fawn, doomed also to die, nuzzles at the cold teats of its mother. The original sketch had been called *Highland Sport!*; a typically half-hearted breath of irony from the schizophrenic humanitarian-sportsman. The picture is, nonetheless, one of Landseer's best deer studies. The pathos is delicately handled, the temptation to show the fawn's grief-stricken bewilderment tactfully avoided. The colour is unusually good: the sun-suffused snow even drew praise from Ruskin who found the picture 'a very beautiful exception' to Landseer's habitual 'falseness and deficiency of colour'. To the critic's somewhat card-index mind it was 'certainly the most successful rendering of the hue of snow under warm but subdued light' that he had ever seen.

A large measure of the success of the deer pictures of the 'Forties and early 'Fifties was due to the formula Landseer had discovered for his preliminary work on them. It was a fresco technique, though far removed from the straightjacketed decorations that embellished the Queen's summer pavilion. Edwin began to practice it in the homes of those with whom he felt most at ease, and whose walls were always at his disposal—Georgiana and the Abercorns. About 1844 Louisa's husband, then the Marquis of Abercorn, had leased from the Highland chieftain 'Old Cluny'. Ardverikie on the southern shore of Loch Laggan in Inverness-shire. There he built a shooting-lodge, cleared the place of sheep and began improving the native stock with deer calves imported from Glenfiddick. It was an ideal get-away-from-it-all spot, described by Victoria as 'very beautiful and extremely wild. There is not a village, house or cottage within four or five miles: one can only get to it by the ferry or rowing across the lake'. The Abercorn's frequent guest Landseer was captivated by the place. 'One of our most favourite resorts' Edwin's close friend the Earl of Tankerville later recalled. Obviously the inaccessible Ardverikie House was constructed of the simplest materials, and it was the bare white walls that inspired Landseer's return to fresco, often with the crudest of drawing materials.

Lord Abercorn was Groom of the Stole to Prince Albert, and Ardverikie was put at the disposal of the royal family for their celebrated 'marine excursion' to the Highlands in 1847. 'The walls' wrote Victoria, who occupied the lodge for a month in that year, 'are ornamented with beautiful drawings of stags by Landseer'. They were said to have been drawn with burnt stick and red brick, though Tankerville's description refined the materials to 'black and red chalk':

The dash and decision with which his touches were put in was

> really astonishing; they seemed quite at haphazard, but it was the
> faultless hand of the master . . .

These rough frescoes had merely been intended to cover the naked
walls: they represented the large virgin space which no true artist
could resist. Yet they became the originals of some of his most famous
deer pictures. Fascinated, the future Earl of Tankerville watched the
germination of *The Stag at Bay*:

> He first sketched in with a few strokes the head and antlers, and
> turning to me said, 'Ossulston, what is this stag doing?' 'Why,
> standing at bay, of course.' 'That will do.' So he went on.

Lord Tankerville had been particularly impressed by Landseer's
ingenuity in adapting the natural flaws on his makeshift canvas to
his own advantage:

> Every irregularity in the rough surface was given its significance,
> and in places where the plaster had holes where nails had been
> driven in, he transformed the holes into the eyes of his deer: the
> dark shadow of the cavity gave such transparent depth to the eye,
> and a mere touch of white upon some prominent edge of it,
> brought out such brilliancy as no pigment could have equalled.

Landseer was no stranger to odd materials. Lord Wemyss reported
that the painter had made a likeness of him, when Lord Elcho, on a
wall of the Ben Alder Lodge, Loch Ericht, in strawberry jam and
mustard, though the noble lord never actually beheld his culinary
portrait. On another occasion, bored and house-bound by bad weather, and without other materials to hand, the artist composed a
picture out of bits of coloured paper stuck on a window. This spontaneous artistic combustion also evidenced itself when Edwin was the
guest in a large house the Abercorns had leased in the Midlands. The
dining-hall was arrayed with 'hideously wooden, full-length portraits
of the family owning it'.* Landseer, who complained that such mon-
strosities put him off his food, one day without permission mounted a
ladder and proceeded to administer highlights in white chalk, making
the dull crusted eyes sparkle. He then heightened the flesh tints with
red chalk, gave the faces some definition and deepened the backgrounds with charcoal. The Abercorns considered the impromptu
face-lifts a great improvement, but the returned owners were furious
at what they considered the wilful desecration of themselves and
their ancestral dead.

The Ardverikie frescoes, however, were of a more inspired order.

* *The Days Before Yesterday*, Lord Frederic Hamilton, 1937.

In the opinion of the deer-stalking writer-artist General Crealock 'these original sketches and ideas are more truthful and lifelike than the finished pictures done later'. A photograph taken by a workman at the lodge shows a rich variety of studies—besides the original of *The Stag at Bay*, there are the sketches later developed into *The Challenge, The Forester's Daughter* and *Children of the Mist*. There was also a fine circular drawing of a stag lying dead in the heather, and one of an eagle sailing up the wind that was never worked out as a painting. The workman with the camera was to achieve at least a nodding acquaintance with posterity. His photograph remains the only existing record of the frescoes. Two weeks after Landseer's death Ardverikie Lodge was burnt to the ground and all the cartoons destroyed. A similar fate awaited the spontaneous artwork on the walls of Georgiana's bothies in Glen Feshie, though their destruction was of a different order and compounded of neglect, misunderstanding and decay.

CHAPTER FOURTEEN

DEATHS WITHOUT GLORY

Now Landseer was certainly not a little of a procrastinator.
—John Callcott Horsley, R.A.

THE KNIGHTHOOD Landseer had refused in 1842 was re-offered and accepted in 1850. Perhaps he considered that he had now fulfilled the 'works of a more important character' that allegedly had not been forthcoming at the earlier date. He had been sporadically engaged on the other cause he had mentioned in 1842 'the equestrian portrait of her Majesty', by now an obsessive and nervous theme that he was reluctant to commit to public exhibition. However, his canine ministrations still involved regular visits to Buckingham Palace. 'Landseer came & showed me how to sketch a dog with a brush & a little sepia,' Victoria wrote in her Journal in March 1850; and Edwin himself made sketches for portraits of two current favourites, the Skye terrier Dandy and the Dachshund Däkel. He was also invited for the first time to Balmoral by his friend, the Queen's Private Secretary Sir Charles Phipps: 'Her Majesty begs that you will come well provided with drawing materials'. Sir Edwin seems to have been slightly anxious about exposing his knees, and Phipps reassured him: 'The usual evening costume is the Kilt, by every body who has any claim to wear one, but at any rate we are not particular in these mountainous districts and many of Her Majesty's guests appear in Trousers'. After Landseer's departure from Balmoral, there was gratifying news for the artist-knight: 'The Queen more than once at dinner said that she wished you had returned, that she would have been so very happy to have seen you again . . .'.

Landseer had reached the age and attained the reputation where some high artistic honour also did not seem overdue, and there was talk of him as a likely candidate for the Presidency of the Royal Academy, vacant through the death of Sir Martin Archer Shee. However, Landseer had already heard the views of the Queen and her Consort on his visit to Balmoral: they greatly hoped the Academy's choice would fall on Sir Charles Eastlake. Later they conveyed the hope in a letter written through Phipps to Landseer. The royals believed Eastlake would make an ideal President 'as a gentleman of erudition, refined mind, and sound theory'. 'It proved,' wrote Eastlake's wife, 'how highly they thought of Landseer that they could address such praises of another to him.' Sir Edwin passed the letter to C. R. Leslie who in turn showed it to Eastlake himself, to help convince a somewhat reluctant candidate. The election of Eastlake was a foregone conclusion. Of some thirty-three members present Eastlake alone had voted for Landseer, two for Jones and one for Pickersgill; otherwise, delightedly recorded his doting wife, 'Charles Lock Eastlake was the burden of each'. Inevitably there were subsequent complaints among members that royal pressure had been unfairly applied in Eastlake's favour; but Leslie pointed out that only himself, Eastlake, Sir Edwin and Charles Landseer had known of the existence of the letter prior to the election. However, by not writing the letter in the first place, the royal couple could more convincingly have absolved themselves from charges of attempting to interfere in the internal affairs of the Academy. Nor was Landseer's role as messenger-boy entirely above criticism. Eastlake, certainly, was much more of an administrator than he was a painter: although he made no great impact as P.R.A. he became a highly distinguished director of the National Gallery, for which he bought 139 important pictures.

Lady Eastlake herself, a diligent hostess, thought a great deal of Landseer. She had indeed taken Ruskin to task for describing *The Old Shepherd's Chief Mourner* as 'a perfect poem or picture', believing it to be a false analogy. However, her own prediction on Landseer that in praise of him 'future generations may rival but will never surpass us' was also not without a certain irony as art criticism. Lady Eastlake had first met Landseer in 1846—'a head of power and strength,' was her impression of him, 'with that early grey hair which looks like the wisdom of age and the strength of youth mixed: he is in very "high society" . . .'.

It was symptomatic of Edwin's increasing age, his doubtful nervous health and his newly-acquired knighthood that he began more and more to frequent ultra-respectable establishments like the Eastlakes', and to discard some of his more Bohemian associations. Of course, that choice had partly been made for him. Lady Blessington and d'Orsay had fled to France, the former already buried at Chambourcy; Georgiana was frail and elderly and subject to respiratory troubles; and the Dickens pack retained certain reservations about the erring royalty-lover. Perhaps Edwin found the douce company at the Eastlakes' restful if nothing else. In her diary in May 1850 the hostess reaffirmed her approval of one of her favourite guests:

'Landseer I like much—he is a fine creature'. Her disapprobation could be equally decisive. On a visit to Turner's home 'the door was opened by a hag of a woman . . . a hideous woman is such a mistake. She showed us into a dining-room which had penury and meanness written on every wall and article of furniture . . .'. Nor was the blue-stocking hostess without colour prejudice, recording of a 'splendid dejeuner' at Grosvenor House: 'The Nepaulese Princes were there, but I have no taste for savages . . .'. Lady Bracknell herself could hardly have phrased it better.

In this year in which Landseer felt closer than ever to his Queen, he was able to serve her in yet another small way—as an artist-reporter, satisfying the royal curiosity about the exotica that arrived from time to time at the Zoological Gardens. Thus in 1850 he was able to preview the hippopotamus on its first appearance in Europe since Roman times. The sketches, in pen and brown wash, tended to corroborate Macauley's opinion: 'I have seen the hippopotamus, both asleep and awake; and can assure you that, awake or asleep, he is the ugliest of the works of God'. But Victoria had heard more exciting reports. 'It is a very sagacious animal & so attached to its various keepers that it screams if they leave it, & that the man is obliged to sleep next to it.' Later Victoria went with her children to see 'this truly extraordinary animal. It is only 10 months old & its new teeth are just coming through. Its eyes are very intelligent'. Unlike so many unknown and exotic animals imported to satisfy Victorian curiosity, the hippo survived happily for another twenty-eight years.

Landseer's offerings to the Royal Academy in that year included the unspeakable '*Good Doggie*'; and a fine if conventional Highland study, *The Lost Sheep,* tarted-up with a biblical text which failed to add much meaningfulness to a picture of a shepherd and his collies struggling to extricate a potential cash loss from a snowdrift. It was a rare upright-oblong canvas painted for one of Landseer's newest businessmen-patrons, Elhanan Bicknell, who paid him £250. Thirteen years later it sold at Christie's for £2,341. 10/-; and made £3,150 at the sale of Sir John Pender's collection in 1897. Landseer's main Academy exhibit of the year, however, was his huge—more than 6' by 12'—*Dialogue at Waterloo,* on which he had been labouring for three years.

Two years before the patron Robert Vernon died, £3,000 of his bequest had reportedly been earmarked for a grand canvas of Water-loo to be produced by Landseer, the painting to be engraved and afterwards donated along with the rest of the Vernon collection to the nation. It was a natural enough artistic dream for a Wellington-worshipping tycoon who had sold thousands of horses into battle. It also illustrated how some of those nearest to Edwin's work seemed to know least about it. Landseer was hardly a painter of battle-scenes: to his brush any more than three people constituted a crowd. Such war scenes as he had painted were generally intimate pictures of its aftermath: a thousand men and horses fighting, slashing, spearing, shying, falling and dying on a battlefield was not Landseer, who just could not manipulate a crowded action scene. Out of loyalty to the deceased patron, he seems to have at least contemplated some kind of affray, since he borrowed helmets and breastplates from T. S. Cooper. But he backed away from this scene, as he earlier had from a great architectural concept suggested by the Duke of Devonshire, substituting his own more mundane (some would say fraudulent) version. Landseer decided to portray the Duke on horseback with his daughter-in-law, the Marchioness of Douro, standing on the old battlefield and recalling the great triumph (an apocryphal scene, anyway) while souvenir sellers try to peddle their wares and a Belgian ploughman (posed by the Scottish painter David Roberts) looks on. To show the Iron Duke, not in the fever of battle, but tranquilly revisiting the scene decades later was hardly an original concept. Haydon had produced a similar canvas several years earlier. But Haydon had not been commissioned to paint an epic.

Whatever else, the venture did not lack financial backing, and in 1849 Landseer reportedly betook himself to Belgium to survey the famous battlefield. By this time there was much curiosity among European artists about the great English painter. Several Belgian artists turned up apparently expecting to find a cheerful bohemian much like themselves, only to discover what to their eyes was a conservatively-dressed *haut bourgeois* closely attended by a champagne-dispensing manservant. However, they had to admit his professionalism, as they watched him make careful studies on millboard. Sir Edwin's millboard studies were generally of a high quality and later acquired value in their own right.

Landseer, of course, knew he was on to a good thing. It was the ambition of every painter to portray the Duke, whom Edwin had already shown reviewing the Life Guards with the Queen. But this would be a much larger work. Its position, if not its success, was assured: already drawing-room walls throughout the land were screaming for the engraving. Despite ups and downs in popularity, curiosity about the Duke could never be assuaged. The minutiae of his daily habits was of absorbing interest to the people of England, or so some newspapers seemed to imagine. Earlier in the century the radical journalist Albany Fonblanque* had mercilessly guyed the

* *The Life and Labours of Albany Fonblanque, 1874.*

breathless journalism with a blow-by-blow account of the events
leading up to the Duke's morning ride:

> The Duke generally rises about eight. The Duke of Wellington
> uses warm water when shaving, and lays on a greater quantity of
> lather than ordinary men . . . The Duke of Wellington drinks tea
> for breakfast, which he sweetens with white sugar and corrects
> with cream. He commonly stirs the fluid two or three times with a
> spoon before he raises it to his lips . . . At eleven o'clock, if the
> weather is fine, the Duke's horse is brought to the door. The Duke's
> horse on these occasions is always saddled and bridled . . . Before
> the Duke goes out, he has his hat and gloves brought him by a
> servant. The Duke of Wellington always puts his hat on his head
> and the gloves on his hands. The Duke's manner of mounting his
> horse is the same that it was on the morning of the glorious battle
> of Waterloo. His Grace first takes the rein in his left hand which
> he lays on the horse's mane; he then puts his left foot in the stirrup,
> and with a spring brings his body up, and his right leg over the
> body of the animal by way of the tail, and thus places himself in
> the saddle; he then drops his right foot into the stirrup, puts his
> horse to a walk, and seldom falls off, being an admirable eques-
> trian . . .

The Duke's ability to stay on a horse was, in fact, a mystery to
many. His seat was insecure-looking to say the least, and when his
mount rose to a stiff trot it seemed inevitable that there must be a
gradual list that would eventually unseat him. Landseer's picture
was much praised for its exact rendering of this unusual seat, which
a later generation might have described as 'glass-assed'. W. P. Frith
found *A Dialogue at Waterloo* 'the only true resemblance of the great
Duke in his later years'. The Marchioness of Douro was notably less
successful. 'That's quite shocking!' Frith overheard the Iron Duke
say to a friend as he looked at the picture. Landseer, admitting as
much, added, 'I wonder the Duke is any better, for he only sat for
half-an-hour'. The painter had had early doubts about the Marchioness. As early as the summer of 1847 he had written in the
beginnings of desperation to Sir William Ross, the famous miniature
painter; but had drawn a blank:

> I would most willingly trust you with a likeness of Lady Douro,
> but I have not one of that beautiful person. It has recently been in
> my hands, but has recently returned to the family.

So Landseer was forced to employ a model with a certain resemblance
to the Marchioness, who claimed that she had to sit to the painter

more than fifty times, and each time Landseer had completely effaced what he had done before. Thus did Wellington's daughter-in-law join the roll of famous faces which Edwin just couldn't get right, which he painted over and over and which added to the sum of nervous despair that eventually helped consume him.

The canvas itself was either admired or deplored; its eighty or so square feet precluded indifference. Similarly mixed reactions greeted the long-awaited engraving by T. L. Atkinson, 'now to be seen in every print shop window'. A Mr. Crossland wrote to the *Illustrated London News* complaining about the pasterns of the Duke's horse: 'If the horse's legs were alive, instead of pictorial, they would snap off just above the hoofs with the mere weight of the body'. Landseer's fellow animal-painter J. F. Herring waded-in with a defence so palpably inept that it probably raised a groan from the *Dialogue*'s creator: '. . . Edwin Landseer is in every sense of the word a gentleman . . . his talent stands unequalled either in the taste or the elegance of his compositions. Yet he is but a man, and therefore liable to err . . .'. To which Mr. Crossland tartly replied by refusing to cross swords with one who 'handles his foils so carelessly'.

It was certainly a fact, as the same Mr. Crossland admitted, that 'our greatest animal painter . . . is not often caught trespassing against the teachings of nature'; but both the controversial pasterns and the tight-as-a-drum belly of the Duke's horse (suggestive of the most acute colic) were transgressions of the kind. Perhaps Landseer had found difficulty in establishing the correct relationship between his eye and the enormous canvas: certainly he was at that time suffering from eye trouble. The weakness was not, however, apparent in a picture shown in the following year, his scene from *A Midsummer Night's Dream*. This had been produced for the great railway engineer Isambard Kingdom Brunel, who had commissioned Shakespearian scenes from several other artists as well, all at 400 guineas a time. Sir Edwin's portrayal of Titania and Bottom was a pleasing and attractive fancy that adorned several generations of schoolbooks, rivalling the efforts of other fairy painters like Dadd and Paton. It was certainly a bargain at 400 guineas, being bought by Lord Clinton nine years later for £2,940. Though hardly an imperishably great picture, it had good pictorial quality, colour, composition, clarity and finish; and Samuel Redgrave went so far as to say that 'it may be (Landseer's) last great work'. It went to Australia, and is now in the National Gallery of Victoria in Melbourne.

Landseer was forty-nine when he painted his famous stag portrait, *The Monarch of the Glen*. It has become the twentieth century projection of his reputation, though vulgarised by over-exposure.

Nevertheless, it is a fine portrait of a noble animal which cleverly obeys the photographic precept, If you aim at dignity aim from below. The three-quarter length *Monarch* occupies a canvas almost four-and-a-half feet square: obviously Landseer waited until his knowledge of the red deer stag was as complete as it was ever likely to be before committing to canvas his definitive close-up. It was admirably engraved by his brother Tom, although he had some trouble in achieving the effect of moistness on the stag's muzzle and it was left to the painter himself to add this touch.

The *Monarch's* history is a chequered one. Her Majesty's Commissioners of the Fine Arts had been appointed in 1841 to look into the whole question of the interior decoration of the new Westminster Palace. In 1850 Landseer had been given the commission to paint in oil three subjects connected with the chase to adorn triple panels in the House of Lords Refreshment Room, £1,500 to be the fee for the set. It was a price which, as Richard Redgrave noted, 'proved that the painter's motives in accepting the commission were far other than pecuniary'. However, politics and aesthetics, then as now, were the uneasiest of bedfellows. The House of Commons were grumblingly dissatisfied with the work the Commissioners had so far secured for them—and no doubt traditionally jealous of the other over-privileged sport-besotted chamber. When the £1,500 was called for, the House, by an adverse vote, struck the figure from the estimate. Their intention had been to show their lack of faith in Her Majesty's Commissioners—but it was Landseer who got slapped. What was to become the most popular of all his stag subjects therefore went privately to Lord Londesborough for a figure alternatively represented as 350 or 800 guineas. It subsequently passed through the collections of two other peers, Lord Fitzgerald and Lord Cheylesmore, before being bought in 1916 by its present owners, the whisky-distilling Dewar family, for almost fifteen times its original asking price.

The year 1852 was an undistinguished one for Edwin. There was nothing of his on view at his favourite showcase of the Royal Academy, although his *Deer Pass* was shown at the British Gallery. In contrast, old John Landseer's interest in engraving had undergone a resurgence. He had apparently ceased exhibiting in the Royal Academy with an engraving after a work of his son's called *Rat Catching* in 1823. However, after a gap of a quarter of a century he showed two works in 1848, four in 1849, three apiece in 1850 and 1851 and *Hadleigh Castle, Suffolk* in 1852, the year of his death. He had remained spry and interested in everything, despite his total deafness. His slightly annoying corrective and argumentative streak had not subsided: after reading *Barnaby Rudge* he even wrote to Dickens questioning his description of the 1780 Gordon Riots at which the engraver had been present as a boy, the great novelist's reply being coldly polite. His behaviour was always apt to be eccentric. Even after attaining distinction both in his own right and as the father of Britain's most popular painter, Mrs. Adams-Acton remembered him issuing regularly from a favourite shop near Fitzroy Square with his dinner tied up in a bright red handkerchief. He never, perhaps, became totally resigned to the fact that Edwin's reputation had outstripped his own. When his only grandson was born he wrote to his daughter Emma, then living in Jersey, a letter in which he complained of being 'sadly plagued with nocturnal cramps':

> Also I want to see that little boy of yours of which I have heard so much. Yet, by what I hear, he is too heavy to be sent for that purpose by post. I find you have christened him Edwin John. It should have been John Edwin. You would still have been at liberty to call him Ned or Jack when he grew up.

In 1848 Edwin had shown an oil sketch of his father. It was a fine little portrait in which the eccentric, shrewd and didactic character of the long-haired and fancy-waistcoated old man is evident. Its main distinguishing feature, however, was the obvious affection with which the painter regarded his sitter.

John Landseer died on 29th February 1852 and was buried beside his wife in Highgate Cemetery. The event can hardly have been unexpected in a man whose age was variously calculated as eighty-three, eighty-eight and ninety-one. But a death in the family, or among close friends, always had a depressive effect on Edwin. The Cunningham *Lives* described him as 'feeling the loss of each friend as a crushing blow, from which only partial recovery was possible'.

If this was the case, there were further crushing blows to come. One of them was dealt in the following year. Georgiana had for some-time been in a delicate physical state, wintering abroad for her health. She and Landseer continued to meet when she was in Britain, and the painter had sometimes been seen in her box at the opera. Although she was now seventy-two, and their sexual dalliance a thing of the past, there was still a considerable bond of affection between them, strengthened by Landseer's continued ties with the rest of the family, especially with Louisa, Duchess of Abercorn. The artist, of course, would have been an ideal advertisement for British tourism. Despite his own variable health, the continental spas and health-resorts obviously meant nothing to him. So he was far from Georgiana when her final illness unexpectedly struck. His painter-friend C. R. Leslie was, however, in Nice at the time, and wrote Edwin on February 22nd 1853:

> My dear Lanny
> I regret very much that I have at any time to write you anything disagreeable but here especially on the present occasion as it concerns one whom we both highly esteem. The Duchess of Bedford has been confined to her bed with influenza and I expect today it has fallen on her chest and she is now dangerously ill.
>
> I fear much from her age and from a predisposition to disease of the chest—it may be serious and we must hope the best in the meantime. I will write you again tomorrow as this night is a great crisis. The change takes place for better or worse this night.
>
> I confess to myself—I have my fears but hope they may not be realised. She has two doctors with her, suffers no pain and is perfectly composed and resigned to anything that may await—her health or death. I cannot write you more now—but will give you another time tomorrow.

In fact, the Duchess's condition gave no cause for hope of any kind. Landseer's friends had learned by practice always to wrap up any unwelcome tidings in several layers of cotton-wool. Even the forthright Leslie had considerately gone out of his way to prepare his good friend for the worst:

> Since I wrote you yesterday a change for the worse took place and with deep regret must be the person who has to announce that this day at 2 p.m. the Duchess resigned her spirit to Him who made it.
>
> She died composed & calm with her children that are here with her. Lady Rachel suffers most acutely. Lady Abercorn also, though in health pretty well. The Duchess expressed a wish to be buried here which will be carried out soon. I will stay for the funeral and then hasten from this sad spot to England.

These sad events helped to precipitate another decline in Edwin's nervous health. Not only had he suffered the loss of his father and the great love of his life; but, in recent years, the loss of two of the patrons who had also been his firm and sympathetic friends; William Wells in 1847 and Robert Vernon in 1849. Another esteemed patron, Sir Robert Peel, had died in 1850 as the result of a fall from a horse. The exiled Countess of Blessington had died broken-hearted in 1849, and Landseer's sartorial hero d'Orsay in the same year as his father. Other morbid factors had for long preyed on his mind, including the sudden descent into insanity of his elegant artist-friend of the 'Twenties and early 'Thirties, Gilbert Stuart Newton, confined to a mental asylum in Chelsea, who had died in 1835. The brilliant young painter Richard Dadd had been another mental casualty, murdering his father in 1843 before fleeing to France where he had tried to slit the throat of a passenger on the ferry: he was now incarcerated for life in Bethlehem Hospital. The popular sporting artist, Luke Clennel, had likewise suffered a decline into madness ending with his death in 1840. It is perhaps not surprising that Landseer's own morbid fears, the slightly self-pitying sense of personal loss and injury that surrounded the death of every friend, the worsening mental and physical hypochondria should become increasingly evident both in his life and in his art.

The crack-up, however, was a gradual one. Landseer was actively engaged on several important deer pictures, three of which were shown at the Royal Academy in 1853. *Night* and *Morning* were two of his favourite type of contrast paintings—the first showed two rutting stags in head-on conflict; in the second the two lie dead on the hillside . . . neither the victor, both the vanquished. The title of his other deer picture of that year deferred familiarly to human feelings. *Children of the Mist* was an evocative canvas showing the contours of a stag and his hinds enveloped in a Highland *har*. Landseer himself said that he received more complimentary letters about this small painting than about any other he had ever painted. It was a triumph also for his eldest brother, who considered it his best engraving. Certainly, it gained Tom a good deal of professional attention, and for obvious reasons. Atmosphere was an enormously difficult quality to convey in a black-and-white engraving. The German-born painter Joseph Wolf complained justifiably that 'Engravers cut out all the mystery—that which makes the painting'. In ordinary hands that would certainly have happened to *Children of the Mist*; but Tom skilfully retained the mystery, even though deprived of the sharp tonal contrasts on which the engraver normally depends.

The Twins, a mawkishly-titled but accomplished exhibit of the same year, pictured two lambs with their mother, guarded by two sheepdogs lying on their master's tartan plaid. It was another picture with railway associations, having been commissioned as a retirement present for the great engineer Robert Stephenson. When Stephenson left the London and North Western Railway Company he was offered a service of plate. He said he would much rather have a picture by Landseer. Flattered by this unusual proposal, the painter declared, 'He shall have a good one'; and *The Twins* was the result. For good measure the grateful railway company also threw in another painting, a landscape by Dickens' best friend, Clarkson Stanfield, *Wind Against Tide—Tilbury Fort*.

In the following year Landseer had two royal pictures on show and in the year after that, 1855, nothing at all. His closest friends were hardly surprised, knowing of the nervousness, the lack of concentration in the painting-room, the procrastination over commissions that had been building-up over the past three years. One of the chief sufferers, whose patience creaked and finally broke under the strain, was the 6th Duke of Devonshire. The two men had known each other for some twenty-five years. *Bolton Abbey in the Olden Time* had been Edwin's earlier response to the invitation to paint the picturesque abbey in the West Riding that had passed to the Devonshire family. Completed in 1834 it had shown, not the imposing structure itself, but a group of clerics and rustics grouped round a collection of dead game. Although clad in period costume, several of Landseer's family and friends were recognisable, including Sir Augustus Callcott, R.A. who had sat for the head of the Abbot. While never critically popular —one critic sneered at 'its shopful of produce'—it had enjoyed a great public success: as the artist later acknowledged to the Duke it 'made me the fashion'. At the time his Grace had confided his reservations about this artistically-convenient digest of a picture to the *Chatsworth Handbook*: 'Landseer's Bolton Abbey might be any other Abbey: its immense success has partly reconciled me to his not having made what I gave him the commission for—namely, a representation of the place'. In the end, however, 'everybody was satisfied, except poor Rev. Carr, who thought it a take-in'—as, for abbey-lovers, it certainly was!

The 6th Duke perhaps did not altogether understand painters. To expect a preponderantly architectural subject from Landseer was to expect the impossible. But his eventual admiration for Edwin's *Bolton Abbey* (and for a painter who was, socially speaking, everything that an artist should be) blinded him to Landseer's limitations. In 1853 he headed a committee to commission from Sir Edwin a companion piece, featuring himself and other members of his circle. The artist had already sounded characteristic notes of caution, reminding the Duke 'that I am more of an animal and beast painter than a delineator of the human form divine!' But the Duke's warm hospitality had already imposed on him a fatal sense of obligation— 'You will understand my eagerness to accept any subject suggested by my first and kindest friend'. The eagerness must have been somewhat forced. Georgiana's death had contributed towards making him (though he did not involve the Duke in causes) 'very unwell, perhaps more seriously than you are aware'. Such events always unbalanced Landseer: coupled with nervousness over a commission, they virtually guaranteed a descent into ill health. The Duke's generous response to Edwin's indisposition was to offer him more hospitality. 'The comforts of your delightful home already begin to revive me,' the painter was writing in April 1853. The Duke was still helping to revive him in July with eagerly-accepted invitations to Brighton—'I have been less well lately and am sure a pinch of salt air will do wonders for me'. Early in 1854 the Duke himself was unwell, though doubtless helped towards recovery by Edwin's repeated assurances of his anxiety to get on with the commission. The artist's letter to Sir Joseph Paxton, the Duke's agent, in May of that year was considerably less assured, reminding him 'that I urged when the Committee did me the honour to select me as their painter . . . that I do not do portrait paintings and . . . cannot *promise* startling success—as there is yet time for the gentlemen to reconsider their choice'. This seems, however, to have been regarded as a further manifestation of the artist's innate modesty.

With the Duke's recovery, Landseer's health lapsed again. 'I have been seriously unwell,' he explained in August 1854, 'and I am ordered out of town. A few weeks in the Highlands normally renews my health. I live in hopes of returning in condition to work at the companion to *Bolton Abbey*.'

The prevarications and protestations dragged on until June 1855, when the Duke managed to pin Landseer down to a date for a personal sitting. Edwin's odd but characteristic conduct was to send out a waffling note all too late to reach the Duke, cancelling the appointment and suggesting that he come to the Duke instead—'I wish to make a drawing that will greatly aid me in the Picture—I take this opportunity to say I am *sincerely* occupied in the Picture—the composition will *I am certain* make a happy companion to the olden time B. Abbey. How ever boastful and conceited you may think me I venture to say when I content my own Eye I please others. I do not promise too much in boldly telling you the scheme pleases me, and that the work goes on *glibly*'. An hour before the Duke was due to appear for his sitting, Landseer turned up at Devonshire House, peddling the same excuses as in the missing note about the splendid progress being made on a non-existent painting. That same evening the Duke of Devonshire (D.D.) was still sufficiently incensed to dictate a memo recording the progress of the interview:

Sir Edwin began, by his wish to see Lord Cavendish and by describing how he had thought of bringing him into the picture, and talking in his usual vague manner about it and above all lamenting that I had not read the note yet which would he said explain everything fully. After a great deal of desultory and very idle talk, D.D., who was naturally not much pleased at continuing to be thus trifled with, may have perhaps shewn some trace of that failing, and later it declared itself freely when Sir Edwin requested him to state his wishes. D.D. said he should like something a little more like progress, that as to the commission, for the execution of which he had now been waiting three years, nothing had ever caused him so much anxiety . . . and it was to D.D.'s great astonishment and great unwillingness that he ascertained that no actual work had really commenced. Sir Edwin again enquiring, D.D. replied thus. 'All I can say is that I urge you to begin in earnest and to conduct yourself like a man of honour and honesty.' Soon after this, Sir Edwin rose to withdraw, saying that the best thing he could do was to go home and work, to which D.D. expressed assent by the word 'certainly'.

Ironically, though, at the height of his dithering and procrastination over commissions, many of which would never be fulfilled, Landseer's name was more insistently before the public than ever before, both at home and abroad. It was the year of the great Paris International Exhibition, with the Fine Arts Jury comprising representatives from all over the world, including Lord Elcho as Vice-President. Richard Redgrave was chosen as Britain's Commissioner, his task being to round-up and send off some three or four hundred examples of 'the rarest pictures of our British schools'. He finally did so, several grey hairs later, at an insurance value of £100,000 for exhibition in a building which he discovered to his horror was of 'timber and paper construction . . . separated only by 2 ft. from a sugar refinery'. However, some of the artists, Landseer among them, proved an even bigger headache than the ever-present risk of fire.

'There were two or three painters who gave us infinite trouble by their procrastination,' complained Redgrave. 'Some painters would not even trouble themselves to name the pictures they wished to be represented by; some would have certain works or none, some named only their unsuccessful works, those that remained in their own possession; while far too many deceived themselves as to what really were their best works. Landseer was one of those who would send and would not, who named certain pictures and then withdrew them, and finally wrote to say he did not intend to exhibit.'

It became necessary to train a heavier gun on the errant knight, and the fiery Lord Elcho manoeuvred himself into position: 'You will I hope excuse my telling you that I think your conduct in this matter to say the least somewhat strange . . . I took it for granted that you would send some pictures to Paris, the only question being which. That I expected would have been decided last night but you bolted after dinner without alluding to the subject!'. Lord Stanley and Redgrave were 'expecting to hear farther from me on the subject . . . Am I to write them and say that you decline to send any? . . . I must beg of you to reconsider your decision . . . all I want is one or two of your *large finished* pictures and some of your chalk studies of which you have hundreds!'.

Landseer's eventual exhibits included *The Sanctuary, Shoeing* and *Jack in Office*, the last-named of which the French found untranslatable, settling for *Jacques en Faction*. As a result he was awarded a large Gold Medal of the First Class, a distinction also accorded to Delacroix, Vernet and the Belgian painter Leys. It was not entirely a popular award in England: some critics thought that Mulready or Leslie had a much better claim to the honour. Dickens, who was living in Paris at the time, was much struck by the contrast between the French and British paintings on view. The British offerings he found 'small, drunken, insignificant, "niggling"'. There were, on the other hand, 'no end of bad pictures among the French, but lord! the goodness also—the fearlessness of them; the bold drawing; the dashing conception; the passion and action in them'. Landseer was equally impressed, particularly by the work of Horace Vernet: his praise of the French painter was, according to Dickens' biographer John Forster, 'nothing short of rapture'. The prizes were given out by the Emperor Napoleon who is said to have stood in a recess so arranged as to produce a startling echo of every word he spoke. He apparently shook Landseer by the hand and said in English, 'I am very glad to see you'. The animal painter had first met Prince Louis Napoleon Bonaparte in very different circumstances, when the exiled Pretender had visited Gore House: the now dead Count d'Orsay had loyally espoused Louis Napoleon's cause and had served briefly under him as Director of Fine Arts. On the evening of the prize-giving, Forster recorded, Landseer dined at the Café Royal with Dickens, Leslie, Boxall 'and three others'.

It had been a triumphant occasion for Landseer—and equally so for the watercolourist George Cattermole, who was also awarded a *grande medaille d'honneur*. Landseer and Cattermole had a great deal in common; both were or had been dandies, sportsmen, skilled mimics and humorists, habitués of Gore House, members of the Athenaeum Club, friends of Dickens and both had declined knighthoods in their time. To the exasperated Richard Redgrave, however, they had something else in common—rank ingratitude towards the man who had forcibly dragged them from their cocoon of artistic lethargy. 'I had compromised myself in both cases,' recorded Redgrave bitterly, 'and therefore, notwithstanding their determination, I made a good show for them, and they both took high awards in medals and honours; but neither they nor others ever thought it worth while to offer me a word of thanks.'

Procrastination was not merely a characteristic of Landseer's art. It overflowed into his life as well. The painter Hollins related to Redgrave the story of Sir Edwin on one of his jaunts to the Highlands. Jacob Bell, as was his wont, had gone to great trouble to get the painter, his manservant and his luggage to the railway station well on time to catch the express to the North, via Glasgow and Perth. Bell paved the way with customary thoroughness, impressing on the stationmaster the elevated status of his passenger and 'bespeaking for him every sort of attention'. The stationmaster was extremely solicitous, taking especial care to see all of Sir Edwin's luggage safely aboard . . . to find a seat for Sir Edwin's manservant . . . and a comfortable place facing the engine for Sir Edwin himself. Finally, after the great painter had strolled up and down the platform several times, the stationmaster informed him that it was now time to take his seat. Sir Edwin thanked him courteously for the information. A warning bell rang. 'Now then, sir, pray step in,' said the stationmaster, 'The train will move on in a minute.' Sir Edwin looked around him, sticking a glass in his eye. 'Ah, a bookstall!' he said, with pleased recognition, 'I'll need a book for the journey'; and he strolled off to make his selection. With a shriek of its whistle, off went the train. The painter spun round. 'It's gone, Sir Edwin,' said the despairing stationmaster. 'Eh, what,' muttered Landseer. 'It can't have? You'll stop it surely?' This, however, was impossible. The great artist could only watch the train, his servant and his luggage disappear in a wreath of white smoke.

The only recourse left was to telegraph for his servant to wait for him at Carstairs. However, like master like man. The message came back that the luggage had been traced, but the servant was missing. He had alighted at Rugby for a quick snack, had mistaken the warning bell and was now as hopelessly stranded as his master.

The year 1855 saw several public reminders of how much Landseer owed, both financially and in reputation, to his engravers. It would finally be estimated (in 1875) that no fewer than 126 engravers had laboured to produce 434 different etchings and engravings of the animal painter's works. Most prominent among them were his brother Tom, C. G. Lewis and Samuel Cousins; but others like T. L. Atkinson, B. P. Gibbon and R. J. Lane were hardly less distinguished. A winter exhibition of 278 engravings from Landseer gave the public the opportunity to see something of the thriving industry that had grown up around him, an industry, of course, that would help to make not only Sir Edwin but engravers like Samuel Cousins very wealthy men. 'A rare honour,' recorded the *Athenaeum*, 'to observe at once the green blade and the harvest, the seed and the fruit, and to trace the growth of a mind from its infancy to its complete development.' 'Among the curiosities,' noted the *Illustrated London News*, '(are) several pieces etched by noble and distinguished amateurs—the Duchess of Bedford, Ladies Elizabeth and Harriet Russell, Miss Wardrop (now Mrs. Shirley) and others . . .' Miss Wardrop, Landseer's occasional pupil, had once complained to him about the difficulties of drawing a horse's hooves; whereupon her tutor had shown her how to overcome the problem, by drawing an extremely attractive little sketch of a mounted huntsman in long grass.

Another event involving the engraving aspect of the Landseer art industry had occurred a few weeks before when Mr. Boys of the print-publishers Moon, Boys and Graves had presided over the ritual destruction of twelve of the artist's most celebrated plates, with an audience invited as though to a public execution. Those marked for destruction included *Shoeing*, *The Sanctuary*, *The Deerstalkers' Return*, *The Return from Hawking* and *Three Hunters*. The virtually indestructible plates had previously been grooved in three-inch spaces to facilitate the operation of breaking. The engraver C. G. Lewis, the *Illustrated London News* averred, 'looked on callously' as a brawny mechanic, placing each plate in turn on an anvil, knocked it to pieces with a sledgehammer. The ritual slaughter occupied one hour; and there were public protests at this apparently monopolistic attempt to enhance the value of the prints to previous purchasers. 'Mr. Boys,' one protester suggested, 'is a vandal of the worst clay!' There seems to have been the implication, in fact, that Landseer prints might alternatively have been distributed, like soup or bread, to the poor. However, more reasonable voices pointed out the melancholy truth behind the public-relations exercise—the plates had been worn-out by over-use, anyway, before being committed to the anvil.

CHAPTER FIFTEEN

THE ABSENTEE LANDLORD

It is delightful to see Landseer's unaffected kindness to his sisters.
—John Constable in a letter to C. R. Leslie

LANDSEER WAS very much the absentee landlord where his St. John's Wood home was concerned. He was too sensitive an individual to be around while the extensive alterations were made to the place: he much preferred to contemplate such operations at long range, leaving others to face the worry and the inconvenience. In 1839 he had written from Scotland to his Aunt, Miss Potts, who was installed there: 'I hope to find the *walls* completed, and the mud removed'; and in a subsequent letter, as winter approached: 'I hope the gardener will put dead leaves out of the way and make the place habitable for my return'. 'Assure Bell of my entire reliance on his taste touching the Stove,' he wrote in another letter in which he also rather pompously enjoined his Aunt and his sister Jessica: 'Let me find *comforts* and Health, *spirits* and contentment on my return and I shall be happy *if* I get to work and keep my present condition'.

Edwin's Aberdonian Aunt was a retiring old lady who spent most of her time incarcerated in a room at the top of the house. The burden of the housekeeping fell on Jessica, and to a lesser extent on Landseer's youngest sister, by then Mrs. Mackenzie. Both women enjoyed a close relationship with their famous brother: in 1832 Constable had written to Leslie: 'It is delightful to see Landseer's unaffected kindness to his sisters'. Nonetheless, if Tom gave too much of himself to Edwin's career, the same might be said of Jessy, an accomplished artist and the most talented of the trio of surviving sisters. Over the years she exhibited ten pictures at the Royal Academy, and many more at the British Institution. She was hardly the first or the last woman to be coy about her date of birth, which she recorded for the benefit of the *Dictionary of National Biography* as 29th January 1810. If this were so, she had been a Royal Academy exhibitor at the age of six, since her *View from a Farmyard, Suffolk* is listed in the 1816 Catalogue, and *Hampstead seen from the fields between Primrose Hill and Kilburn* in the following year. Such precocity (had it been credible) would have made Edwin, an Academy exhibitor at thirteen, look like a late developer. As it was, her baptismal record gives her year of birth as 1807 which would make her (potentially) the most prodigious of all the Landseers. Her later contributions to the R.A. and the B.I. included several landscapes and a rare canine portrait in 1863 of *Lassie, the property of Sir E. Landseer, R.A.* She had also etched plates of Edwin's work, including one of the Scotch terrier *Vixen* in 1824 and another of *Lady Louisa Russell feeding a Donkey* in 1826. In 1839 she made a copy in ivory of *Beauty's Bath*, a portrait of Miss Eliza Peel with her dog Fido, which highlighted yet another of her skills, as a miniaturist. She seems, however, to have shared Edwin's tendency to procrastinate: in 1837 the normally even-tempered Duke of Bedford had written several letters pressing Landseeer about an unforthcoming miniature of the Abercorn children, an intended present for the Duchess. When the miniature finally materialised he huffily deemed it 'somewhat glaring and offensive to the eye', complaining, too, about Landseer's and Jessica's time-honoured reluctance to name their price.

Jessy might well have become an artist of some note, but ladies who painted professionally (the private water-colour album was another matter) were rather frowned upon. Edwin could easily have encouraged her to greater things, but in artistic matters he was scarcely an emancipationist—his involvement with the theatricals at Woburn, for instance, did nothing to ameliorate his view that acting was *not* a profession for a young lady. The mild-mannered Jessica seems therefore to have been content to sun herself in her famous brother's reflected glory. Algernon Graves described her as 'a meek, amiable little body who looked after her brother's house in a very quiet and unostentatious way'. She usually dressed plainly in a poke bonnet and a long shawl which swept the ground at the back; and was said to have been the chief sufferer from Edwin's frequent shortage of the ready, sueing in vain for more housekeeping and money for repairs to the ultimately rather dilapidated house. The youngest surviving child, Emma Caroline, Mrs. Mackenzie, was reputedly as haughty as Jessy was self-effacing, an impression partly borne out by Edwin's portrait of her. Early on she had antagonised Edwin by copying his pictures and signing them *E.L.* She exhibited twice at the Royal Academy when she was in her early forties—a *Study from Nature* in 1852 and *The Twa Dogs* in 1853—and outlived the brothers and Jessica to become the heiress of them all.

According to near-neighbours, as the Landseer property developed

its rambling beauty and its distinctive character steadily diminished.
It was perhaps a little hard on Landseer, as a famous painter, to
expect him to retain a pretty country cottage in its pristine state: it
would have been incompatible with his growing social and professional status. The main alterations had been put in hand in 1840
when Edwin, characteristically, had left for the Continent and could
thus be sure that none of the inconvenience and upset would devolve
on him personally. He became increasingly obsessive about his
privacy, seeking both to protect and extend his boundaries. One
letter from an adviser hinted both at territorial problems and the
anti-semitism so prevalent at the time—'Have your agreement
signed before you put property in shape of backing upon his ground.
He is a Jew. You have already paid much too Dear for the slice of his
backside which you have obtained'. In its finished state, the house
itself was a sizeable two-storey white mansion, said to be in the
Italian style of architecture. It perhaps reflected over-ambition in
its owner—several of its rooms remained closed and unfurnished.
The chief studio, according to the *Illustrated London News*, measured
40′ × 24′ × 15′ high, with an ante-room and a sketch-room adjoining, and opening onto the terrace and gardens. One end of this large
studio was paved and enclosed to accommodate the painter's animal
models. There was a lesser studio on the first floor—26′ × 17′ × 12′
high. There was also a large paddock to contain Landseer's four-
footed sitters, which might range from a small herd of deer to a lion.
The whole character of the place was largely determined by its
owner's profession of animal painter. The epic painter John Martin
had been a frequent visitor to St. John's Wood in the 'Thirties; and
his description of the original place, recorded by his son Leopold,[*]
indicated an easy informality, largely animal-induced:

> It was a long low house enclosed in a secluded garden. The studio,
> its chief room, was long, low and dark, the floor covered with the
> skins of lions, tigers and deer. The windows—none of which
> faced the north—the usual aspect selected by artists—opened
> onto the garden, which was quite a zoological one. There was an
> eagle, chained to the branch of a tree; a fox, also chained not far
> off; more than one dog, all splendid of their sort—an Alpine
> mastiff, a Scotch deer-hound (a present from Sir Walter Scott), a
> Dandy Dinmont, and other terriers. In a loose-box might be seen a
> really beautiful pony of Turkish breed—quite a study—one often
> painted by its master, but hardly the horse such an animal painter

[*] *John Martin*, Mary L. Pendered 1923.

would be expected to ride. Landseer, however, was an indifferent horseman ...

The architecture and the animal occupants might change, but it was to the same address that Landseer, safely removed from the dust and the rubble, would convey his endless instructions and his pious hopes for his future comfort. A growing worry was the encroachment of other building on his property. The intention to raise a school next door to him was a real blow to Landseer, never notably sympathetic towards the patter of tiny feet and the hubbub of youthful voices. In October 1850 Jacob Bell was writing to the absentee owner/occupier of 1 St. John's Wood Road at one of his favourite Highland retreats:

> We had a consultation this week (Ashton, Jones and myself) at St. John's Wood and we are putting the work forward as much as possible. We hope the old painting-room will be ready for your reception the middle of the coming week ...
>
> The garden looks very ruinous and must be until Spring ... I shall be glad when all our operations are completed. It has been a heavy job and attended with unusual difficulties and expenses.
>
> It is of no use wishing that we could have known before the house was built that the other ground would have been available. All we can do now is make the best of it.

The best was perhaps worse than two such wealthy and class-conscious bachelors could have imagined. The institution raised next door to Landseer, and which deprived him of his title of Number 1 St. John's Wood Road, was a Special Asylum for Female Orphans.

There may have been more than purely social considerations behind Edwin's constant absenteeism. Mid-nineteenth century London was not always considered the ideal place for anyone, particularly a hypochondriac like Landseer, to live. Cholera had come to the city in 1832, with later epidemics between 1846–49, 16,000 people dying of it in the metropolis in the last year alone. As the homely cup of tea rose to popularity on the certainty that the water in which it was brewed had been boiled, the 1840 *Annual Report of the Register of Births, Deaths and Marriages* was asking: 'Are cities then necessarily the graves of the race?'. Such dread diseases, of course, struck twice as hard at the poor as they did at the rich: in 1830 the average age at death was twenty-two for labourers and their families as against forty-four years for professional men and *their* families. But the thought of being only half as like to perish of cholera or one of Old Father Thames' other diseases as a Houndsditch road-sweeper may not have put Edwin completely at ease, and strengthened the appeal of the English country-estates and the Highland deer-forests. Despite the frequent absences, however, Landseer remained deeply attached to the home which (orphans notwithstanding) he never seriously considered leaving in fifty-one years. The attachment remained equally strong to his two brothers, Tom and Charles, both of whom now shared a common affliction.

John Landseer's deafness had unfortunately been hereditary, and his children came in for more than their fair share of the infirmity. Mrs. Adams-Acton somewhat exaggerates when she says of the family that all its members 'would have remained unconscious of any noise had a cannon been fired beside them'. But at least three of the brothers and sisters became very deaf. The eldest son Tom was the chief sufferer. The middle brother Charles became progressively more deaf, as did his sister Anna Maria. Although Edwin was not as hard of hearing as his brothers, he didn't entirely escape the family blight. It says much for him that he was able to retain almost to the last his reputation as a raconteur and mimic, though it partly explains his tendency to engage people in *tête à tête* conversations, a habit which the rest of the assembled company often found rude. This deafness was a particularly burdensome cross to Tom, whose great love was music. Frith recalls a rather pathetic scene at a *soirée* when, after observing a great round of applause after a song, Tom approached the singer at the piano, asking him to be so kind as to sing 'just a verse or two' into his ear trumpet.

If Tom was excluded from many of the world's pleasures, he certainly did not let it embitter him. His habitual expression was a beaming smile—almost as though he was basking in the endless tributes to his benignity. 'Dear old Tom' was the expression most often applied to him. 'Everyone quite loves (him) for his sweet nature under a most deplorable infirmity,' wrote Dickens to Macready. 'A universal favourite' opined G. D. Leslie who was reminded of 'a large very amiable purring tom cat'. 'A most amiable and happy man' thought Algernon Graves who, as a child, remembers the broad-faced kindly man pressing upon him a bag of sweets that had partly melted in the engraver's pocket. 'They are fishes in a per-spi-ra-tion!' boomed the ever-fanciful Tom. As an adult Graves was able to return such small favours. Whenever he visited Tom he would spend the entire evening writing out all the art news on bits of paper.

It is a pity that so many people should have gone out of their way to avoid such a man—but perhaps inevitable. When walking down Bond Street or Regent Street his fellow artists and engravers counted themselves lucky to see Tom before he espied them, hastily dodging into some convenient doorway. They had all been through the embarrassing ritual before. In fact, Tom's customary reaction to meeting friends in the street was to throw his arms wide, sometimes half-turning away with an incredulous whinny as though such sheer good fortune could hardly be possible: at the same time he would execute a capering dance of pleasure and bellow a rapturous greeting which froze passers-by in mid-stride. The Victorian art-set, hardly notable for its bohemian eccentricity, can perhaps be excused for taking evasive action to avoid the subsequent one-sided conversation conducted in Tom's loud staccato tones amidst a growing knot of amused and fascinated spectators.

Inevitably, such conduct often embarrassed Edwin, always so anxious to make his mark as the essence of laconic sophistication. In his biography G. D. Leslie recalls the occasion when he, Orchardson and Tom Landseer were elected Associates of the Academy. Both Edwin and Charles were that year on the Council, doubtless heavily conscious of the gravity of the event and seated with the President Sir Francis Grant and other members in the Council Room. The 'Boots' for the evening, Calderon, accordingly introduced the three new Associates to this august body, at which 'dear old Tom, seeing his brothers and his friends thus seated in formal array, raised his hands up above his head and gave forth a loud and playful exclamation of recognition, very much resembling the crow of an exultant baby, whereupon Edwin and Charles shook their heads at him with disapproving frowns'. The ceremony thereafter pursued its frigid and decorous course. Afterwards, returning home in a cab with Leslie, the downcast Tom confided his disappointment, detonating every syllable as was his way: 'Did—it—strike—you—that—there—was—some-thing — unnecess-ar-ily — grim — about — the — whole — affair? Edwin — and — Charles — looked — *very* — cross'.

It is perhaps regrettable that Tom was not much more the elder brother. He had the natural fellow-feeling and lack of affectation that might have served to puncture Edwin's vanity and social seeking at a crucial stage of his development. But the besetting sin of extreme amiability is often weakness of character, and Tom's no doubt lacked its bit of steel. Many critics maintain that he submerged his own career in the interests of Edwin's, choking-off the fine artistic talent evidenced in *Monkeyana* in order to become the most frequent engraver, along with Samuel Cousins, of his brother's work. Certainly John Landseer, a much stronger personality than any of his sons, had apprenticed his oldest boy to the graver at an early age, while he was still hopeful that engraving would be an Academically-honoured career. Engraving was, besides, considered a much more solid, less risky vocation that painting. Ten years later, Landseer Senior might have been inclined to allow Tom (as he did Edwin) much more scope with the pencil and brush. But by then Tom was a fully-fledged engraver; and, despite the several eminent painters who began or doubled as engravers, it was seldom that the transition could be happily made from one to the other. The Academician Uwins was one who believed that his painting style had been irrevocably cramped and crippled by his early training as an engraver, and there must have been times when Tom felt the same. 'Tom ought to have been a painter,' insisted William Bewick, 'as he is vigorous and spirited, and draws well.' It is possibly a little harsh to make Edwin the whipping-boy for his brother's aborted artistic talents. Tom's down-to-earth character, his deafness and his eccentricity would scarcely have gone down as well with the rich patrons as Edwin's charm of manner, his brilliance as a dinner-table and weekend guest. In fact the partnership of painter Edwin and engraver Tom worked extremely well, achieving an almost intuitive quality. And if Tom gave a dangerously large dose of himself to the adolescent Edwin, his youngest brother certainly repaid that loyalty in later years.

In appearance Tom was short and stout, built like a barrel, with curly reddish-brown hair. He was the only one of the Landseer brothers who ever married, and that match was something of a disaster. His wife was unfaithful to him, presenting him with a child by another man—an event rather heartlessly celebrated by Haydon in his diary:

> Tom & Edwin are brothers well known
>   But there's a great difference betwixt 'em
> Tom loves to have horns of his own
>   And Ned on his Patrons to fix 'em.

Mary was, by all accounts, a shallow and rather fickle woman, though guests would often find her warm and welcoming. Algernon Graves recalls visits by his father Henry to Tom's studio in Cunningham Place near to Edwin's home when he was engraving plates for Graves Senior:

He was very conscientious in his work, but his wife was not so particular. She often brought down a half-finished plate . . . before opening the parcel she would dilate for half an hour on the splendid qualities of the newest plate which, by her account in every case, was the finest he had ever done. My father, who was used to it, merely looked at the plate and said, 'Take it back and tell Tom to finish it. It is a splendid first proof'. Mrs. Tom, who wanted a new dress, was always in the hopes that she would get the plate passed and draw the money at once. Tom would afterwards tell me he knew the plate was not finished, but she said, 'Oh, you leave it to me. I will get Graves to pass it'. But he never did. My father was too wily an old bird for that.

Tom excelled in another capacity (the one in which Turner was the past-master) as an arbiter of pictorial taste; or, more facetiously, as a 'picture-doctor'. Artists who couldn't get their pictures right would call in Tom who would seat himself silently in front of the canvas, peering intently for up to an hour, before announcing the steps necessary to achieve the missing balance. Having delivered his verdict, the genial Tom would be unceremoniously bundled off the stool by the bottom of the enlightened artist, and usually left to see himself out.

Charles Landseer was the least talented of the three brothers. 'I hate all he does,' said Constable; adding, 'This Landseer is a common man'. (He certainly enjoyed spitting in the fire.) His father had encouraged him both as engraver and artist: he chose to be a painter. Ironically, he was the only one of the brothers who, in his fashion, remained true to Haydon, becoming a painter of historical themes. As a young man he had shown signs of developing into an artistic *emigré*: he travelled in the suite of Lord Stuart de Rothesay to Portugal and South America, and his resulting studies and sketches were much admired. Instead he became very much part of the English artistic establishment, enjoying a full social life, partly by hanging on to Edwin's coat-tails. He first exhibited at the Royal Academy in 1828, was elected A.R.A. in 1837 and R.A. in 1845—a steady progression that argued diligence rather than genius. In 1851 he was appointed Keeper of the Royal Academy, where he seems to have enjoyed only limited success. One of his students, G. D. Leslie, testified both to his unshatterable good nature and to its predictable side-effect, his inability to maintain discipline. The staccato mode of speech induced by his deafness was much mimicked by the students, and no great retribution seems to have descended on them when he walked in on such impersonations. Indeed, it was during his term of office that curators had to be introduced for the purpose of keeping order, sitting in with the unruly pupils in the Schools. Leslie seems to have found his remarks and criticisms of very little help, deriving much more from the advice of the occasional Visitors like Dyce and Cope. Charles's output of paintings decreased after 1850, ostensibly because of his heavy commitments in the Schools. There were, perhaps, other reasons. The dual-role of Keeper and exhibiting artist was an uneasy one, and reviews like this one in the 1861 *Art-Journal* of the Royal Academy Exhibition cannot have done much for his confidence:

> No. 153, *Births, Marriages and Deaths*. C. LANDSEER R.A., is, without exception, the most perplexing picture in the exhibition. Upon the claim of right to the line assumed by academicians, the picture is hung where it cannot fail to attract attention; but how shall it be described after it has been seen? In a former article we referred at some length to the state of the Academy school, and endeavoured to point out the disgrace of being unable to produce students worthy of receiving the usual prizes. Mr. C. Landseer is keeper, *i.e.* teacher of drawing in the Academy, and it is impossible to overlook these two facts after this picture has been so ostentatiously forced upon public attention. It is admitted that a man may be a good teacher, up to a point, without being able to produce good pictures; and it is also admitted that the mere drudgery of teaching tends to destroy an artist's works who continues to combine exhibiting with tuition. And these admissions are frankly made, to help in some measure to account for the qualities of this picture; but after all is said that can be conceived in extenuation, it is difficult to see how the school can be otherwise than bankrupt of ability if this be a fair sample of the instruction given to the students . . . If a fourth-form student produced drawing like the arms, legs, hands and feet of these women and children, Mr. Landseer's righteous soul would feel constrained to apply the birch with vigour, and not spare for the delinquent's crying.

There was rough justice in the criticism. When Charles had succeeded to the keepership, there had been no shortage of tongues to suggest the influence of the (newly knighted) Sir Edwin, whose fame was then at its height. When Charles resigned, aged 72, it was to an almost universal sigh of relief, and his successor Pickersgill found his popularity assured in advance. Twenty years had been a long time in which to make a sinecure of a post which was, in theory at least, vital to the state of British art.

Poor Charles found relief from his critics in unremitting pursuit of the pun, the art by which he is today most remembered. The pun was, of course, virtually a Victorian institution. Periodicals like *Punch, Judy* and the *Mask* could scarcely have survived without it, any more than could many of the newspaper headline-writers of our own day. When the French painter Delaroche in 1839 uttered his famous *cri de coeur* on the invention of sun-pictures—'From today painting is dead!'—Charles Landseer was not found wanting. 'Foeto-graphic art' was his (all too accurate) description of the new phenomenon.

He was most in his element at art exhibitions—for his fellow-artists a 'pun-tour' round the major art shows with Charles was at one time almost a *must*. A weakly-executed painting of some cows standing in a stream, he dismissed as 'a milk-and-water picture'. When the small *Portrait of a Gentleman* by Corbet of Shrewsbury was found vandalised with the eyes gouged out, Charles boasted that he was able to help baffled detectives by narrowing the range of suspects to 'a schoolmaster in want of pupils'. Another flaw, this time of the artist's doing, showed in a romantic picture of two lovers: the gentleman, about to ride off, is exchanging tender farewells with his girlfriend who is leaning out of a window immediately over the door—with no room between window and door-top to accomodate her lower half. 'She's the man's sweetheart, *notwithstanding*,' punned Charles philosophically. He was probably also responsible for the retort to a young artist with a badly retroussé nose who bitterly complained about people deliberately making his proboscis a subject of conversation—'No, my dear fellow, I assure you—we merely picked the first subject that turned up!'

In fairness to Charles, he was not the only guilty man in the Royal Academy, where the running-pun was very much *à la mode*. Richard Redgrave records a typical example of the genre with Charles Landseer, of course, in the thick of it:

> During the dinner a discussion rose on the respective merits of Harrow and Eton as public schools. 'And yet,' said Grant, 'Peel was educated at Harrow; and then consider the poets—Byron was a Harrow boy.' 'Yes,' chimed in Landseer, 'and Burns was a *plough*-boy'—a groan from Creswick. 'There,' said Eastlake, 'you have *furrowed* Creswick's brow again', upon which Knight added, 'Aye, but you have had your *share* in it . . .'

The unfortunate Creswick was the butt of many of Charles's puns and conundrums: 'I say, Redgrave, do you know why that carpenter is uglier than Creswick? . . . Because he is a *deal planer*!'. There is little to be said for all this badinage as a diversion for artists, except perhaps that it was marginally less harmful than drinking absinthe and seducing midinettes.

Even Charles's appearance lent itself to double meanings, involving him in at least one visual pun. He had inherited the family mop of thick unruly hair; and he liked to relate the story of his visit to an extremely picturesque old house in Kent, Ightham Mote, which artists loved to paint. Unfortunately, it had to be a clandestine operation. The house was owned by a bad-tempered and continuously suspicious old crone, and painters who went there were forced to rely on the kindness of a chambermaid who would admit them to the inner courtyard while her mistress was asleep. One morning, when Charles was stooping over his work, the querulous head of the old lady appeared above. Charles instantly froze. 'What is that by the fireplace?' she screeched. 'I believe it is a man?' 'Lor', mum,' chirped the maid reassuringly, 'why it's only the old kitchen mop lying against the chair.' At which the sleep-tousled head withdrew, satisfied.

In the mid-Fifties, however, the Academy was treated to a much more interesting diversion than Charles's never-ending puns, when France's best-known animal painter crossed the Channel. Rosa Bonheur's dual-reputation had preceded her: she was known to be a great painter and also (it was rumoured) a lesbian. She already knew and admired Landseer's Scottish scenes, and was determined to see the Highlands in all their purple-tinted glory. She was not disappointed, exclaiming in her excited English, 'Oh, magnificent! Oh, beautiful! Oh, grand! Oh, *very well*!'. She also very much looked forward to beholding a Scotsman in a kilt, but was disappointed until at Callander her wish was suddenly fulfilled—a fine figure of a man was striding down the high street with the tartan swinging round his legs. He turned out, however, to be the English painter Millais, who hinted that he probably wouldn't be wearing the garb much longer since the (sensibly betrousered) Scots kept staring in rigid fascination at his legs.

Her dearest wish, however, was to meet the great British animal painter. 'It was the dream of her life to see Landseer,' reported Lady Eastlake, the wife of the Royal Academy's President, 'and I sent them down to dinner together.' Sir Edwin appears to have taken the meeting rather less seriously than the little Frenchwoman:

> Landseer was full of impudence, counted up eight bachelors present and invited Munro to head a deputation of marriage to her. He told me to tell her that he would be very happy to become 'Sir Edwin Bonheur'.

Frith seemed to take the joke seriously (or perhaps he merely wished to extend it), calling on Landseer to offer him 'my congratulations and best wishes'.

'Who am I going to marry?' asked Sir Edwin, reasonably enough.

'Well, I understand that Rosa Bonheur is to be the happy woman?'

'This is the first I've heard of it,' said Landseer, 'but it's not a bad idea, and I must think it over.'

Despite the nudges and innuendos with which their friends surrounded the relationship, it is a little difficult to imagine a successful marriage between the greatest animal painters of England and France, particularly since (although Rosa was twenty years younger than Edwin) both were slightly past the ideal age for founding a dynasty of little animal artists. Obviously, however, Sir Edwin struck an unusually responsive chord of sheer femininity in the hickory-tough little woman, whose cropped curly hair and horrifying habit of riding horses astride did little to dispel her 'butch' reputation. Frederick Goodall, who painted her while she painted him, had a slightly pathetic recollection of how the Frenchwoman put her foot out 'and begged me to notice it, as it was so small'. Goodall denied her much-publicised masculinity: 'her hands and feet were *petites*; her face was not strictly beautiful or fine or handsome, but her expression (was) vivacious and intelligent . . .'. His somewhat measured gallantry fell largely on deaf ears. Rosa's huge masterpiece *The Horse Fair* perhaps had not helped; its size, its sweat-steaming horses and sinewy men hardly squared with the conventionally delicate image of the lady-painter. Nor, of course, did her violent daily quarrels with her female companion, in which they would 'call each other dreadful names', ending with Rosa falling dramatically on her knees to beg the other woman's forgiveness. 'How very French!' commented Goodall, his gallantry undimmed.

If would-be matchmakers were at work, Lady Eastlake was probably the most prominent among them:

Yesterday I took her to see Munro's gallery, and then by appointment to Landseer. This was the *comble* of her happiness; her whole sympathy and admiration as an artist, and her whole enthusiasm as a woman have long been given to Landseer. Engravings of his works were the first thing she bought with the money she earned; and in his house, surrounded by most exquisite specimens of his labour and his skill—studies without end of deer, horses, Highlanders, tops of Scottish mountains &C: and with him pulling out one glorious thing after another, calling her first into one room and then into another—his dogs about him, and a horse, as tame as a dog, handed into the painting-room—she was in a state of quiet ecstasy. Then he presented her with the two engravings of his spendid *Night* and *Morning*, writing her name with his upon them, and then pretended to call her attention to the excellence of his brother's work. This was too much for the little great-hearted woman, who is only a man in her unflagging work, and renunciation of all a woman's usual sources of happiness, for one great end;

and her face crimsoned and eyes filled. As we drove away, the little
head was turned from me, her face streaming with tears . . .

The two painters collaborated on a predictably skilled but otherwise unremarkable oil painting of a dead deer. It was inscribed *Etude
de Sir Edwin Landseer de Madmse. Rosa Bonheur*, and is now in the
Sheffield City Art Galleries. Called *A Stray Shot*, the half-life-size
canvas pictured an all too common sporting accident when the
stalker, who has perhaps been missing sighted shots all day, bags
some undersized antlered innocent as he casually empties his gun
into the distance. Plainly Rosa felt anything but disappointed by her
meetings with the man who, in Lady Eastlake's words, had been 'a
kind of God in her imagination'; and whom the French artist herself
repeatedly described as 'the poet-painter of animals'.

More than a decade later, Frith went with Millais and the dealer
Gambart to visit her at her chateau in the Forest of Fontainebleu.
They were met at the station by a ruddy-faced white-haired coach-
man in a long black habit who, to Frith's amazement, appeared not
only to be a priest but was also undoubtedly a red-ribboned member
of the *Legion d'Honneur*. Perhaps Frith's earlier naivity in the
matter of Landseer's impending nuptials had been genuine, after all
—the coachman-priest was, of course, Madamemoiselle Bonheur!
Later, at the chateau, they spoke of Sir Edwin. 'Gambart repeated to
her some words of praise given by Landseer to a picture of hers then
exhibiting in London. Her eyes filled with tears as she listened . . .'.

Whether Rosa Bonheur could have abandoned her eccentric ways
and her lady-friend in the interests of matrimony is perhaps about as
fruitless a speculation as whether Sir Edwin could have given up *his*
spoilt-boy bachelor routine on the same account. He remained until
his death a somewhat ageing Prince Charming to several women;
some of them plain, some of them beautiful; but gallantry rather than
sensuality was the keynote. The lovely Caroline Norton was one
with whom he carried on a long but mainly platonic flirtation. Not
for him the carnal speculations of another of her artist-admirers,
Haydon: 'Mrs. Norton's grand majesty of beauty is sublime, but her
mouth is not sufficiently voluptuous to kiss with *inner lip*'. The
beautiful grand-daughter of the playwright R. B. Sheridan had at
the time of her correspondence with Landseer left behind her the
notorious court action brought by George Norton against Lord Melbourne for allegedly seducing his wife. The case was so flimsy the
jury had decided against Norton without leaving the courtroom.
Although the action failed in its object of destroying Melbourne's
political career, the lovely Caroline subsequently paid dearly for her

infatuation, turning her status as a deprived wife and mother to good account, however, by helping to bring about the Infant Custody Bill and the Marriage and Divorce Act. Three years after the 1836 scandal had subsided, she wrote a long poem called *Dedication* inscribed to Landseer, some of the lines of which perhaps reflect her feelings about the artist as an unswervingly faithful friend:

> ... For easy are the alms the rich man spares
> To cheer the hour of poverty and pain;—
> But Thou gav'st me what Woman seldom dares
> Belief when others doubted; when in vain
> I strove with that dark deluge which rolled o'er
> My soul, and left me wrecked upon a barren shore.

> ... Thou gavs't me that *the poor do give the poor*
> Kind words, and holy wishes, and true tears;
> The Loved, the near of kin could do no more,
> Who changed not with the gloom of varying years,
> But clung the closer when I stood forlorn
> And blunted Slander's darts with their indignant scorn ...

Landseer made several sketches of the lovely Lady Caroline, among them a chalk drawing from memory and another in a low open dress which, as Mann demurely noticed, showed off her 'well moulded figure'. Her relationship with the painter was clearly an informal and confessional one. She had (undated) sent her son to Landseer to sketch, obviously whilst in the bitterest depths of her protracted marital feud:

See the bearer—Paint his picture Do!
Dear Sir Lanny
I send you a 'Prodigal Son'. I'm so glad I met him before his Father killed the fatted calf. I pray you sketch him, and you can find the pigs yourself. Give him a friendly little dog (in the picture) as a link to home and love, in the midst of indifference and hoggery.
                                        Yours truly
I say—whatever attitude you draw them in when you draw them, pigs may be said to be looking up!

She seemed to find in artists a refreshing social relief from the stern world of suffragettist politics into which she had been so forcibly propelled. Thus, in another letter to Sir Edwin:

Pray catch me your brother Artists. I will write to Eastlake. Be my tame elephant and entrap them into the jungle. I will treat them gently afterwards.

At another time she had suffered from Landseer's petulance over one of his likenesses of this universally admired beauty:

I have received your note on my return home. It would take more to offend me than a huffy note from you—as I have seen too much gentlemanlike and generous feeling in you not to forgive you for being touchy, even when I think it unjust. I *did* not wish to have the picture you did of me . . . *to give away*: you may not think that a compliment—but at all events it is the only picture of me I have ever wished even to do *that* with . . . If you do not wish to look upon your sketches of me in this business like way—if you want them as studies for yourself—I am equally ready to sit—at any time—that you wish it—and have leisure.

Do not write huffy notes; no one you have known, or are yet to know, can have more sympathy for your talent that I . . .

Caroline's sympathy for his talent extended to sending him suggestions for pictures, each one of almost endearing fatuity:

Spring:	Spring Flowers. Shepherds Carrying Lambs over the Hills. Children Gathering Primroses. Driving the Plough. Birds Nesting and Shewing the Young Ones. Rabbits Sporting.
Autumn:	Vintage. Corn Reaping. Hunting, etc.
Summer:	Boats on a Lake (swan). Orchard with Children Playing . . . Lovers in a Bower (a most popular subject, but make them *reading* for the sake of propriety).
Winter:	Children with Small Snow Balls. Waifs at Midnight in the Street, Houseless and Homeless. Shepherd and Dog—Track Lost, Holy Family.

Landseer did not apparently avail himself of any of these original themes—partly perhaps because he had one or two good ideas of almost equal banality stowed away along with the good things in his own locker.

CHAPTER SIXTEEN

THE UNKIND STAR

I have simply to state that my source of income during a considerable period has been chiefly from copyrights.
—Landseer in a letter to his patron Bicknell

LANDSEER'S OFFERINGS to the Royal Academy in 1856 reflected the feeling of emotive tenderness that would increasingly display itself when he was nervously at a low ebb. Both were dedicated to humanitarianism. *The Nurses*, inscribed to Florence Nightingale, showed a wounded stag high on a hillside whose hinds are gathered around him solicitously licking his wounds. The stag had reputedly been the victim of a stray shot, when the painter had carelessly emptied his gun: later that day a gillie had asked Landseer to accompany him to a spot where, creeping the last few yards, both had watched the scene the artist afterwards portrayed. It is to be hoped that the heroine of the Crimea did not see the dedication as a trivialisation of her great mission, since the tribute was undoubtedly sincere. To Landseer at least there was some allegorical connection between the wounded soldiers of the Crimea and the wounded stags of the Scottish Highlands. And the link between soldiering and deer-stalking was not entirely tenuous—in Victorian times the sport was regarded as excellent military training.

Saved! was dedicated to the Royal Humane Society, and pictured a large Newfoundland dog, slobbering with exhaustion, crouched over the body of a little girl it has rescued from the sea. Rather unexpectedly, Ruskin half took its part, complaining that the painting had been placed too high to allow full appreciation of Landseer's 'bold handling'. However, he added (pertinently enough) 'I never saw a child fall into the water, nor a dog bring one out; but under such circumstances are not the clothes usually wet, and do not wet clothes cling to the limbs?'. Certainly *Saved!* was a tableau not only over-dry but too neatly arranged. It was much appreciated, however, by those admirers who had always hoped to see the magnificent quayside-lolling Newfoundland of *A Distinguished Member of the Humane Society* finally get its bathing-suit wet. 'Good enough to have made the reputation of another painter,' said F. G. Stephens of a canvas whose over-dramatisation would today only make us smile. The original sketch, which allegedly had been done on a page of *The Times*, was said to have had all the qualities of front-page immediacy lacking in the finished canvas. But Landseer's liveliest concepts so often evaporated between the sketch and the final exhibit.

The following year saw the exhibition of a fine Highland wildlife study dominated by a defiantly-bellowing stag. *Scene in Braemar* was a large and universally admired work, whose praises Ruskin also sang. Because of its size it was hung 'above the line', an unenvied position which meant that the picture was 'skied' and viewers had to strain their necks to see it. Ruskin echoed the general complaint: 'Good work should be put near us, whatever its scale: and we ought to be able at our ease to study the wonderful execution of the fur in Landseer's large grey mountain hare'. Another immense ($7\frac{1}{2}'$ by $9'$) work of the same year was the red, black and white chalk cartoon, *Browsing*, which showed stalkers creeping up on an unsuspecting herd of deer. Landseer completed it at the Holme Wood, the Huntingdonshire home of William Wells, the agriculturalist and politician nephew and heir of his departed patron. The huge cartoon was only moved with great difficulty to the Trafalgar Square gallery where further trials awaited it. A heavy downpour found a defective skylight, and rain actually passed between the glass and the chalk cartoon. Fortunately the damage was not irreparable. Landseer had clearly felt excited both about the execution and the size of *Browsing*, refusing to allow anyone into his room until it was finished.

One wishes that feeling of excitement could have been maintained. Not surprisingly Landseer and the oil medium were going sour on each other. The attachment had been a long one, dating from before Sir Edwin's teens. If oil had secured him his reputation, it was also associated with those miserable health-eroding portrait commissions that would never come right. In chalk he found an obvious pleasure and release. 'His chalk and pastel were the best materials he used . . . probably his best pictures,' said Landseer's fellow-Academician Goodall; an opinion in which the *Mask* concurred: 'We confess we would sooner possess one of those large chalk drawings . . . than almost any of his paintings'. Time and again his magnificent preliminary chalk studies would become mere travesties of themselves when transferred to the canvas—nowhere was this more evident than in his chalk portraits of the gillies John Grant, Charles Duncan, Peter Coutts and John Macdonald for what was at that stage known as the 'Large Boat Picture', a protracted torture of a commission that would become one of the last great fiascos of Landseer's life.

Among his contributions to the Academy in 1858 was the rather pretty-pretty *The Maid and the Magpie,* whose story was equally quaint. Jacob Bell had sold for £2,000 a picture for which he had paid Landseer only £100. Magnanimously, he lodged the money in the painter's bank account. Curious to know where the unexpected bulge in his fortunes had come from, Landseer approached Bell who told him the story, though suppressing the names of the partners in the transaction. The buyer, Bell, explained, had refused to pocket the money but wished to have another picture in its stead. 'He shall have a good one,' agreed Landseer, in a characteristic phrase. It was only afterwards when Sir Edwin pressed his business manager for the name of his generous patron that Bell confessed it was himself. The picture, on a theme also used by Rossini, showed a Belgian milkmaid in a red cap, and was no doubt designed to recall their times together on the Continent twenty years before.

As the Eighteen-Fifties drew to a close Landseer looked back with reluctance on a decade that had undeniably witnessed the slowing of his powers; years that could not compare in any way with the frenetic output of the 'Thirties and 'Forties. In a letter to his patron Elhanan Bicknell, he could not hide the disappointment and anxiety he felt:

> Could I have *done* that which would have best suited and pleased my inclination—you would have had ere this a *choice* of something from my hand—the *completion* of many things begun *now* depends on my health, for the last year I have been quite unable to give mind and energy to my profession—(the Picture now in the R.A. was begun 8 years ago and *nearly* finished)—to go into my difficulties would be tedious—I have simply to state that my source of income during a considerable period has been chiefly from copyrights . . . *

In the same letter he complained of being 'in a state of prostration from a bad throat attack and cannot take advantage of invitations kindly given by friends'.

Landseer's health was by now a matter of intense speculation among his patrons, his fellow-artists and his friends: his four Royal Academy exhibits of 1859 served both to raise their hopes and confirm their fears. *The Prize Calf* had little to recommend it. The second offering, *Doubtful Crumbs,* was predictable enough: a miserable starveling puppy dubiously eyes the bone outside the kennel of a large St. Bernard who is sleeping off his feast. The content was time-worn, the technique competent, the canine expressions perceptibly

* *Letters of British Artists of the XVIIIth and XIXth Century—Part VI,* A. N. L. Munby, *Connoisseur,* December 1948.

humanised. However, it was *The Kind Star* that most appalled
Landseer's more intelligent admirers: a dying hind lies on the shores
of a lake with a star-haloed spirit bending tenderly over it. Pictorially it was almost pure Walt Disney, and it showed such an
alarming lack of artistic self-criticism that some regarded it as proof
positive of the impending disintegration of Landseer's mind. They
turned with a shudder from this work to another that rejoiced in the
title of '*Bran will never put another stag to bay; and Oscar will no make
out by himself. The deer will do fine yet!*' (perhaps a further instance of
flawed judgement), and more conveniently known as *The Hunted
Stag*. What met their eyes, however, was not entirely a relief. *The
Hunted Stag* is a cruel, stark and uncompromising study of a stag and
the two deerhounds Bran and Oscar being swept to their deaths in a
Highland torrent, one of the legendary scenes of deer-stalking.

In his feeling of tragic self-pity, of being deserted and abandoned
through the deaths of friends, of being assailed by unaccountable
ailments and occasional critics, the painter seemed to identify more
and more with the stag. 'Landseer *was* his stags,' declared Jonathan
Mayne,* 'in a way that he was never his sheepdogs.' The fact showed
itself in the ambivalence of his attitude: he was at once their antagonist and their protagonist, their slayer and their mourner: he
could exalt the sport of deer-stalking yet portray its consequences
with a savage debunking irony; in a single painting he could both
eulogise and expose it. Occasionally he treated the stag with sentiment, but always with reverence. There may have been *Comical
Dogs* dressed up in bonnets with clay pipes in their mouths: there
were no comical stags. The nearest approach to the comic was in
pictures like *Missed!*, with a rapidly retreating deer re-enacting a
scene all too familiar to a mediocre shot like Landseer. But there the
joke was entirely on the stalker. As man and as artist, it never ceased
to impress him that a creature so shy and inoffensive in the wild
should turn on its adversaries and defend its life so courageously to
the last. The nature of Landseer's adversaries is not always clear—
but he obviously saw himself as standing at bay for the last twenty
years of his life.

Yet he continued to find his best months and his most successful
themes in the Scotish Highlands. The Queen and the Prince Consort
were now established there in Victoria's 'Dear Paradise' of Balmoral, which Albert had leased from Lord Aberdeen in 1848 and
finally purchased in 1852. Victoria shared with her favourite artist
an almost migratory annual urge to get to the Highlands and an
equally overwhelming reluctance to leave again. 'The Queen always

* *The Listener*, October 14, 1948.

9 Landseer in Middle Life

10(a) Tom Landseer

10(b) Miss Ellen Power

11(a) The Challenge

11(b) 'Good Doggie'

12(a) The Stag at Bay

12(b) Queen Victoria Sketching at Loch Laggan (reproduced by gracious permission of Her Majesty the Queen)

13(a) The Monarch of the Glen

13(b) Dialogue at Waterloo

14(a) Sir Edwin Landseer sculpting his Lions, by John Ballantyne

14(b) Study of a Lion

15 'Man Proposes, God Disposes' (detail)

16(a) The Connoisseurs

16(b) Landseer in his Last Years

clings to the healthful and free life of this beautiful place,' wrote the royal secretary Phipps to Landseer, 'as the period to lay in a stock of strength for the rest of the year.' The thought of being painted by Landseer with her family in these much-loved and relaxing haunts greatly appealed to the Queen. In 1847, while she was a guest of the Abercorns at Ardverikie, Edwin had painted her beside her small portable easel with two of her children, the Princess Royal and the Prince of Wales. *Queen Victoria sketching at Loch Laggan* had, like the others painted at Buckingham Palace and at Windsor, delighted Victoria. 'It is quite a new conception,' she wrote in her Journal, 'it will tell a great deal.' Victoria was among the first of monarchs to realise the limitations of the stiff and formal court portrait, and the value inherent in the painted holiday family snapshot. 'They say no sovereign was *more loved* than I am (I am bold enough to say) and *that* from our *happy domestic home*—which gives such a good example.' However, the burden of royal propagandist obviously lay too heavily upon Landseer. The attractive cosiness of *Loch Laggan* was later replaced by the portentous People's Republic pose-striking of *Queen Victoria landing at Loch Muich*.

Nor was Landseer alone as an earnest recorder of royal events. Several other lesser artists appeared from time to time at Balmoral, including one Carl Haag, whose portrayal of the royal party fording the River Tarff on Highland ponies perhaps gave another clue to the popularity of Scotland with Victoria and Albert. They are accompanied by two pipers and a guide on foot, the chill waters already lapping at his armpits: one catches a whiff of Darkest Africa, a feeling among the intrepid party that they are being explorers and colonisers by proxy. The venturesome Queen and her Consort had a soft spot for their Highland ponies which, next to their dogs, were the most pampered of their pets. Landseer would later exhibit his portrait of *Brechin*, the Prince's favourite pony; and Victoria's Highland Journal bristled with references to her own favourites—'good little "Lochnagar"', 'dear "Fyvie" is perfection', 'good "Inchory" who went admirably'. They lived a sybaritic life, eating their heads off, with only occasional exercise to disturb the even tenor of their days. There is, in fact, a well-known photograph of the Queen with John Brown, in which Victoria is seated on a veritable Billy Bunter of a Highland pony. The wayward Prince Edward once brought extreme odium upon himself by prankishly tying the tails of the Highland ponies together; but that was before he, too, had succumbed to deer-stalking fever. 'That Prince of Wales,' the gillies would say, 'ye cannae get him off the hill!'

The Queen herself sketched the Highland life around her as well and as often as she was able. 'I wished for Landseer's pencil,' she had written in September 1850, after happening on some wildly picturesque scene. It was, however, another ten years before she visited Glen Feshie—'a most lovely spot—the scene of all Landseer's glory'. But there was onimous news as well. The 'little encampment of wooden and turf huts, built by the late Duchess of Bedford . . . alas! all falling into decay. . . '. Inside the huts were the wall frescoes in coloured chalk that had been Landseer's contribution to their decoration. However, with Georgiana dead, the painter's interest in them had no doubt decayed also. Saddened, Victoria urged on her pony: 'We met Lord & Lady Alexander at a small farmhouse, just as we rode out of the wood, and had some talk with them. They feel deeply the ruin of the place where they formerly lived, as it no longer belongs to them . . .'. The destruction of some valuable, if unconventionally sited, works of art was due in part to a typical demarcation feud between two fiery Highland lairds. Georgiana had merely leased the land, the responsibility for which was now a matter of dispute between Macpherson Grant and The McIntosh. Meantime the rising damp and the leaking roofs were eating at Landseer's frescoes.

The cartoons were probably not as remarkable as those at Ardverikie; but their preservation might have been a matter of some concern, at least in a century which expressed almost unanimous praise of all Landseer's works. General Crealock was another who visited Georgiana's ghost-village long after its founder had been laid to rest amidst the gentler scenery of the south of France:

> The chief bothy, where the Duchess had lived, had had some charming drawings on its walls; but alas! when I was there the place was in sad ruin, and but a few remnants of these pictures remained. In the hut which served as a dining-room, however, there was one large drawing of a deer in good condition still, and fresh in colour—a charming sketch, and it was grievous to think that such a work of art was doomed to destruction, the more so as it might have been saved by removing it bodily from the wall . . .

Crealock, a fine amateur artist, did his best to preserve a record of the last large deer fresco, drawing a faithful copy of it which was probably, he noted sadly in 1892, 'now all that remains'. The Ardverikie frescoes had been destroyed by fire; the loss of those in Glen Feshie was even more reprehensible. In 1954 a falling tree destroyed the last of Georgiana's huts, exposing the final faint traces of Landseer's joyfully spontaneous wall-cartoons to the hungry Highland winds.

CHAPTER SEVENTEEN

THE COLOSSAL CLAY

If I am bothered about everything and anything, no matter what,
I know my head will not stand it much longer.
                    —Landseer in a letter to T. H. Hills

I N HIS early fifties Landseer had begun to complain of failing
eyesight. The timing of the disability could hardly have been
more ironical. As the *Daily News* was later to write:

It was one of the sorest trials of his life that he had to paint in
glasses just when the rage for Pre-Raphaelite finish was rising.
While his eye served him he could have held his ground with any
of the Pre-Raphaelite school in regard to accuracy and finish. As
it was he was blamed for slovenliness just when he was striving
after finish more than ever before.

As a younger man Landseer had delighted in putting a magnifying
glass in the hand of a friend and inviting him to admire his painting
of the eye of a bird, so proud was he of his own eye. It was, indeed, a
treatment he tended to employ himself on other men's paintings,
somewhat to their chagrin. T. S. Cooper complained that Landseer
'examined my work with a magnifying glass, which I thought was
very unfair'. At first Sir Edwin was philosophical about his deteriora-
ting eyesight. The painter Joseph Wolf quoted him as saying to a
young artist: 'You young fellows will never be able to paint a decent
picture until your eyesight begins to fail'. None, of course, knew
better than the liberally-gifted Landseer that an artist's limitations
can often be his strengths. The dimensions of his canvases began
perceptibly to grow. In 1853 he had greatly admired an extra-large
easel designed by his next-door neighbour Lucas for one of the portrait-painter's earlier pictures of the Duke of Wellington: Lucas had
immediately offered to have one made for Sir Edwin. On receipt of
this 'Great Treasure' Landseer had written in acknowledgement: 'I
shall paint no more small pictures—so that you will improve my
Eyes as well as my Head'.

Landseer's colour sense had always been in grave doubt, a lack for which his father was sometimes blamed. As an engraver John Landseer's interest in colour had been merely academic: Edwin, in his turn, had learned to see and paint pictures with the eventual end of a black-and-white engraving in mind. It had not been the best intro-duction—nor was it the best kind of professional commitment—to colour; and Edwin's paintings were increasingly criticised for colour-ing variously described as cold, clayey and chalky. The cloudiness of ageing eyesight certainly did not help, nor did the attitude of some strapping young Pre-Raphaelites who already regarded Sir Edwin with a mixture of reverence and contempt. 'Landseer has drivelled his time away in another group of the royal family in Highland cos-tume,' airily wrote Burne-Jones to a friend after seeing one R.A. exhibition. Holman Hunt's animals were thought to put Landseer's in the shade. His famous allegorical painting *The Scapegoat* (which seems to contain echoes of *The Challenge*) was an idea that Hunt had at first thought of passing on to the older painter: after its completion Sir Robert Peel had wanted to buy it to hang beside one of his Land-seer's, but since £250 was his offer for all the sun-baked trials and tortures that Hunt had endured, the Pre-Raphaelite understandably refused.

Edwin had little call to be jealous of the Pre-Raphaelites, who might spend as many years on a canvas as Landseer spent days. Few, moreover, had the older painter's enormous range of accomplish-ment—in oil, watercolour, fresco, gouache, chalk, crayon, pencil and pen-and-ink as well as in etching and engraving. He also painted successfully on linen, a technique later perfected by the fine Nor-thumbrian animal artist Joseph Crawhall, who would be hailed as 'the coming Landseer' and who acquired at least one of Sir Edwin's works.

Landseer had begun mainly by painting on canvas. In the 'Twen-ties, however, he had started to establish his own style and to use his own materials, favouring wooden panels and millboards coated with a preparation of gesso, size and lead white. It was not an easy surface to paint on, necessitating the finest of brushes and a more than liberal use of oil paint, though it allowed a smooth and delicate finish. Attempting the same effect on canvas did not always end in success, resulting in painted surfaces which, from the 1840s onwards, became progressively coarser and deader, especially as his eyesight dimmed.

Landseer disliked having anyone looking over his shoulder as he worked, and usually banned other artists from his studio. His neigh-bour Lucas believed that this shy secretiveness was due to more than his extreme nervous sensibility:

Many of the singularly realistic representations of the furry coats of the animals he represented so wonderfully were largely assisted by the use of some 'dodgily constructed' brushes which he had contrived, and the design of which he desired to keep to himself.

This impression was borne out by another artist, William Bewick, in a sprightly memoir compiled and edited by Edwin's brother Tom.* Bewick's comparison, in a letter to his friend Davison, between Landseer and Turner showed that at least the reputations of those two stars burned with something like equal brightness in the Victorian heavens:

> Landseer is sensitive and delicate—with a fine hand for manipulation, up to all the *finesse* of the art; has brushes of all peculiarities for all difficulties; turns his picture into all manner of situation and light; looks at it from between his legs—and all with the strictly critical view of discovering hidden defects—falsities of drawing or imperfections. See to what perfection he carries his perception of surface—hair, silk, wool, rock, grass, foliage, distance, fog, mist, smoke—how he paints the glazed or watery eye! Turner could never paint any of these details!

For all his eye for detail, however, Landseer could be less than particular about the materials he used. It had, of course, been the practice of artists well into the nineteenth century to mix their own colours. But the convenience of using pigments manufactured in tubes largely replaced the habit, especially among painters like Landseer whose social life and lack of assistants left him little time for such mundane and time-consuming tasks. As Sir William Gilbey recalled:

> It is said of Landseer that he was singularly careless about the colours he used. When a vendor of pigments brought his wares for trial with a view to sale, he would straightaway try the paint on whatever picture he had on his easel at the moment, irrespective of the fact that he knew absolutely nothing of the visitor and the quality of his goods. These reckless experiments sometimes produced bad ultimate results in the shape of unsightly cracks and fading tints on his canvases.

Sir Edwin might have been forewarned by the example of David Wilkie, many of whose later pictures, as Uwins recorded, 'are going to pieces like old ships, cracking so that the cracks cannot be filled up . . . it is quite a marvel how paint could so split up into small square bits . . .'. Deterioration shows even on some of the works to

* *Life and Letters of William Bewick*, 1871.

which Landseer himself attached greatest importance. Nor is the unsightliness always the Landseer's fault: there is a tendency to consign Victorian works of art to the basement and a frequent reluctance to improve or clean them, and it is sometimes necessary when viewing a Landseer painting to remind oneself that the smoked-kipper patina cannot entirely be laid at the artist's door.

Considerably more remiss, however, than Landseer's occasional misdemeanours in technique and materials was his painting philosophy—or the apparent absence of one. His remark to Frith, 'If only people knew as much about painting as I do, they would never buy my pictures', had been a disquieting one, reflecting not only over-modesty but a kind of professional sourness, the result perhaps of having been apprenticed to art at an uncomfortably early age. Richard Redgrave related a story told him by Landseer that had its origins in the artistically barren reign of William IV. ('King Billy doesn't know a picture from a door-shutter,' had been the painter Uwins' comment.) As the sailor-king, William was interested only in seascapes and pictures of ships, which he set about substituting throughout the palace for works of much greater merit. It was on such a picture-hanging junket that (according to Landseer) William appointed the future Inspector of Palaces, Saunders. Having enquired after the name and artist of an obscure Italian picture, and the presiding expert Sequier having been unable to supply the answer, William asked the same question of the man who was cleaning the walls. Of course, the man did not know and said so, and this blunt honesty so took his Majesty's unstable fancy that he hired him on the spot. It was the same Saunders whom Landseer came across several years later cutting a magnificent Gainsborough in half so that it would fit above a door. A horrified Redgrave, to whom Landseer years afterwards told the tale, suggested that the animal painter should have insisted to the young Queen that the pieces of the picture (showing the Princess Royal with the Princesses Augusta and Elizabeth) be kept, so that the painting could later be relined and restored. But Landseer had apparently never thought of such a thing. Ever the journeyman, he had no very marked bump of reverence for works of art as such; and had clearly been more intrigued by Saunders' boorishness than by the possible loss of an important picture.

This airy negligence was also apparent in his attitude to the young artists whom his interest could have helped so much. Royal Academicians were expected to appear from time to time, usually for one month, as Visitors at the Academy Life School, so that the students could take advantage of their prestigious presence and their advice. It was a task which Landseer, no friend to sweaty and boisterous students, postponed for as long as possible. He was not, of course, unique. Few Academicians looked forward to the dubious pleasure, which one of them, Cope, described as 'a tedious drudgery'. To Landseer, with his high connections, it was positively distasteful, and he did little to disguise his boredom. He antagonised the students by habitually arriving late for these evening sessions, and then kept them waiting outside the door while he arranged the model in what seemed to them a deliberately aggravating way. Once in the classroom he immersed himself in a book, taking no interest in what the students were doing. However, his spell as Visitor might have passed over without much incident but for the unexpected appearance one evening of his father. John Landseer, at that time at the height of his eccentricity, shuffled into the room in slippers with his ear-trumpet under his arm. Frith, then a student, witnessed the scene, as Landseer, who had been languidly reading, rose to meet the father whom he loved, but who caused him frequent embarrassment:

> 'You're not drawing then; why don't you draw?' said the old man in a loud voice.
> 'Don't feel inclined,' shouted the son down the trumpet.
> 'Then you ought to feel inclined. That's a fine figure; get out your paper and draw.'
> 'Haven't got any paper,' said the son.
> 'What's that book?' said the father.
> '*Oliver Twist*,' said Edwin Landseer, in a voice loud enough to reach Trafalgar Square.
> 'Is it about art?'
> 'No; it's about Oliver Twist.'
> 'Let me look at it. Ha! it's some of Dickens's nonsense, I see. You'd much better draw than waste your time upon such stuff as that.'

Naturally the students were much amused by this unexpected diversion. They tittered, 'and deepened the frowns that had been gathering throughout the interview on the brow of the great animal painter'. Thereafter, it seemed, the uncertain relationship between Visitor and students could only get worse. On the following evening Landseer kept the pupils waiting for such an untoward length of time that they began to stamp and jeer. The animal painter, even then a power in the Academy, made his objections known to the Keeper, Mr. Jones. By the next evening an order had been posted forbidding the students to ascend the many stairs to the 'pepper-pot', as the central cupola of the National Gallery was known, until they had been summoned by a bell. The body of students buzzed with angry

protest—one of them wrote *Humbug* across the offending notice. There
were threats of expulsion. Landseer completed his honorary term of
office in an atmosphere of chill unpopularity and was never Visitor
again. Frith's is a telling little recollection of a man who seemed
unable to equate his high life with a low duty (albeit a strictly temporary one). Landseer's celebrated wit and charm could so easily
have smoothed his own path as Visitor, but he chose from the start
to set himself in a wilful and petulant way against the students.
Amongst them was at least one firm friend of the future; but there
were others who would invest the name Landseer thereafter with
varying tones of contempt and scorn. However, the artist at that
time was at the height of his social success. The contrast between the
stately homes and the 'pepper-pot' had clearly been too much for
him.

'There is nothing to teach,' Landseer once said. Yet he made
conscientious efforts to tutor Victoria and Albert in both drawing and
etching, and his lady-love the Duchess never went short of an art
lesson or two. In fact, in this important respect, Landseer laid himself wide open to charges of snobbism and self-interest. The case most
often quoted against him was that of Alfred Stevens, whose patron
approached Landseer to take the young artist into his studio as an
apprentice. The animal painter, however, asked a premium of £500,
obviously well beyond the means of the poor Dorset lad. Instead,
through the efforts and sacrifices of his clergyman-friend Best, the
youth went to Italy where (Landseer's critics infer) he was blessed
with a much more inspired artistic education and, indeed, could
subsequently count his unfruitful dalliance with Landseer as a lucky
escape.

There is no doubt that a formal master-pupil relationship would
have been irksome and embarrassing to Landseer, and an informal
one impossible. Moreover, if he lacked altruistic motives, he lacked
ulterior ones as well. Such was the demand for his work that he might
well have set up an art factory in the style of Rubens or Doré, taking
on several likely apprentices to help cover the canvases for which
there was always a long and eager queue. But this was not his way.
Landseer always wore his faults on his sleeve—his social opportu-
nism, his vanity, his petulance. He had always been too innocent to
exploit the obvious advantages presented by a public agog for his
paintings—just as he had become the despair of his financial advisers
by making ludicrously inadequate and self-effacing deals for some of
his best work.

Nevertheless, he genuinely helped many other animal artists, if in
a sporadic way. The self-taught John Bateman, son of a Billings-

gate fish-dealer, was one of them. Thirteen years younger than Landseer, he gave up his clerical job on the strength of an unusually magnanimous offer from two gentlemen 'of £100 for all the pictures he could paint in a year'. He sometimes worked in the same studio as Landseer, absorbing a good deal of his style, so that engravings of his work were occasionally mistaken for Sir Edwin's. According to Sir William Gilbey, the great painter sometimes rendered Bateman 'kindly assistance'. On one occasion, painting a landscape with river, Bateman found himself short of a Newfoundland dog model with which to animate the scene. He went in unsuccessful search of one, and on his return found that Landseer had pre-empted him by the beautifully-painted addition of a Newfoundland's head emerging from the water. Self-help advocates would hardly approve the method, but it was characteristic of Edwin's many small efforts to help younger painters. Bateman himself, an accomplished though somewhat over-dramatic painter of dogs, foxes, stags and hunting scenes, died of consumption at the age of 35, having been privileged to follow his chosen profession for only nine years.

Thomas Woodward was another contemporary whom Landseer helped, both by recommendation and with his brush. Edwin, who had done several portraits of equine favourites for Sir Thomas Wigram, eventually advised him to go to the other man, confiding on another occasion to an artist friend that he 'wished he could paint a horse like Woodward'. There was certainly an impressively spirited quality about Woodward's horses, doubtless helped by the fact that he was himself a fine horseman. However, it was in a dog-painting that Landseer's ever-ready brush has been recorded as coming to the rescue. *Foxhounds waiting to be fed* was a favourite hunting subject, apparently completed, but with which Woodward remained dissatisfied. Peering over Woodward's shoulder, Landseer himself declared it unfinished. 'Thereupon (recalls Gilbey) Sir Edwin took a brush and rapidly touched in an old red coat hanging from a peg on the kennel wall. Thus lightened by a cunningly introduced dash of colour, the painting gained the look of finish which Woodward required.' Like Bateman, Woodward's potentially brilliant career was circumscribed by ill-health and premature death.

The German-born bird and animal painter Joseph Wolf also profited from Landseer's help. Wolf arrived speculatively in England in the 1840s. Both Edwin and Thomas Landseer were immediately taken by his work. He sent his *Woodcocks taking shelter* to the Royal Academy in 1849 and was delighted not only to receive his varnishing ticket but to find his picture admirably placed 'on the line'. It was only afterwards he discovered that Edwin, having first rescued the picture from the committee's condemnatory chalk cross, had then taken great pains to ensure that it was hung to fullest advantage. Predictably enough, the result was not so much to establish Wolf's general reputation as to embroil him in endless commissions for pictures of woodcocks. However, Landseer's praise of Wolf was always unstinted. H. E. Dresser, author of *The Birds of Europe*, maintained that Sir Edwin had told him he considered Wolf without exception the best all-round animal painter that ever lived. 'When a good many artists of the present day are forgotten,' Landseer had added, 'Wolf will be remembered.' The remark hardly rates very highly as prophesy, but it was a generous tribute from a man sometimes accused of being obsessively jealous of his reputation.

The nearest Landseer ever got to a regular pupil and studio assistant was another foreign artist, the Belgian painter Friedrich Wilhelm Keyl. Edwin introduced him at Court, and he subsequently painted dogs, cattle and other subjects for the Queen. His gratitude was of a somewhat unctuous order and even Landseer, who was not altogether averse to flattery, must at times have found him a little cloying. Thus, writing from Westmorland in 1850:

> I am afraid I must give up Scotland for this year. I could not think of spoiling one impression with the other. You know, dear Sir Edwin, that I never feel so sure doing right as when I do as you bid me; therefore I trust that if you have a different idea about my movements you will tell me. I shall trouble you occasionally with an account of my doings. To receive a line from you would be delightful, but I must not expect it . . . I have so much to say and am so afraid of becoming a bore by a long note . . .
> Forgive me, dear Sir Edwin, and believe me
> Yours ever obediently

Landseer, of course, was no stranger to deference. His contemporaries were noticeably chary of entering into direct rivalry with him. T. S. Cooper (known as 'Cow' Cooper to distinguish him from Abraham or 'Horse' Cooper) not only seemed pleased to concentrate on cattle and sheep (occasional subjects as far as Edwin was concerned) but even deferred territorially to the great man. 'I preferred (North Wales) to Scotland for two reasons,' he wrote in his *Life*. 'First, because Landseer was that year painting in Scotland . . .' At other times he stopped short at the Cumberland Fells, wistfully looking further north, it seemed, at the cohorts of shaggy cattle and puff-ball sheep that Landseer was merely *shoo*ing out of his path on his way to the deer.

The painter who most directly challenged Landseer was Richard Ansdell, whose paintings often bordered on sheer imitation. Even the titles, *The Death of the Deer*, *The Combat* and (final indignity!) *The Stag at Bay* proclaimed Ansdell's determination to snap at the Master's heels. Imitation, in this case may not have been the wisest form of flattery. He was 55 before he was elected R.A., having temporarily abandoned the Highland and sporting scene to go with John Phillip to Spain. He thus acquired a wider range than Landseer, though he was never quite able to step clear of the great man's shadow. 'If we had no Landseer,' wrote one critic in 1860, 'Ansdell would unquestionably occupy the very foremost place in this department of art.' It was a very formidable *If*, and one under which many sporting and animal artists fretted for more than half a century.

Being mistaken for Landseer didn't always work to an artist's advantage. The sporting painter Frederick Taylor was, like his more famous contemporary, an amusing companion and mimic always welcome in the homes of the wealthy. His love for Scotland and the deer led him along many of the same fern-lined paths as Landseer, and doubtless also led to similarities in style. Passing a print-seller's window one day, he noticed a prominently-displayed engraving of one of his works, *Weighing the Deer*. He stopped to admire himself in the window, as it were, and was disconcerted to see the print described as 'this beautiful engraving from the original by Sir Edwin Landseer'. Naturally he stepped inside the shop to inform the haughty proprietor of his mistake. 'If you will be so good as to mind your own business,' Taylor was tartly told, 'we shall be glad to follow your example.' Such was the inviolability of Landseer's reputation.

Similarities in style helped to fuel the boom in unauthentic renderings of the most commercially successful painters. Frith tells of visiting a manor at Blackheath belonging to a retired tanner, who proudly showed off his gallery of alleged Turners and Wilkies, all of them 'the vilest daubs'. The would-be connoisseur then produced a 'Landseer', 'which I only show to my particular friends'. It was a picture of a girl feeding dogs in a Highland cottage on which Frith himself and Ansdell had collaborated several years before. This canvas was at least by painters of repute: the other 'Landseers', including one of *Daniel in the Lions' Den* were merely 'vile'. One, in fact, *was* a genuine Landseer; a life-size picture of a lion painted by Edwin's brother Charles, who had used it as a chimney board in his home such was his estimation of its relevance to posterity. Now it occupied an exalted position in a superb frame with a curtain in front of it. Landseer himself visited Blackheath to confirm the fakeries, a melancholy but familiar chore to well-known artists of the day.

The redoubtable Thomas Sidney Cooper was even more bedevilled by unscrupulous imitators than Edwin; and, in fact, made quite a profitable sideline out of certifying 'Coopers' one way or the other at five guineas a time. Of the 199 certificates he issued only 16 referred to genuine Coopers: a further 200 to 300 doubting Cooper owners, he noted disparagingly, refused to pay the fee. One of the patrons he was forced to disillusion was Gladstone, though with 'deep distress' rather than the uncompromisingly-worded certificate with which he shattered the hopes of more modest patrons. It is possibly a little to Cooper's discredit that he was so easy to imitate. 'No wonder his pictures are all alike and all equally bad,' Orchardson said of him, 'he has perfected his imperfections.' Cooper was another whose titles derived inspiration from Landseer's. *Monarch of the Meadows* was shown at the Royal Academy in the year of Sir Edwin's death; though even Landseer might have winced at the title appended to a large painting of a foreground bull, his cows in the far distance— *Separated, but not Divorced.* Poor Cooper, few well-known painters have been damned with such faint praise. He goes on, said Mrs. Adams-Acton, 'eternally painting the cows lying down in his meadows, stolidly chewing the cud, and selling these pictures for enormous prices, and after all, when you have once mastered the technique, there is very little drawing required in a cow'. The late T. S. R. Boase noted 'the unforgettable woolliness' of his sheep; and even H. G. Wells could not resist a tongue-in-cheek reference to him in *The Invisible Man* when, during the siege of Dr. Kemp's, a revolver shot 'ripped a valuable Sidney Cooper'. Fortunately Cooper had a good opinion of himself. 'Cuyp will have to look to his laurels,' said a brother-artist by way of encouragement. 'Cuyp,' intoned the offended Thomas Sidney. 'Cuyp couldn't draw a cow like that!' In a way, he had the last laugh. By eschewing the company of what he called 'roisterers' and 'fast' men, he survived all his contemporaries, dying in his hundredth year, the longest-lived Academician.

In 1859 Jacob Bell died. Two weeks before he had sat to Landseer for his portrait, his hands in their characteristic finger-tip-touching pose: it was a rather stiff and tentative portrayal completed in two hours, perhaps reflecting the painter's unease in the presence of impending death. He presented the portrait to Thomas Hyde Hills, with the inscription: *Given to his very worthy successor T. H. Hills by his friend the author.* Hills had joined Bell & Co. as a junior, and became head of the firm after Jacob's death. There may have been cupboard love as well as respectful affection in Edwin's gift of the Bell portrait, since Hills was the man who would take over from his deceased partner the not always enviable task of managing Land-seer's financial and business affairs. Without a John Landseer, a Bell or a Hills, Edwin would have been lost; but at least his father and Jacob Bell had known the painter in his younger days when a bit of good cheer had leavened the bouts of melancholia. The faithful Hills had, in many ways, the worst of the bargain, as Landseer struggled mournfully and self-pityingly to cope with the process of growing old—and, even worse, with the unspeakable tragedy of gradually losing his precious foothold in society. His physical afflictions and his nervous irritability were growing markedly worse. These were facts which must be concealed as much as possible from the *haut ton*, for whom the remnants of his plausible charm were reserved. It was his own family and Hills who would have to listen to the endless com-plaints and worries and apprehensions.

Soon Hills was inundated with problems great and small, real and imaginary. He must explain to a certain art publisher what Landseer wished, and did not wish, done with an engraving plate; he must step in at once to prevent a firm of photographers from selling prints made with alleged illegality from one of his pictures; he must also 'smooth the feathers' of a friend Landseer thinks he has offended 'so that he may fly back again'; he must drop everything and come to lunch to talk over 'those bank and investment matters'.

When it is remembered that Hills was a man with heavy business commitments of his own, his patience and resource can only be wondered at. He must always, it seemed, be at the painter's beck and call; but his attempts to involve Landseer in the details of business did not always fare so well, leading to ominous masochistic threats:

I am much surprised by your note. The plates, large vignettes, are all *the same* size. The sketches from which they were engraved for the deer stalking work being done in a sketchbook of a particular shape and size. Those of the O form all the same, as also the others. I have got quite trouble enough; ten or twelve pictures about which I am tortured, and a large national monument to complete. . . . If I am bothered about everything and anything, no matter what, I know my head will not stand it much longer.

Many of the letters read as though he were addressing a humble employee rather than a wealthy businessman: 'I cannot even leave off to read Gosling's letter. If you will call at three you will find me': and again: 'Have the kindness to read the enclosed. Perhaps you could kindly call on the party'. At other times he seemed to feel remorse over his brusqueness, realising his dependence on Hills' kindness, which went far beyond the ordinary calls either of business or of friendship:

> I have just heard from your friend P. . . . I told him you were an object for plunder in this world, and that I was ashamed of living on you as others do.

Yet the same letter showed acute prevarication of mind. He wants to make alterations to his home, but seems uncertain what to do and where to start and whether to go ahead at all: he feels he must go somewhere, but can't make up his mind where. Nor was Hills the butt only of his business and domestic worries. A similar sense of complaining persecution marked his attitude to the critics.

Landseer had always been sensitive to criticism, though generally able to swallow his resentment. Yet with age he found hostile criticism increasingly difficult to digest. Rather pedantically he complained to Hills about critics 'who through fearful ignorance perpetrate most disgraceful cruelty to deserving and patient originality of mind'.

Of all the gadflies, the one whose sting went deepest was Ruskin. 'Mr. Ruskin's fine English is often extremely mischievous', Millais later wrote to Hills, apropos of the critic's treatment of the animal painter. Landseer had always felt ill at ease in the presence of pure intellect, and no doubt his own lack of scholastic training often stared back balefully at him over the years. The future Oxford don enjoyed the occasional sly dig at Landseer's shortcomings in the matter of a classical artistic education, particularly at the fact that he had never made the pilgrimage to Italy. 'It is not by the study of Rafael, but by a healthy love of Scotch terriers that he achieved his eminence,' he wrote—the word *healthy* cannot quite counterbalance the patronage of the tone.

It is a pity that Landseer should have taken him so much to heart. By the time Ruskin's influence had begun to bite, *his* reputation at least was impregnable against the critic's barbs, which is more than many another artist could claim. As the rhyme ran:

> I paints and paints
> Hears no complaints
>   And sells before I'm dry:
> Till savage Ruskin
> Sticks his tusk in
>   And nobody will buy.

Ford Madox Brown was only one whose career suffered badly from Ruskin's personal dislike of him; though his most tragic victim was probably Windus, whose painting *Burd Helen* he had praised; but its successor *Too Late* he dismissed with a few curt sentences beginning 'Something wrong here' which, like some sadistic head's rebuke to an over-sensitive pupil, caused the promising artist to lose heart and give up painting altogether. Ruskin's well-known horror of non-idealised nudity also led him to categorise Mulready as 'degraded and bestial' and to reject his fine nude studies as 'most vulgar' and 'abominable'. His later decision to slug it out, toe-to-toe, with Whistler, to the ruination of them both, seemed to reveal how little he had learned from his hero Turner about the essential freedom of art from established canons and principles. But by the time of that legal *cause célèbre* Landseer was dead. In animal painting Ruskin was probably out of his depth—or found the waters too shallow for his serious consideration. His myopia in the presence of a great animal draughtsman like George Stubbs perhaps indicated lack of interest rather than ignorance. Immediately after meeting the famous critic, Rosa Bonheur had delivered her opinion of him to the dealer Gambart, casting a dash of feminine intuition on the subject: 'He is a gentleman,' said she, 'but he is a theorist. He sees nature with a little eye—*tout à fait comme un oieseau!*' Unfortunately Landseer did not have her detachment. He took all criticism cruelly to heart, and Ruskin's more than anyone's. Even his irony when he could bring himself to mention the self-appointed Messiah of Victorian art was tight and unhappy. Thus, in a letter to the collector Bicknell:

> Your friend and neighbour Ruskin will not recommend you to invest in any modern works unless the pre-Raphaelite or the gt. Turner! I am sure it is but honourable in any painter to remind a patron of the fine arts of the gt. importance he should attach to this wonderful man's instructions!

In his fifty-sixth year Landseer had clearly felt that his heavy-weight crown was slipping slightly, and it was now time to embark on something really grandiose. The huge crowded six by ten foot canvas *Flood in the Highlands* was two years in the making. It showed a crofter family and their animals beset by the torrential flooding of the River Spey. Landseer had thrown everything, human and animal, into the large detail-filled canvas; a beautifully-drawn seated woman nursing her youngest child; her other two terrified children; the bearded grandfather, resigned to anything the elements can produce; their dogs, cats, chickens and ducks, horses, cattle, sheep and goats. There is even a hare that pathetically struggles to find its place on a small islet of temporary safety besides its natural enemies. So detailed was the canvas that it invited the kind of

criticism that was not really criticism at all: one commentator
solemnly pointed out that the shattered egg which a hen has laid in
her panic would not in fact have been brittle at all, but soft-shelled.
F. G. Stephens considered it the painter's last great work, but many
who knew him felt that Sir Edwin's rediscovery of the epic was taking
its toll of his health.

Landseer's approach to his work at that time was characterised by
an irritable anxiety amounting almost to a mother-hen complex. In
1861 he finally completed a series of drawings on which he had
laboured since 1849. There were twenty of them—some done in
coloured chalk, others in crayon and three cartoons in distemper—
under the general title of *The Forest*, the great majority of them
concerned with deer-stalking and not a few of them concerned with
death. The set included pictures of a stag lying with his hinds on a
hill, the stalkers beyond; of a stag hiding from its pursuers; of stags
in a deer-pass; of a stag missed by the marksman beating a hasty
retreat; but most of them dwelt either on wounded stags or on the
grisly aftermath of the shoot—a comment perhaps on Landseer's
depressed state of mind at the time. *The Grealoch* was in many ways
the most macabre of the drawings (in Scottish deer-stalking parlance
the process by which the stag's innards are removed): the stag is
shown lying on its back with a knife-wielding gillie hovering over it
in a way which (even to the purest mind) would suggest some kind of
gruesome sexual assault. Another drawing, *The Fatal Duel*, of stags
fighting, aroused the interest of the biologist Frank Buckland, who
questioned the accuracy of a blob of blood at the break in one of the
deer's antlers. It was Buckland's theory that Landseer's 'bit of red'
was the equivalent of 'the white horse of Wouwerman';* in other
words, a kind of psychological trade-mark. Certainly one can quote
many examples of the telltale bit of red—very often gouts and
smears of blood; sometimes a red dog-collar, a red crayon, a red flag,
the gills of a fish and so on. The original intention had been that
letter press for *The Forest* should be written by Lord Alexander Russell
(the painter's alleged son); Alexander had entered the Army as a
youth, rising to be a Colonel in the Rifle Brigade, was afterwards
Aide de Camp to the Governor-General of Canada and later appointed
Deputy Assistant Quartermaster-General at the Cape of Good Hope
—to which Landseer sent at least one of the drawings for his approval. But the proposed collaboration came to nothing.

Rather foolishly Landseer decided, despite the parlous state of his
nervous health, to superintend the work on the prints himself, commissioning the engravers (most of the work going to his brother Tom,

* Philips Wouwerman (1619–1668), Dutch animal and landscape painter.

however) and watching over the prints to ensure that none went out independently or prematurely. His rather fussy concern was understandable. The drawings for *The Forest* are among the best work he ever did. Though hardly of uniform excellence, they do fulfil at least one important artistic criterion in that it is quite impossible to imagine any other artist of any other age who could have done that particular subject-series any better. The quality of the draughtsmanship was variable—they would not have been by Landseer otherwise. But the best of them are inimitably fine. The painter himself was fully aware of the commercial value of his large detail-crowded oils; but he, and his most discerning critics, knew that his chalk drawings were among the best of his work.

In 1855, when the jealously-guarded project was at the halfway stage, C. G. Lewis who had already executed some of the plates had held a sale of a complete set of engravings after Landseer, and accidentally two or three from *The Forest* were included among them. Landseer at once threatened an action to have them withdrawn. Confusion over the precious prints was almost inevitable—they differed very little in subject-matter and style from many another of the artist's Highland drawings. In 1862 the print-seller Henry Graves acquired two, without being aware of having done so. By chance Landseer called on him to sign a parcel of proofs. He had almost completed the mundane task when he came across the two sacred *Forest* prints. In a towering rage he hurled them across the gallery, and refused to sign any more that day.

For all his almost paranoic husbanding of the venture, Landseer discovered when the twenty plates were finally engraved that he was unequal to the task of publishing them. Hills therefore suggested that Graves acquire the plates on the understanding that only one hundred sets would be published, that the sets would be sold unbroken and that Landseer would personally sign all two thousand proofs and design the portfolio. Painter and printer agreed the transaction. There was no difficulty in finding one hundred discerning subscribers willing to pay thirty guineas for a set. But when Graves went to St. John's Wood carrying the two thousand prints for signature, Sir Edwin fell into a fury. He was an artist—this thing Graves was asking him to do was sheer pot-boy drudgery. He threatened to cancel the entire transaction, stamping out of the room with his bucolic complexion at its most livid.

Perhaps it would have been better if Graves had held Landseer to their agreement. But most people gave in to Sir Edwin's tantrums, apparently fearing to induce the apoplectic stroke that would deprive the nation of its best-known painter. After further petulance from Landseer, it was finally agreed that he need sign one print only in each set, entrusting Graves with his signet ring so that a stamp (E.L.) might be made and the remaining 1,900 proofs marked with the somewhat abbreviated evidence of Sir Edwin's authorship. Even then the arguments were not over. Landseer wanted to put his signature to the first plate, *Wait till he rise*, since the incident shown was the logical opener to the set; but Graves insisted he sign *The Fatal Duel*, in his opinion the best of the series. To the horror of Sir Edwin's family, another emotional tempest seemed about to break. But the painter apparently decided to pay homage to Graves' earlier climb-down. It was agreed that he should sign twenty-five of his own choice and seventy-five of Graves', and on this faintly ludicrous note of compromise the matter was settled. In relation to the general excellence of the prints themselves these were niggling and unimportant points: most of the originals were retained by Landseer and fetched high prices at Christie's in the year after his death.

A few years before Graves had found himself on the antlers of a similar dilemma. A print of one of Sir Edwin's pictures had required the artist's signature of approval before it could be published. Landseer was at that time recovering from one of his bouts of nervous illness at Mr. Wells' place, so Graves decided to enlist the help of a doctor-friend who was also staying at Redleaf, begging him to look for a quiet and convenient opportunity of obtaining the painter's signature. After dinner one day, Sir Edwin seeming to be in tranquil mood, the doctor gently broached the subject. To his embarrassment Landseer rose without a word from the table and left the room, refusing to be coaxed from his bedroom for the rest of the evening. On the following day the doctor carefully avoided the subject, but in the afternoon Sir Edwin brought it up himself. 'You wished me to sign Graves' print yesterday,' he announced. 'Now if you will cover it up so that I cannot possibly see it, and leave just the space where I am to sign, I will do it. But I could not look at the subject without being quite ill again.' Accordingly some paper was found to cover the hated representation whilst Landseer, with a shudder, quickly signed.

Nor were such self-indulgences entirely confined to business. Lady Louisa Wells told Manson of another occasion when Landseer was their guest at the Holme Wood, confined to his room by one of his attacks of melancholia. One late afternoon the sun poured into the drawing-room falling directly onto the painting, *None But the Brave deserve the Fair*. The effect was startling, heightening the already impressive effect of the storm in the glen among the hills. Thinking that this natural illumination of his work would be as intriguing to the artist as it was to her, she asked him to hurry down. Landseer, however, begged to be excused, declaring that such a sight would be altogether too much for him in his state of nervous depression. There was sometimes more than a touch of exhibitionism about such woeful pleadings: the exposed nerve-endings were too obviously on display. His artist-friends tended to treat him with some circumspection. Nonetheless, there were trivial and stiff-necked quarrels. He fell out with the landscape painter F. R. Lee over accusations of cheating at a game of billiards: the two men never spoke to each other again. He had also quarrelled with Sir William Russell, whose gun-locks he had offered to adorn, writing him an incensed letter accusing the sports-man of having spread defamatory remarks about him; that he was 'untrustworthy, never kept to his promises, had no notion of punc-tuality, etc. etc.'. In this instance, however, the day was saved by a little ritual backing-up and shaking-down of the feathers on the part of both egos. Landseer was normally more inclined to throw tan-trums than to hold grudges.

In 1861 a Landseer picture was, all unwittingly, the sensation of the Royal Academy's Annual Exhibition. *Taming the Shrew* showed a lovely young lady in a straw-strewn stable reclining against the sweat-glistening body of the spirited thoroughbred mare she has just dominated into submission. The model had been, ostensibly, Miss Gilbert, a refined and accomplished young horsewoman who had figured in several canvases including Frith's *Derby Day* and who shortly afterwards died of consumption. Miss Gilbert may well have posed at some stage for the picture, but those familiar with the *demi monde* were quick to recognise in the overdressed and excessively be-jewelled shrew-tamer the courtesan Catherine Walters, otherwise known as Skittles.

Landseer was careful not to make his denials too vehement. As the *Annual Register* tut-tutted over a painting 'suggestive of one of the social scandals of the hour', it quickly acquired its natural title of *The Pretty Horsebreaker*. The term *horsebreaker* was, in fact, an extension of the word *whore*: the 'pretty little horsebreakers' of song and poesy were the high-class prostitutes who disported themselves in Hyde Park's Rotten Row. With direct access to society otherwise denied them, especially for purposes of advertisement, some of the more active and able prostitutes took to riding in the Row. A high-bred and spirited horse was a natural adjunct, and the pretty horse-breakers were sometimes the daughters of local livery-stable pro-prietors or horse-copers who would at the same time advertise their own wares and their fathers'. Catherine, a Liverpool docker's daughter who had somehow learned to ride extremely well, was sponsored by one Roberts, a Bruton Mews livery-stable keeper, whose stock she rode and sometimes drove wearing the 'horse-breaker's' official uniform of a thin tight-fitting costume with nothing underneath—a dress into which the whoring equestriennes were sometimes sewn before being hoisted into the saddle. The effortless domination of a difficult horse was part of the attraction to the young and not so young bucks who congregated in the Park: no doubt the suggestion of forthright erotic initiative was an exciting contrast to the passive sexual role enjoined on respectable Victorian women. Strange, in fact, were the uses of advertisement. Cora Pearl, a British-born horsebreaker who left her hoofprints in the Bois de Boulogne rather than in Rotten Row, would regularly and publicly subject her wheeling and cavorting horse to a sound whipping for some imaginary misdemeanour, apparently as an incitement to any well-heeled masochist among the male lookers-on.

Landseer's involvement with Catherine no doubt related much more to his profession than to hers. If it was more than that, he chose well, since Skittles was (apart from occasional lapses) the most discreet and ladylike of whores. It is much more likely, however, that he admired her for her equestrianism. In the Row could be seen some of the finest horse-flesh in London: an animal painter certainly needed no excuse to be seen loitering there. Skittles was at that time the mistress of Lord 'Harty-Tarty' Hartington, a keen if erratic sportsman who enjoyed the unique distinction of having once bagged with a single shot a cock-pheasant, the retriever following it, the retriever's owner and an innocent bystander. Two years after the showing of her controversial picture, she became the mistress of the poet-traveller Wilfred Scawen Blunt, then a young attaché at the British embassy in Paris. Whatever her shortcomings Catherine deserved a Landseer portrait: she was an enchantingly honest whore, not given to the exotic extravagences of her sisters—except perhaps in the matter of the luxuriously-padded w.c. which earned her the title of The Girl with the Swansdown Seat. It was not a part of her anatomy that she habitually pampered. When a gallant Master of Foxhounds congratulated her after a hard run on her delightfully rosy cheeks, Catherine yelled after him gaily, 'That's nothing. You should see the cheeks of my arse!'.

Even those well-born young ladies who did not know of Skittles still found the picture made them uneasy. 'It is not,' reported Miss Hall,* a young lady whose diary was her closest companion, 'a pleasing picture . . . The young lady is unpleasing, her expression disagreeable, her attitude ungraceful and unartistic . . . The idea of her

* *Two Victorian Girls*, O. A. Sherrard, 1966.

having been pacifying the horse in such a dress is ridiculous and impossible . . .'. There had already been public complaints about the horse-breakers disporting themselves in Hyde Park; and there were those who felt that Catherine had, in effect, taken a few square feet of advertising space on the almost sacred walls of the Royal Academy.

Despite his age and his unendingly-expressed infirmities, Edwin did not lose either his attraction for women or his own need for female companionship. Throughout his life, and even into his sixties, he had been considered an extremely eligible bachelor; though his liaison with Georgiana, and his running with the fast d'Orsay set, had no doubt kept some of his more respectable female admirers at bay. Like most lifelong bachelors he had grown extremely covetous of his freedom and independence, but in his sixties he seems to have looked back with some nostalgia. In his youth and middle-age he had made a number of proposals of marriage, most of them only gallantly and half-seriously. Probably he had hoped to be refused, since until his late thirties he had fondly cherished the idea of being affiliated by marriage to the aristocracy.

One proposal that was genuine was to a young woman who was later to become a close friend of the Thackeray family, Kate Perry. She had, it seemed, turned Landseer down on the grounds of ill health when she was twenty, though she appears to have lived almost till the end of the century; she also at times suggested to others regret over her decision, talking in a melancholy fashion of Landseer and of her 'Autumnal life'. Her true reasons for rejecting the hand of the great painter are not apparently on record. Kate, the daughter of a former editor of the *Morning Chronicle*, was described as 'a pretty, animated lady who saw a great variety of company, and commented with a neat mixture of sentiment and irony on the vagaries of the London world'. Whether her knowledge of those vagaries embraced Edwin's reputation as a young stallion let loose among the aristocracy is not known. Certainly Kate Perry was also a douce and proper lady who would probably not have been tolerant of the extra-marital activities so commonplace among the upper echelons of Georgian and early Victorian society. She lived in Chesham Place, Belgrave Square with her sister, Mrs. Frederick Elliot, the wife of a prominent figure in the Colonial office. She was credited by Thackeray with making 37 Chesham Place 'a kind, amusing home, full of welcome and interest and discussion'. Although charming hostesses, she and her sister eschewed society, devoting most of their energies to a board school where they looked after three hundred neglected children. Together they fed, taught and clothed the poor mites and, as Miss Perry herself related in rather Lady-of-the-Lamp prose 'with the help of other kind souls, preparing them in some degree to join the battle of life, in which there are many crosses —but few Victoria ones'.

Kate is the unobtrusive heroine of Landseer's romantic saga: she would have been much better for him, one can almost hear the London gossips infer, than that fast Duchess of Bedford or that over-emancipated Nellie Power or that close-cropped long-striding French animal painter. She was certainly capable of establishing a rapport with creative genius. Thackeray had met her at Brighton whence he had repaired seeking solitude to work on *Vanity Fair*. She became his confidante, being the first to learn of how the title of his greatest novel, for which he had 'ransacked his brain', came on him suddenly in the middle of the night, causing him to leap out of bed and run round the room muttering, 'Vanity Fair, Vanity Fair, Vanity Fair'. Thackeray himself knew of the unfulfilled romance. Since his allegedly satirical but in fact heavily sarcastic attacks on Edwin's royal pictures in the 1840s, the two men had become firm friends; though Landseer only ever illustrated one piece by Thackeray, a short story called *The Black Sheep* that appeared in 1861 in *The Cornhill Magazine*, of which the novelist was then editor.

Landseer and Kate remained friends and correspondents. In 1863, before she left for a tour of Italy, he wrote to complain that R.A. business 'prevents me kissing hands before your departure. Don't become too Italian; don't speak broken English to your old friends on your return to our village, where you will find no end of us charmed to have you back again; and amongst them, let me say, you will find old E.L. sincerely glad to see his unvarying K.P. once more by that old fireside'. A few years later she wrote him complaining of illness (almost predictably, since it was the official pretext for their having to communicate by letter at all) before adding 'when you are in this quarter late in the afternoon do come & see me. It will be a perfect pleasure to show you my little home. Your sincere and affectionate old friend . . .'.

Throughout his sixties, Landseer had other women writing to him in similarly affectionate terms—among them the handsome Lady Emily Peel and a Mrs. Lehmann who would send him flowers, being gallantly thanked by the artist for 'leaving your rosy tints at my gate' and 'scattering flowers in my path'.

As a young man Edwin had naturally encouraged the attentions of physically attractive women, like the still beautiful Countess of Blessington and her pretty niece Ellen Power. Even as an elder, he still retained an eye for a pretty girl. Returning from Windsor with John Bright one day he told the well-known reformer: 'If I were a young man and a Prince I should never rest till that lovely girl (Princess Louise) had promised to marry me!'. However, from middle-age onwards he had begun to find apparent reassurance in the company of women whose attraction was anything but physical. One of these was Marianne Skerret, the private secretary and close confidante of the Queen, and the daughter of a Colonel who had distinguished himself in the Peninsular Wars. 'There was,' declared Goodall, 'less of her than I ever saw in any woman; under 5 feet in height and as thin as a shred of paper.' Her plainness of feature was 'almost comical'; yet she was a creature of keen intelligence, widely read and cultivated and a devout Christian. 'She is the dearest and most wonderful little woman I ever knew,' said Landseer. 'If anything goes wrong in Buckingham Palace, Balmoral or Windsor, whether a crowned head or a scullery maid is concerned, Miss Skerret is always sent for to put it right.' Clearly such a paragon posed no threat to Edwin's bachelor status: they struck up a long, lively and mutually illegible correspondence (fifty of her sprightly letters were included in a sale of the artist's sketch-books and effects at Christie's in 1961). She became the forerunner of other close female companions of sterling moral qualities, whose features would nonetheless be likened to 'a monkey', 'a wizened apple' and so on.

There is always, of course, speculation about any attractive and accomplished man who fails to marry. A semi-frivolous excuse must normally be found. In Edwin's case the answer was ready-made— his obsession, indeed his consanguinity, with animals; the realisation among Victorian ladies that, in the unlikely event of Landseer's being hooked, the lucky woman would have to share his home (and his affections) with a menagerie. On St. Valentine's day 1861 such apprehensions were wistfully conveyed to the artist by an unknown admirer—though it is not impossible that the lines could have emanated from one or more of his more jocose male friends:

A beautiful young lady's complaint Addressed to Sir Edwin Landseer

> Oh! were I but a Puppy dog
>   Or e'en a playful Kitten
> A Badger rough, or Grunting Hog
>   Your fancy I had smitten!
>
> Had I but antlers or a mane
>   Or claws, or Feathers bright
> I might your admiration gain;—
>   Find favour in your Sight.

But I'm a thing of gowns and caps
　A talking, laughing creature.
A Laughing Hyaena had perhaps
　Some more attractive feature!

Had I a 'Brush', your brush perchance,
　Had added grace to mine.
Bristles my beauties might enhance
　Or Scales have made you mine.

Alack! Alas!—I'm not a brute!
　I'm smooth, and human faced.
Your Palette I should never suit
　I am not to your taste.

Farewell, Sir Edwin! Wondrous Man!
　A second Comus though
For he could change (the story ran)
　To Horse, Dog, Goat or Sow.

The final verse of a long poem summed-up the frustration felt by dozens of pet-loving women who sometimes found themselves jealous of their own dogs:

I cannot hope to win your eye
　Unless your magic wand
Should change me into *Spitz* or *Skye*
　To sit at your Command.

Ever since the days of Lady Caroline Norton's *Dedication*, Edwin seemed to have inspired verse. Another anonymous (and undated) poetess calling herself the Lady in Black Velvet had written him a kind of dental love ode (adaptable, she noted, to the air of *Queen Mary's Lamentation*):

I sigh and lament me forsooth
These Walls do partake of my grief
My Edwin has broken a tooth
And how shall I give him relief.

Through those lips with what pain do I see
The gap which must let in the air
My life! that it had but been me
To suffer this woeful affair.

But the Gem that once dwelt in thy pate
I cherish more dearly than those
Which fortune allots to my State
Still I prize but this Stump of my Beau's.

As he entered his sixtieth year Landseer no doubt treasured any and every message of comfort. In 1862 and 1863 his health and spirits were again at a low ebb. His commission to help model the Nelson monument involved a great deal of hard physical effort and a multitude of distractions in a medium with which he was unfamiliar, and he sent nothing at all to the galleries in those years. But he was engaged on another large canvas, determined to prove himself an independently-minded epic painter instead of an obedient patron's pet.

While attending the Highland Games at Balmoral in 1859 (where, it was noted, the leading male dancer had been disqualified because he danced 'too well'), Queen Victoria had heard the sad news of the finding of the explorer Sir John Franklin's remains—'or rather of the things belonging to him and his party'. Sir John's party had disappeared in the Arctic in 1847, but it was not until twelve years later that a few skeletons and other relics had been found. The tragedy impressed itself on Landseer's mind and by 1864 he had produced his *'Man Proposes, God Disposes'*, a pictorial epitaph which, though full of potential bathos as a picture of successful polar-bears dining off unsuccessful explorers, achieved a genuine eerie pathos. The chill colouring (the painter's normal tendency now) was for once effective. By the Catalogue Notes in the special Royal Academy Exhibition the year after Landseer's death, *'Man Proposes, God Disposes'* was 'according to our judgement, his greatest picture'. Most critics praised it, though the *Mask* affected to recognise 'our old friends the two bears at the zoological gardens' and to find that the ice 're-sembled canvas and powdered alum but *not* frozen water'; and certainly Landseer was not the kind of painter to expose himself to sub-zero temperatures in search of on-the-spot realism. Another who allegedly disapproved of it was the great explorer's widow, Lady Franklin, who may have objected to her courageous husband's being featured on the walls of the Academy as a polar-bear's dinner. This want of pictorial tact was a growing feature of Sir Edwin's work, supporting the contention that his mind was failing. His *Queen Victoria on Horseback in Windsor Park*, showing her Majesty on a fat bay pony contemplating the carcase of a fallow deer, incorporated the figure of a gamekeeper with his disembowelling knife at the ready and a deerhound avidly licking the wound in the dead animal's neck. The unbearably arch, *Piper and a Pair of Nutcrackers* (a bull-finch and two squirrels) reflected another kind of misjudgement, being a Royal Academy exhibit with all the weight of a children's book illustration.

In 1865 Sir Charles Eastlake died during one of his trips to Italy to

secure paintings for the National Gallery. On sheer wealth of experience as a practising artist there was only one possible successor as
President of the Royal Academy, Sir Edwin Landseer. Besides, it was
rumoured that once again Victoria had stated her gently persuasive
preference. What Haydon might have called the Mock-Election was,
by all accounts, a moving scene. Tearfully Landseer thanked his
fellow-artists for the honour but explained that he could not accept
the post. He recovered sufficiently to suggest the name of Daniel
Maclise, but the burly Irishman declared himself the worst possible
man for the appointment, which finally went to the fashionable Sir
Francis Grant. Sir Edwin's tears had no doubt been mixed: if he
had been deeply moved by the almost unanimous acclamation of his
fellow-Academicians he was also aware that the prize had been
offered all too late: he knew, as most of the others present knew, that
he no longer had the energy, either nervous or physical, to make a
success of the appointment. Nor was his variable mental condition
any secret. Such a Presidency, in fact, could only have been a
macabre farce.

In the same year Landseer had sent to the Academy's annual
exhibition *The Connoisseurs*, a rare self-portrait with his sheepdog
Lassie and the retriever Myrtle (the connoisseurs of the title) looking
critically over the painter's shoulders at the sketch-pad on his knee.
When compared with a photograph taken at around the same time
it can only be regarded as a somewhat glamourised portrait—a noble
brow, fine curling hair, a luxuriant moustache and whiskers, the
proudly disdainful aspect of a noble squire softened by the flopping
cravat and casually crumpled shirt-collar of the artist. Landseer
presented the original to the Prince of Wales. It was engraved by
Samuel Cousins, and numerous prints sent by the artist to his friends.
Lady Emily Peel was one of them: 'How more than kind and good of
you to have remembered one of your chief admirers, and to have
bestowed upon her your own Portrait with the favourite old dogs'.
Kate Perry was another grateful recipient, thanking him for 'the
likeness of one whose friendship is *very valuable* to me, and it was
indeed a surprise & a delight when I opened the long white roll & saw
your kind face peeping out of it—the likeness is perfect . . .'. It was,
indeed, too perfect; and it is significant that in the same year in which
Lady Emily and Kate received their copies of *The Connoisseurs*, Sir
Edwin was in almost panic-stricken fashion trying to absolve himself
from other likenesses. At Lady Eastlake's he had met an unnamed
female French photographer and promised to sit to her for his
portrait, but a horrified disclaimer to his hostess quickly followed (a
letter described by Lady Eastlake herself as 'characteristic'):

It is always embarrassing to refuse a lady anything. I had not pluck enough the other evening to say 'no' at the right time: it is a nasty, discourteous syllable. Dare I trust to your good nature, and ask you to get me out of the dilemma, which my want of courage has got me into with your foreign friend, Madame -----, who did me the honour to ask me to sit to her? At the risk of your laughter, I tell you I am shy, and dislike passing printshops where my sins are exhibited: if, in addition to these misfortunes, I saw a photograph of myself exposed to view, I should leave the country. In one word, I cannot part with the copyright of my own phiz. I have had the same flattering proposal from no end of English friends. Say to your foreign friend that I am unworthy the highly flattering compliment she proposes—say that I am crazy—only pray release me from the scrape the appearance of 'yes' has got me into.

Landseer produced little in the following year to extend his reputation. Victoria visited his studio in March 1866, and a few days later wrote to her daughter, the Crown Princess of Prussia: 'I think you might like to hear what I saw at Landseer's the other day. Such beautiful unfinished things. A 'Lady Godiva' most charmingly treated, on a dun pony (of course, nude but, so simply arranged— you see her back and she has her arms outstretched, offering up a prayer to be supported in this terrible ordeal), an old Duenna standing by, closing her eyes'. *Lady Godiva's Prayer*, dismissed by F. G. Stephens as 'unfortunate', was shown at the Academy in the same year.

One or two wealthy patrons had stepped eagerly into the breach created by the deaths of Wells, Sheepshanks, Vernon and Bicknell, among them H. W. Eaton, later Lord Cheylesmore, whose acquisitions included *The Monarch of the Glen, A Flood in the Highlands* and *Taming the Shrew*. Another was Mr. E. J. Coleman, a fellow deerstalking enthusiast, at whose fine home, Stoke Park near Stoke Poges, Landseer was a frequent guest. He had commissioned '*Man Proposes, God Disposes*' and the much admired dogs-and-game picture, *Well Bred Sitters who never say they are bored*. In 1866 Landseer produced for him *The Chase*, a spirited study of a deerhound in pursuit of a stag. Lord Elcho was so impressed with the figure of the fleeing stag that he asked the painter to make a life-size model of it as a target for the annual Running Deer shooting competition then held on Wimbledon Common and eventually at Bisley. The same definitive running-deer figure later graduated to road-signs.

Landseer had been given the government commission for the

Trafalgar Square lions in 1859. It was eight years before they were placed in position. *Punch* had been sceptical all along: 'Nor can we place reliance / Upon the four stone lions' ran one of its inimitable couplets. The original intention had been for John Graham Lough to sculpt them, but his designs were considered unsatisfactory, and the government cast around for another modeller. The expectant smiles of the sculptors turned to frowns when the Tory Prime Minister Lord Derby finally appointed Landseer, a painter. Whatever Sir Edwin's shortcomings as a sculptor, he was undeniably a 'lion-man', with experience ranging from his early menagerie studies, through dissection to the monster van Amburgh canvases; and this no doubt bore heavily in his favour.

The main worry to Landseer's friends, however, was not over any lack of specialised skill (no artistic medium had so far defeated him), but whether his physical and nervous health would be equal to such a colossal undertaking. Not long after he had accepted the commission, F. G. Stephens visited him in his studio where he was engaged on the large canvas, *A Flood in the Highlands*. Although the painter seemed in outward appearance fairly normal, Stephens felt an almost indefinable, even slightly ominous, sense of unease about Landseer's physical condition:

> He looked as if about to become old, although his age by no means justified the notion; it was not that he had lost activity or energy, or that his form had shrunk, for he moved as firmly and swiftly as ever, indeed he was rather demonstrative, stepping on and off the platform in his studio with needless display, and his form was stout and well-filled. Nevertheless, without seeming to be overworked, he did not look robust, and he had a nervous way remarkable in so distinguished a man, one who was usually by no means unconscious of himself, and yet, to those he liked, full of kindness. The wide green shade which he wore above his eyes, projected straight from his forehead, and cast a large shadow on his plump, somewhat livid features, and in the shadow one saw that his eyes had suffered. The grey 'Tweed' suit, and its sober trim, a little emphatically 'quiet', marked the man; so did his stout, not fat nor robust, figure; rapid movements, and utterances that glistened with prompt remarks, sharp, concise, with quick humour, but not seeking occasions for wit, and imbued throughout with a perfect frankness, distinguished the man.

During the years of the commission, Landseer had produced a fairly steady stream of other work, including several large canvases; so the long gestatory period did not reflect slowness or laxness of working. He had approached the task, in fact, with considerable thoroughness; studying, sketching, dissecting and modelling in miniature. Of course, he haunted the Regent's Park zoo. He had even wanted to spend an entire night by himself watching the resting lions; but permission had been refused, understandably and mainly in the interests of his own safety. Wild cats are apt to be discomposed by having too much of the 'eye' fixed on them; Landseer had already unwittingly induced big cats to throw themselves maddened at the bars of their cage after he had held them for too long in his steady gaze. Perhaps the authorities also had in mind an earlier experience involving the painter Mulready, who is said to have entered the enclosure at Regent's Park one day in the absence of the keeper to find a fully-grown lion loose and on the prowl. For three-quarters of an hour until the keeper returned, according to Linnell, 'Mulready kept the lion at bay by the power of his eye'.

Landseer also contrived to work from a live model at his home. The Duchess of Abercorn's son Frederic recorded the dismay of his mother on visiting the painter one day to find him up a step-ladder against a great mass of clay. Even more offputting was the sight of a large lion stretched out on the lawn. The animal in question was a particularly elderly and docile lion that had been brought to his house in a furniture van attended by two keepers. The senility of the lion may have had something to do with later criticisms of the model's anatomy: much of the musclature is certainly somewhat flaccid and consistent with an elderly and underexercised *felis leo.*

Nor was Sir Edwin any stranger to lion cadavars. He had, of course, studied Haydon's anatomical drawings and dissected his own lion carcase while he was still in his teens. Other opportunities had occurred throughout the years. In 1848 the Secretary of the Zoological Society of London had written to him from Regent's Park:

> The lion who has been for so long the most noble ornament of the Society's collection is now suffering from so acute an attack of inflammation of the lungs that I fear there is little chance of saving his life.
>
> As he is certainly the finest example of his species now in Europe, and it is scarcely possible to expect that we shall ever obtain another equal to him, it has occurred to me that a study from this animal might be desirable to you. If the event which I cannot but regard as most possible should unfortunately occur, I shall be happy to send him to your studio while yet warm, and leave him with you for two or perhaps three days ...

This cadavar became the subject of a true story which Dickens loved to quote. A party of guests had been dining with the artist at St. John's Wood when Landseer's manservant entered and solemnly enquired: 'Did you order a lion, sir?'.

The carcase that Landseer acquired while modelling the Trafalgar Square prototype was quickly past its best. Edwin had unfortunately been in the country when it died. 'Pity the beggar takes it in his head to die when Sir E. is out of town,' wrote the artist's studio assistant F. H. Keyl. It was therefore in a state of near-decomposition before Landseer could set to work making plaster-casts from the carcase. It was brave of Edwin to take such risks. Possibly he was inspired by the example of George Stubbs, his nearest approach perhaps to an artistic hero, who had sometimes worked for up to eleven weeks on the putrefying carcase of a horse he had manhandled up a flight of stairs. As Landseer well knew, the wages of studying decomposing carcases could be death. William Duffield, a still-life painter who often used dead game in his compositions, succumbed at the age of forty-six to the dreaded *putrid miasma* after working too long over the corpse of a stag. But poor Duffield had lost his sense of smell, which Edwin clearly had not:

> Anything as fearful as the gasses from the royal remains it is difficult to conceive even in spite of friend Hills nostrums for the renewal of healthy atmosphere. We have shut our eyes to nasty inconvenience and opened them to the importance of the opportunity of handling the dangerous subject whilst in a state of safety. With the experience of the Animal photographs, Casts in Plaster and Studies you may believe that I shall neither disappoint you, my Country or the brave Nelson in my treatment of these symbols of our National defences.

The man chosen to cast the four lions in bronze from Landseer's giant clay model was Baron Marochetti, an experienced but uninspired creator of equestrian monuments for public squares. Like Sir Edwin, Marochetti was an enthusiastic sportsman, though his hunting expeditions occasionally lent themselves to anti-climax. That other sportsman Millais recalled a visit to the Baron's estate in France near Passy with the whole party setting out one morning in gorgeous Lincoln green coats, feathered hats and girt about with circular hunting-horns. Millais was greatly caught-up in the excitement of the occasion until he discovered that the role of each hunter was to sit on a kitchen-chair in front of his allotted rabbit-hole and blast-off with a large gun as soon as one of the denizens of the warren had the temerity to show its twitching nose. A successful shot was greeted with stentorian blasts on the horn, suitable to the demise of a bull-elephant. Marochetti was paid £11,000 to help maintain his mock-heroic life-style, while Landseer received only £6,000. As the *Art-Journal* noted, however, 'it appears that one body only has been modelled, while two heads were made, each of which served for two bodies. Thus the same body was cast in bronze four times, and the heads twice each'.

The first lion, heavily swathed in calico, was placed in position on the 25th of January 1867. *Punch*'s punsters had been straining at the leash: 'The first Lion intended for the Nelson Monument has broken loose from its distinguished keeper, Sir Edwin Landseer . . . A poet has already begun a poem entitled *A Dawning of a Roarer . . .*'. The critical reaction to their combined appearance was mixed. The most violent was from a man who pelted them with stones, and who was arrested as a madman. Much of the criticism was, of necessity, almost self-contradictory. 'Their power is irresistible,' said the *Art-Journal* 'they have crushed everything around them'—and it is certainly true that they are 'too large to compose with the column'. Many felt that by modelling one couchant lion Landseer had pulled-off another *Bolton Abbey* or *Dialogue at Waterloo*—he had accepted a difficult commission and taken the easiest way out. The lions were unfavourably compared with, among others, Thorwaldsen's famous lance-pierced lion at Lucerne and Canova's at the tomb of Pope Pius VI: nearer home, it was even suggested that 'the old lion at the top of Northumberland House would not acknowledge them as brethren'. The arguments over anatomy have never died. They surfaced again in 1943 in the *Illustrated London News* when the naturalist and private zoo owner Sir Garrard Tyrwhitt-Drake maintained that the Landseer lions were inaccurate since a resting lion does not have its forepaws flat on the ground but right-angled inwards. Doubtless a more volatile sculptor might have included this peculiarity which would have added a touch of realism, but photographs of zoo lions published in the *Illustrated London News* showed that the flat-pawed position, if not habitual, was both possible and natural.

The greatest praise, of course, came from Landseer's friends. 'They seem to me to combine the two greatest qualities of Art—Majesty and Repose,' Brinsley Morley assured him; whilst Algernon Graves suggested that 'had the lions been erected in the Egyptian desert, they would have attracted travellers from all parts of the globe'. In Lord Elcho's view Sir Edwin's model was 'a real stunning roaring success—cheap at £6,000'. Sir Charles Gray wrote from Cannes about 'that wonderful creation of yours! . . . Most heartily do I congratulate you upon your most *complete Success*! . . . I only wish you could have worked in a glass hive, like the industrious bees, that the public who found fault at the time it took, might have seen the great fatigue, labour and wonderful skill required to bring the four King of Beasts to such *astonishing perfection* . . . I trust now that going up and down that ladder has ceased, you will feel all the better and stronger for it. . . '.

Landseer, however, was no doubt aware that he had come to sculpture too late in the day. Like his large freely-conceived commissions in oil in which he seemed at last to have cut himself loose from the apron-strings of aristocratic patronage, it required the physical strength he no longer had. He did produce one other piece of sculpture of *The Stag at Bay*, shown at the Royal Academy in 1866. The Duke of Abercorn had wanted Landseer to sculpt a group of deer and hounds to be cast in silver as a centre-piece. But it was modelled too large for translation into such a precious metal. Instead it was cast in bronze, overpainted by Landseer and bought by the future Lord Cheylesmore.

Sir Edwin's reputation as a sculptor lingered on. Three years after the appearance of the lions, Hugh Lupus Grosvenor, the First Duke of Westminster wrote to Landseer inviting him to model a great equestrian statue of his heroic ancestor, the Norman Earl of Chester. The artist's reply was that 'perhaps at my time of life it is better not to have too many irons in the fire. The equestrian statues I am conversant with remind me so much more of art than of nature that I give up my wish to try something original with reluctance. Hereafter, however, I may amuse myself trying a new treatment of the horse and his master'.*

Landseer, of course, by that time knew that he would never set another ladder against another mound of clay. The days both of amusing himself and of attempting new treatments were fast running out.

* *Victorian Duke*, Gervas Huxley, 1967. The commission was eventually accepted by another painter, G. F. Watts, whose characteristic pomposity over the matter was in contrast to Sir Edwin's modesty. It was fraught, however, with some Landseer-type delays over the choice of a model, as an attempt was made by genealogical hindsight to breed a typical Norman warrior's charger. The sculpture, a good one, was thus not completed until 1879.

CHAPTER EIGHTEEN

FAREWELL TO THE HEATHER

Flogging would be mild compared to my sufferings.
— Landseer in a letter to his sister Jessy

THE TIME had obviously come for Landseer to give up his yearly trek to the Scottish Highlands. But he stubbornly refused. His motives in persevering with his annual migration were no doubt complicated. In his morbid death-obsessed sixties he genuinely feared that he might never see the Highlands again. They were, after all, one of the great loves of his life. There was much more than mere politeness in his address on his election to the Royal Scottish Academy in 1866 when he remembered Scotland as the place 'where I have spent the best years of my life'. To him stalking was also a manly ritual, one whose continuance proved that he was still scarcely more than middle-aged. Nor was he able to resist the invitations to shoot the great deer forests where, after a long day on the heather, he could fleetingly pretend that he was still the irrepressible *bon viveur* he had always been. The fact was that he now tended to repeat his stories, his mimicries sounded a little cracked, he sometimes nodded-off at table or had to retire early or spend whole days resting in his room. That the invitations were getting fewer each year no doubt made them all the more precious. One of the gillies had earlier remarked, looking at the artist's white hair, 'Sir Edwin, you're becoming like the ptarmigan!'. Perhaps he should have seen it as a hint. But Landseer seemed determined to postpone for as long as possible the approach of winter.

'The long long walk in the dark, after the shot is fired, over rocks, bog, black moss, and through torrents, is more than enough *for twenty-five!*' he wrote to Hills; and again on October 7th 1866 from Kinrara House, Aviemore:

I returned here last Wednesday October 3, and have been out every day since in the Forest. Some very good stags have fallen to my rifle—as yet have only missed *one* shot when it was nearly dark! I have unintentionally taken too much out of my already weak condition. I can't keep my hand steady. This is Sunday, and perhaps to-day's rest may restore me.

Several days later he was still pushing his strength beyond endurance:

> Yesterday I was at it (after riding nine miles to the ground) from 6 o'clock—the hour I was called—till 7 in the evening, having the same distance to ride home. The whole day passed in rocky ground, long heather and unceasing rain. I killed my stag at 150 yards towards the gloaming and have the bill to pay to-day—tired and very shaky. I have not got over the great shock sustained by the awful shoot out of the dog-cart downhill—this style of accident.

The accident, from which Landseer had emerged badly shaken, was illustrated in a characteristic sketch appended to the letter. It showed a bolting horse, a smashed vehicle meeting an immovable object and the artist somersaulting head over heels through the crisp Highland air. It was scarcely recommended exercise for a sixty-four year old, and had been his second drama that year. Earlier he had sailed from Dunrobin, one of a party of guests on the Duke of Sutherland's yacht. But the vessel had encountered rough weather and had been wrecked on some rocks. Although all the party and the crew were eventually taken off safely, the experience had done little for Sir Edwin's already overwrought nerves.

Such incidents seemed at times to bring him face to face with himself, especially since he could so effectively caricature an elderly man pushing himself beyond his physical means:

> *Reaction* (after exhaustion) may give me boldness. My *Hart* is in my art. I long for meditation in my painting-room and for the quiet and repose necessary to an old gentleman's revival. Some things make age older as in youth some things make youth younger.

But the painting-room never remained occupied for long. The Continent beckoned, as it had in 1840, but with the same result; a curtailed visit, no recovery in his health and nagging worry about the work awaiting him at home:

> I have made up my mind to return, to face the ocean! The weather is unfriendly—sharp wind and spiteful rain. There is no denying the fact, since my arrival and during my sojourn here I have been less well. The doctors keep on saying it is on the nerves; hereafter they may be found to be in error . . . I desire to get home. With this feeling, I am to leave this to-morrow, pass some hours in Paris

. . . take the rail to Calais at night, if it does not blow cats and dogs; take the vessel to Dover; hope to be home on the 6th before two o'clock.

He might have been more ready to cut short his trips to the High-lands had not the Queen unexpectedly revived her interest in Land-seer as a guest and as a painter. When Albert died in 1861, she had given up invitations to all but her most intimate friends. Landseer, however, seems to have taken as a personal slight his dismissal from her guest-list. In his depressed state he was unable to separate cause from effect: the absence of invitations meant that he was out of favour. There was some truth (as well as a good deal of self-lacera-tion) in the surmise. The Queen had not *entirely* forgotten about pain-ters. Winterhalter, he knew, was not only much in demand to paint Victoria's grown-up children, but was actually playing hard to get. The Paris-domiciled German painter had first been summoned to the British Court in 1841: twenty years later he was no longer answering summonses. 'Winterhalter is most provoking,' the Queen was writing to her daughter the Princess Royal (then the Crown Princess of Prussia) in 1863, 'saying he won't come to England, that he has Russians and Poles to paint, that he is very ill and that he will paint me in Germany'. The following year he was finally persuaded to come to England but 'refuses to paint full lengths of Bertie and Alix'. What's more, he was naming fees that caused Victoria to baulk—a further reflection, Landseer no doubt felt, on an old and trusted family-painter who would have travelled anywhere on the shortest of notice to paint the Queen and her descendants for a nominal fee. To add to his chagrin, the Queen was also toying with an obscure sentimentalist, A. Graefle—'I think after Winterhalter his like-nesses are by far the best'. Sir Edwin might have consoled himself with the thought that at least he was no longer regarded as a reliable hack—his erratic record in the matter of polite likenesses was by now a matter of legend.

When, three years after the Prince Consort's death, Landseer was finally invited to Windsor to meet the Queen, the occasion was too much for him. 'I saw Sir E. Landseer for the first time on Wednesday,' wrote Victoria to her daughter, 'and he cried dreadfully.' Perhaps partly out of pity, she later invited him to paint her on horseback at her Isle of Wight home. *Her Majesty at Osborne in 1866* was shown at the Royal Academy in the following year, and became something of a scandal picture. At a casual glance, it was a picture of almost stultifying conventionality, showing Victoria reading despatches from the back of a glossy black pony, attended by the inevitable

begging dog (by now almost a Landseer trademark). But the painting
was remarkable for two things—its almost stygian gloom (the result
of Edwin's increasing melancholia and fading eyesight) and the presence at the pony's head of John Brown, the Queen's Highland fac-
totum. Brown had previously been little more than a shadowy public
rumour, yet here he was (in a black kilt and wildly overgrown
sporran) jaunty, self-confident, protective, having all the appearance
of the Queen's most intimate counsellor and companion. The tongues
wagged, half-hinting at a relationship that the Queen's own open-
ness totally disproved. 'An imprudence has been committed,'
breathed the *Saturday Review*. 'We respect the privacy of her Majesty,
but when Sir Edwin Landseer puts the Queen and her black favourites
into what are, during the season, the most public rooms in England,
he does her more harm than he imagines.' The *Illustrated London
News* was in total agreement—'Not one of her Majesty's subjects will
see this lugubrious picture without regret'. The *Art-Journal* merely
pursed its lips: 'It is not a theme for criticism. We pass it by'. The
satirical magazine *Tomahawk* took a less serious view of the cave-
dark painting. 'All is black that is not brown', it punned.

It was the public reaction that had most scandalised the journals.
Some onlookers frowned, but many tittered. One delicate young
Victorian diarist found the picture 'absurd and disagreeable', and
repeated rumours that Brown on a rail journey to Scotland had been
'so utterly drunk that he had to be smuggled into a carriage the best
way they could'. Soon there were further stories of the ex-groom's
gross over-familiarity in the presence of the Queen. On a royal picnic,
when rain threatened, Brown advised a hasty return to the lodge:
when Victoria ordered a maid to brush the crumbs from her dress,
Brown had interposed irritably, 'Och, jist gie yersel' a shak' like
a'body else!'. Strictly for the lower atmosphere of the smoke-room was
a tale about the Scotsman's legendary physical prowess. Having
single-handedly lifted the wheels of the Queen's carriage out of a deep
wayside ditch, Victoria expressed spontaneous admiration for his
enormous muscular power. 'Aye' the great Brown allegedly (and
wistfully) agreed, 'and if it were not for the perneecious habit of
wanking my doodle, I'd be a veritable Hercules the noo!'

It was not so much that Brown ignored protocol: he did not know
what it was. But he was forgiven little. In common with many of the
Queen's close associates and her son the Prince of Wales, Landseer
disliked him intensely. It is said that he more than once complained
openly of the Scotsman's insolence during the painting of the Osborne portrait. Brown himself was rattled by the spate of critical
rumours sparked-off by the picture. Only Victoria remained above

the controversy. She was delighted with the portrait, desiring Land-seer to make an engraving of it, though suggesting certain altera-tions. Through her secretary Caroline Gordon she sent photographs showing her beloved Highland retainer with 'a short beard. She wishes much to know if this could be introduced into the Engraving— and whether you would think it an improvement'. The task of tidy-ing-up John Brown's facial hair (even if only artistically) cannot have greatly appealed to Landseer. He filed the letter under *Royal Fus-series*; a file already fairly full of royal complaints about sketches for which 'the Queen has no particular fancy' or were 'too slight' and of suggestions about what should come out of them and what should go in.

In the same year he was invited to Balmoral, from which Victoria wrote, not without a degree of pleased surprise, that 'I never saw him more amiable or more *en train* and amenable to observation'. Writing to Jessy from the Queen's Scottish home, Landseer, des-pite poor health, could not resist preening himself a little at his restitution:

> The Queen kindly commands me to get well here. She has to-day been twice to my room to show additions recently added to her already rich collection of photographs. Why, I know not, but since I have been in the Highlands I have for the first time felt wretched-ly weak, without appetite. The easterly winds, and now again the unceasing cold rain, may possibly account for my condition, as I can't get out. Drawing tires me; however, I have done a little better to-day. The doctor residing in the castle has taken me in hand, and gives me leave to dine to-day with the Queen and the 'rest of the royal family'.

If Jessy hoped for polite reassurances, however, they were scarcely forthcoming:

> Flogging would be mild compared to my sufferings. No sleep, fearful cramp at night, accompanied by a feeling of faintness and distressing feebleness . . . All this means that I shall not be home on the 7th.

He returned to Scotland again that year. His letters to Jessy were the usual blend of complaints about infirmities and descriptions of the feats of endurance he was nevertheless forced to accomplish. But enforced by whom? It is at times difficult to believe that Landseer is his own master. There is a heavy sense of duty about his junketings, almost as though someone *else* was putting him through his trials. He knows that it is time to settle at home, but he cannot. Any suitably monogrammed invitation that presents itself must be accepted. The invitation to Chillingham was at least from old and loyal friends, the Earl and Countess of Tankerville, who had promised him 'any room you like to paint in':

> I made out my journey without pausing, starting on the eve of Thursday the 3rd, arriving here the evening of Friday (700 miles) the 4th. I confess to feeling jaded and tired. The whole of hills here present to the eye one endless mass of snow. It is really cold and winterly. Unless the weather recovers a more *generous* tone I shall not stay long, but at once return south to Chillingham. I was temped yesterday to go out with Mr. Coleman to the low ground part of the forest, and killed my first shot, at deer. I am paying for my boldness to-day, Sunday. All my joints ache; the lumbago has reasserted its unkindness; a warm bath is in requisition, and I am a poor devil.

Mr. Coleman, with whom he had been shooting in Ross and Cromarty, was another all-weather friend. From Coleman's home at Stoke Poges, he later writes again to Jessy, contemplating further feats of derring-do . . . expressing nostalgia for the scenes he need never have left:

> It is on the cards that I try my boldness by a run up to my home and back here the same day. It is quite a trial for me to be away from the meditation in the old studio—my works starving for my hand.

In 1868, while travelling in the Highlands, he was involved in a train crash which hurtled him across his carriage. The result was a badly gashed forehead, the scar of which remained clearly visible for the rest of his life. Physically he was badly shaken; mentally it seemed to be further evidence of the cruel nemesis that was stalking *him*. His health, by now an indefinable phenomenon, suffered another 'relapse'. The Highland fairies that had lashed him with wind and rain, shot him out of a dog-cart, shipwrecked him and finally opened up his head began at last to reduce the extent if not the frequency of his travels. In the following year, writing from Chillingham Castle, he is still pursuing renewed health and peace of mind with all the restlessness of a globe-trotting businessman:

> Very mortifying are the disappointments I have to face; one day seeming to give hope of a decided turn in favour of natural feeling, the next knocked down again. If my present scheme comes off, I shall not be at home again for ten days. If on my return I find

myself a victim to the old impulsive misery, I shall go on to East-well Park, as the Duchess of Abercorn writes she will take every care of me. Since I last wrote I have been on a visit to the Dowager Marchioness of Waterford, Ford Castle, a splendid old edifice, which C.L. would enjoy. Love to all.

In fact, Landseer could not bear to be alone: in convivial company he could still shine a little and forget the woes which crowded in on him when he sat down to write a letter. The artist P. G. Hamerton, who knew Sir Edwin only as a guest at social gatherings, a raconteur and bon viveur, one day unexpectedly confronted Landseer walking alone in the street. To his shocked astonishment he found the great painter 'the image of profound melancholy'.

Yet Landseer still managed to fulfil some commissions. The notorious portrait of Victoria had overshadowed two other works shown in the same exhibition. *Deer at Chillingham Park* and *Wild Cattle of Chillingham* had been painted for the Earl of Tankerville. The famous Chillingham herd of cream cattle, numbering between sixty and seventy head, had roamed the Caledonian forests since pre-Roman times. Landseer had closely studied these rather intractable animals, sometimes through a telescope, sometimes from a hide, on his frequent visits to Chillingham Castle. On one occasion the Earl (then Lord Ossulston) had decided to kill one of the bulls from the herd in order to allow his artist-friend closer study. But the operation to cutout the animal from the rest of the herd went wrong. The bull charged, goring Ossulston's horse which fortunately bolted several hundred yards with its master before dropping dead. It then turned on and tossed a keeper, breaking four of his ribs and piercing his chest with its horn. The hero of the occasion was the deerhound Bran which distracted the infuriated bull until the badly injured man could be rescued. The beast was finally shot, and its carcase figured with Lord Ossulston, Mr. Wells of Redleaf and the heroic Bran in *Death of the Wild Bull*, an 1836 Royal Academy exhibit. The picture was posed and peaceful, considering that Landseer's desire to study a wild bull at close quarters had resulted in a dead bull, a dead horse and a hospitalised keeper.

The two pictures which joined this one on the walls of Chillingham Castle were even more revealing in their way than the Osborne portrait, in that they showed the difficulty Landseer was now having in painting freely and keeping the appearance of his subjects alive. The lineaments of both family groups of deer and cattle are familiar enough, the treatment is professional, but the animals are trans-fixed, lifeless and overworked—somewhere *under* that paint, you

feel, are the true portrayals. Landseer's handling of oils was becoming increasingly moribund. He still possessed a certain spontaneity in a whole range of other media; but oil, of course, still dominated
artistic thinking, an attitude reflected in the official attitude to
water-colour—or 'paper-staining', as the mighty oil-painters would
patronisingly call it. The Royal Academy was extremely reluctant
to elect a water-colour painter, and a professional artist with a penchant for that particular medium generally resigned himself to being
poor. Sir Edwin's boyhood friend, J. F. Lewis, who in Ruskin's view
ranked next to Turner in the English school, had complained in 1858
to the secretary of the Water Colour Society: 'I work from before 9
in the morning till dusk, from half-past 6 to 11 at night always
. . . And for what? To get by water colour £500 a year, and this, too,
when I know that as an oil painter I could with less labour get my
thousand'. It was this harsh fact of life that caused Lewis to abandon
the medium to which his great talent most truly belonged—this, and
the continual prompting of Ruskin who warned him of another
aspect of water colour's impermanence: '*Are* you sure of your mat-
erial? If one of those bits of white hairstroke fade—where are you?
Why don't you paint in oils only, now?'.

It would never have been necessary to give any such advice to
Landseer. No one knew better than he what the rich patron wanted
—the solidarity of oil on the permanency of canvas, the whole enclosed in a stout gilt frame. He had, of course, from the eighteen-
thirties onwards gained a great facility in oils, the better to keep up
with the volume of his commissions. In his youth he had been by
nature something of a niggler: his acquirement of spontaneity in oils
had been less a matter of artistic policy than of private necessity, an
attempt to prevent his painting interfering with his social life. Now
he returned to the 'niggling' against which David Wilkie had warned
him as a youth. Oil had been the medium in which his considerable
reputation was enshrined: it would increasingly become the substance in which that reputation would be embalmed.

Yet the painter still had a shot or two left in his locker. *Rent Day in
the Wilderness*, one of his two Royal Academy entries on 1868, was
unsatisfactory yet not easily dismissed: one of these composites in
which the parts do not fuse but remain interesting in themselves. Sir
Roderick Murchison commissioned the painting, which he bequeathed
to the National Gallery of Scotland. *Rent Day* portrayed an incident
in the history of the owner's family when, after the defeat of the
Stuart army in 1715, bold Colonel Murchison, to whom the Earl of
Seaforth had entrusted his confiscated estates, continued loyally to
collect the rents from the people for transmission to his exiled chief-

tain—despite the bristling presence of the Redcoats, seen in the distance on the far shore of Loch Affric. The picture's elongated narrowness is one of its less satisfactory aspects, and the *Mask* of the time thought it had been 'unkind to cut off the colonel and his reverend friend at the waist'. But there are fine individual touches—the dogs, a Highland boy, Murchison himself impersonating his sagacious ancestor, a recumbent Highlander with a spy-glass, the tortuous and mist-hung banks that serve as concealment for the defiant clansmen.

His other exhibit of the same year had one of those endless titles with which Landseer on occasion liked to show off his knowledge of gillie vernacular. Admittedly it was neither quite as long nor as labyrinthal as the title of an 1859 picture—*'Bran will never put another stag to bay; and Oscar will make out by himself. The deer will be fine yet!'* This more modest text ran, *'Weel, sir, if the deer's got the ball, sure's death Chevy will no leave him!'* The title recorded an event which Landseer was (as any stalker would be) somewhat ashamed. He had wounded a stag, following it 'over rocks, bog, black moss and through torrents', but finally losing it and no doubt using age and infirmity, hunger and cold, as his excuses for returning home to a warm fire and a hot toddy. But the tracker-dog has been trained never to give up. It follows the stag that has 'got the ball' until the wounded animal drops of exhaustion and loss of blood, then lies beside it, huddling closer for warmth as the dead deer gradually loses its body heat. Landseer is said to have given a fine chalk drawing of the same theme to Mr. Ellice at Invergary in rather shamefaced atonement for leaving the latter's best collie tracker-dog out all night with a stag the painter had shot and lost. He had painted a similar scene in 1825, and was clearly no stranger to the business of abandoning the trek after a wounded deer and condemning the tracker-dog to an icy night-shift on the hill. W. M. Rossetti was sensitive both to the skill and the cruelty in *Chevy*: 'A masterpiece of Landseerian art (but) a work of brute ability, excellently repulsive as all brutish pain must be if duly rendered'.

If there had been any cause for celebration that year, it was Thomas's election as Associate Engraver of the New Class of the Royal Academy. It seemed an inexcusably tardy piece of recognition. He was seventy-two and had been before the public for more than fifty years. It would be another six years before he became Associate Engraver, and finally A.R.A. in 1876 when he was over eighty. He had produced a volume of work that was always highly professional and often distinguished, working in both line and mezzotint, and not only for his brother. His mezzotint engraving of Rosa Bonheur's *The Horse Fair* was considered by many to be his best plate; and most of his engravings of Edwin's works, particularly the deer studies, were of a high order. Where engraving was concerned, the name Landseer seems to have remained anathema to the Academy. John Landseer had been safely dead for three years before the first engraver, Samuel Cousins, had been elected Academician in 1855. The two events were perhaps not entirely unconnected. Ironically it was not until 1928, when engravers had ceased to be a power in the land, that they received full equality of status with artists.

It is, of course, hardly unusual for honours to be awarded to a man whose best work is behind him. From his sixties onward Tom had become increasingly dependent on his brother to find him work. Despite occasional differences, the Landseers remained a close-knit and loyal family. Edwin's influence had, of course, helped Charles become Keeper of the Royal Academy, the post which he held for twenty years. Tom had served Edwin well, and when age began to catch up with him his youngest brother wasn't half-hearted in returning the compliment. The extent of Edwin's loyalty was shown when Graves wanted from him a companion picture to his highly successful *Lost Sheep*. The painter consented for only one reason: 'I do not like being tied down to companion pictures, but I will do so for once in order to give Tom a plate'. As a result he produced *Event in the Forest* in 1864. On another occasion, when Tom was hard up and clamouring for a plate, Mr. Graves regretted politely that he had none to give him. Edwin waded in without preamble. 'If anyone has the right to the benefit of my signature it is my brother, the engraver of your fortune. This you must be well aware of.'

Tom's *forté* was the depiction in black-and-white of atmosphere and the elements. His interpretation of Edwin's *Children of the Mist* had been one of his most impressive achievements. Like many another virtuoso, he tended with age to indulge himself in what he did best rather than bothering too much about the range expected of him. This habit, at which Edwin connived, naturally incensed the publishers. Thus Edwin's painting of *The Hunter and the Hounds* (1862) represented these animals in the subdued light of a stable. Edwin sold it to Mr. Graves who made it over to Tom for engraving. When Graves got the picture back the animals were standing outside in a snowstorm—snow being one of Tom's specialities. 'I would give anything to engrave snow like Tom Landseer', Samuel Cousins had told Graves; but on this occasion the print-dealer did not see the point. *The Hunted Stag* was another picture that suffered a transformation of convenience. It had been originally set in a calm lake scene. Edwin altered it for Tom to engrave, replacing the tranquility with a wild storm, an effect that Tom was good at and enjoyed doing. Graves would often suggest a younger and more vigorous hand for some of Landseer's later pictures, if only in an attempt to counterbalance rather than underline Edwin's own ageing hand. But Edwin remained staunchly loyal to his eldest brother; and in his nervously irritable sixties he was a difficult man to thwart. Graves could only concur grudgingly with such filial loyalty, while privately expressing the view that Sir Edwin's 'management of his own affairs is not satisfactory to those who have dealings with him'.

Graves could at least complain about the Landseer brothers all the way to the bank: Hills did not have such obvious compensations. However, Sir Edwin's gratitude towards his business manager occasionally took a tangible form. In 1869 he gave him two fine paintings of lions shown that same year in the Royal Academy, both of them dating from his days wrestling in his lion studio with the 'colossal clay': one of these vigorous studies is in the Tate Gallery; its companion was destroyed in the flood of 1928. They were not the first animal portraits he had presented to Hills. A few years before he had wanted to make the businessman a present of a dog, but Hills had insisted that, being so seldom at home, he wouldn't be able to give the animal proper attention. 'About a month afterwards,' Hills recalled, 'he came to dine with me, and when he arrived he brought me a beautifully-finished picture of a dog, saying, "Here, Hills, I have brought you a parlour boarder. I hope you won't turn him out of doors".' This had been his portrait of *Pixie*, painted in 1860.

However, Landseer's mood in his sixty-seventh year was perhaps more accurately conveyed by a canvas of unsettling intensity which he also sent to the Academy in 1869. *A Swannery Invaded by Sea Eagles* had lain for years unfinished in his studio: it was a rape of a painting in which there was nothing but cruelty and violence. Next to man himself, the eagle had long been the chief predator in Landseer's art; floating in slowly towards the dead stag on the hillside, tearing at the entrails of its prey. In 1833 his small painting of *The Eagle's Nest* had shown the grey, bleak and uncompromising landscape that was the great bird's home: that, too, had been a landscape totally without rest or pity which seemed to reflect the beginnings of Edwin's *angst*. But *A Swannery* was the most agonised of them all. It is unlikely that Landseer ever witnessed such a scene; indeed naturalists have pointed to possible inaccuracies in it, including the fact that the eagles appear to be attacking the swans with beak as well as claw. Whatever its faults it had largeness and boldness of style: pictorially it was Landseer's last great scream for help—as more than one critic suggested, his 'swan-song'. Queen Victoria found it 'not pleasing' and hurried on. Some commentators believed that the painting symbolised the Franco-Prussian War. But Landseer's symbolism was usually subsconscious, and the struggle in this case was being waged within himself. The soft downy whiteness of the swans bespoke purity and innocence: the sea eagles, it seemed, were the spectres of his own insanity.

'My health (or rather condition) is a mystery quite beyond human intelligence,' Landseer had written to Hills. It was certainly the subject of much speculation. His early biographer Manson suggested one reason for the fact that the painter 'became the prey of hallucination and delusion to an extent that bordered on actual dementia. I have heard that a fall from his horse did cause injury to his brain, not suspected at the time nor known till after his death; and this indentation of the skull was doubtless at the root of his mental trouble'. Permanent mental damage, and worse, through falling from a horse was certainly an ever-present hazard in these days before the adoption of the crash-helmet. Peel had been one fatality, and the youthful Edwin's admirer Géricault had himself died young as the result of his addiction to spirited horses. Landseer was, according to Leopold Martin, 'but an indifferent horseman', whose vanity nonetheless demanded blood horses. In May of 1850 Sir Charles Phipps had written to him from Buckingham Palace anxiously urging him to get rid of an Arab he had acquired from Victoria: 'The Queen and the Prince would be very sorry that you should keep a horse that was not safe for you to ride . . . The Prince will, I expect, call at your house today'—though whether to visit Landseer on a bed of pain is not stated. Yet riding accidents do not appear to have figured in his catalogue of woes; though driving, yachting and rail accidents did. The 'indentation of the skull' might as easily have been a result of his rail accident in 1868, which certainly seems to have intensified his inconsistencies of behaviour without, however, being the cause of them. Whatever the cause, the effect was disquieting and the behaviour classically schizophrenic: almost to the last he would move unpredictably from light to shade, from a wry self-debunking charm to wild fits of hallucination and egocentricity. Victoria would wonder how the man who had painted little Dash and Islay and her parakeets and herself and her handsome husband and fine family could produce a tortured 'black' painting like *A Swannery Invaded*. In Victorian times, of course, the unmentionable usually went unmentioned. Landseer's other biographer, F. G. Stephens, also pursed his lips, gathered up his voluminous skirts and hurried by—'The closing years of Sir Edwin's . . . life were darkened in the manner we have already indicated rather than described.' Old friends like Kate Perry could only reminisce sadly beneath their treasured likenesses of the

great painter: ' "Landseer will be with us" was held out as an induce-
ment to join many a social board, where his wit, gaiety and peculiar
powers of mimicry rendered him a delightful guest. But I am speaking
of him as he appeared before the fine spirit was darkened by one of
the heaviest of calamities!'.

Landseer himself had long been aware of the rumours circulating
about him, judging from a story he liked to relate about himself.
One day, riding down Bond Street, he saw a notice in a picture-
dealer's window: *A fine Landseer on view within.* Curious, he dis-
mounted from his horse, gave a boy the reins to hold and went inside,
enquiring after the *fine Landseer*. The dealer, taking Landseer for a
wealthy customer, ushered him into a back room and proudly produced the work, an early one.

'And how much do you want for it?' the painter asked.

'Two thousand guineas,' said the dealer.

'Two thousand? That seems a long price for such an early work?'

'I couldn't take a shilling less,' replied the dealer, touching the side
of his head significantly. 'He's gone, sir, you see. He's out of his mind.
He'll never paint another.'

'Is he indeed?' said Landseer respectfully. 'I'm very sorry to hear
that.'

On his way out he noticed a large picture in a corner by his friend
Clarkson Stanfield.

'How much do you want for the Stanfield?' he asked.

'That, sir, is also two thousand guineas.'

'My God,' said Landseer, tapping his own forehead. 'Has Stanfield gone too?'

CHAPTER NINETEEN

A VACANCY AMONG THE ACADEMICIANS

'I shall never see these green leaves again!'
—Sir Edwin to his sister Emma

LANDSEER HAD begun to drink heavily to anaesthetise his pain and his nervous apprehensions. Though never exactly abstemious himself, he had always tended to be critical of drunkenness in others. As an attitude it was classically Victorian. T. S. Cooper recalls a dinner of Academicians at the Star and Garter, Richmond, with Cousins, rather the worse for wear, stretched out on the floor while his friends tried to revive him sufficiently to pack him on an omnibus. Landseer had viewed the scene with Olympian distaste, declaring that he just couldn't understand how any man could sit down to dinner with friends and drink wine to such excess as to render himself 'helpless and degraded'. Alas, Cousins apparently never repeated the lapse whereas rendering himself 'helpless and degraded ' not long afterwards became habitual with Landseer.

There had doubtless been a solid enough base on which to build his later alcoholism. Heavy social drinking was part of the life he had chosen to lead. For more than fifty years he had regularly dined over some of the best-stocked cellars in the land. His habitual nightcap was 'a Lager and a glass of grog'. Millais talked of accompanying him home one evening and passing four hours in pleasant conversation over brandy and water. Sherry and soda water was another favourite club tipple, and he was also known to be a fine judge of port. His taste, though hardly modest, seemed suitably controlled and catholic. The level, and the temptations to raise it, was no greater than that contemplated by many another man whose professional and social lives tended to merge at times; but his extreme nervous sensitivity, his adoption of more work than he could handle, his fatal habit of procrastination, his worry over unfulfilled and late commissions, over his failing health and fading eyesight—all helped to drive him towards the point where drink seemed the only comforter.

When his drunkenness got beyond family control, Charles Landseer sent his younger brother to 'dry out' in a home near Carshalton
in Surrey. One Sunday T. S. Cooper went to visit the sick painter
accompanied by Charles who warned him in advance that Edwin
was 'a perfect wreck' suffering from D.T.s and eternally craving drink.
Cooper found that Charles had not exaggerated:

> I was indeed shocked when I saw him so changed. He was always
> crying out for more drink, and was to all appearance half out of his
> mind. He said to me:
> 'Oh, Cooper, you do not know how ill I have been, and still am!
> And they don't care anything about me; they leave me alone and
> they do nothing to help me; they will not even give me anything
> to drink when I am dying of thirst!'
> It was too sad to hear him continually groaning and mumbling,
> and to feel that no one could do anything to help him. I tried to
> console him, but it was of no use. He did not seem to understand
> what I said . . . The whole place was in dire disorder—beer and
> porter bottles, dishes, pipes, cigars, newspapers strewed about the
> room; but no Bible, nothing to calm his mind, or to lead him to
> think about death and eternity! . . .
> He dined with us; but his whole talk was of himself and his
> troubles, groaning and complaining and calling out for more drink
> . . .

In another month or so Edwin was released. Cooper was in the
Athenaeum Club when Edwin and Charles came there to dine. When
Cooper went to the butler's table to choose his dinner, Edwin was
already there, 'tasting' by his way of it 'some fine old brandy . . .
to try if it is really good'. The connoisseur already seemed half seas
over, and Cooper later observed him 'walking about more than half-
boosy; his nose of a purple-brown colour, and looking altogether
repulsive . . . everyone in the place made remarks about him, either
in derision or in pity'.
Avoiding Sir Edwin had become a habit among his fellow
Academicians. Later that same day, on hearing on the steps of the
Athenaeum that Landseer was within, Sir William Boxall R.A., an
old friend who had known Edwin since boyhood, could not bring
himself to go in—'It would be too much for me, Cooper!'. So the two
artists walked up and down Pall Mall until Sir Edwin finally emerged
and clambered unsteadily into a cab. This was the last time Cooper
ever saw Landseer; whilst Boxall, close to tears, delivered himself of
sentiments that were doubtless much more moving than Cooper,
with his cloth-ear for dialogue, could make them:

'What a wreck! That one beloved by Royalty, petted by those in high station and noble in name, and so highly esteemed by all lovers of art, should have become the victim of so debasing a habit, is truly sad!'

Landseer's troubles with his exhibited pictures had also been growing. In 1870 one of the five pictures he sent to the Royal Academy was *Queen Victoria meeting the Prince Consort on his return from deerstalking in the year 1850*. The painting was as appealing as its title, being a re-hash of a work exhibited by royal command at the Academy in 1854 while still unfinished. In both versions it was a piece of unashamed royal-family idolatry of the kind that would have future counterparts in the Soviet propaganda pictures which adorned the walls of politbureaux and collective farms. Even the composition was sheerly propagandistic; the Queen (her head forming the apex of the grouping) descends a tartan-covered gangplank from her boat with dead deer at the foot in such a position that they could only have tripped her up; her husband (on a suitably lower level) hands her down; two deerhounds look up at their monarch in adoring reverence; the young Prince of Wales sits his pony with a gillie beside him who proudly holds up a fish of dubious ancestry.* Perhaps the most ludicrous touch of all is the four Highland servants steadying the shallow boat as her Majesty alights whose expressions, though meant to convey awesome respect, suggest instead an uneasy mixture of treason and indigestion. Even here Landseer did himself a typical injustice—the original chalk sketches of these same gillies had been extremely accomplished.

By 1870, according to G. D. Leslie, Sir Edwin never attended varnishing days himself, but sent his pictures in covered with a cloth, which was the way they stayed during these three preparatory days. However, early on the morning of the private view day, Landseer appeared. The canvas, too, had only just arrived. The empty frame had previously been sent in with a cloth over it, the Queen herself having granted the painter permission to keep the canvas at home until the last possible moment. Canvas and frame were joined and re-covered, whilst Landseer prowled in another room. Then the royal painter reappeared. Pickersgill and Leslie stood by the draped picture while Sir Edwin frowningly positioned himself on the other side of the room. He hesitated. Then, at his nervous signal, the two men removed the cloth. Landseer took one agonised look at his picture, shuddered and stalked out of the room. As Leslie records 'the

---

* In the biologist Frank Buckland's opinion, 'The fish is neither grilse, salmon nor trout; and if meant for either the fins are wrongly placed and there is no adipose fin'.

canvas was a failure and he knew it. For sixteen years this picture had been haunting Sir Edwin's studio. It was far finer in every respect when first exhibited, in the unfinished state, in 1854. I feel sure that the worry and trouble it had given him during those sixteen years did more than anything else to hasten the breakdown in his health which ended in his death . . . And yet people continually remark, "What a delightful occupation painting must be!"'.

No one knew better than the ageing Landseer that the critics were about to have a field day. Some of the more august journals deferred to the artist's age, his fading health and his past glories, but the smaller, less reputable publications spared him little. *Judy* commented:

> The connoisseur will not in the whole 'land see a' better Landseer than 'The Doctor's Visit to his Poor Relations'* nor a *worse* than a group of Royal Portraits to which Sir Edwin Landseer has not been ashamed to affix his name, but which it is only charitable to hope he did not paint.

And *The Period*:

> Apropos of Sir Edwin's work, the intelligent reader will derive much amusement from the faces of the gillies in the background who are gazing at the meeting of the Queen and her husband with unmitigated disgust as if they would like to pitch the Prince Consort into the Loch.

The lion lying down with the lamb was a theme that had obsessed Landseer from an early age—there were suggestions of it in the lion-dog partnership at Polito's Menagerie and in van Amburgh's beasts. The outcome of this obsession was *The Lion and the Lamb*, painted in 1871, at the height of his mental suffering. He had seen a lamb that he kept as a model lying down beside the large cast of a lion in his garden, and the scene had apparently impressed him as an illustration of the millenium as described in Isaiah. Immediately he had expressed a desire to paint the theme; and his family, only too eager to distract him from his suffering, had placed a large canvas on his easel. In two days, according to G. D. Leslie, he had produced 'a wonderful picture; so complete that if he let it alone it would rank with his best works'. 'But,' added Leslie, 'I know how it will be. If he paints on it again he will muddle it, and re-paint it and spoil it . . . that is how he spoils half his pictures.'

In his present nervous state, with so many tongues declaring him finished, Landseer was reluctant to miss a year at the Royal

* A small much-praised picture of zoo monkeys in the same exhibition.

Academy, lest it be interpreted as a public testimony of his impotence. When the pictures were all but hung, he decided to send in his
lion and lamb painting for exhibition. Although at that stage against
regulations, he asked the Queen if the laws might be bent to allow the
picture's admission. The Queen, very properly, replied that if the
Academy was agreeable, she would sanction the rules being broken.
But the Academy were not agreeable—it was an unfinished picture,
it could only now be squeezed into an unfavourable position and so
on. The President Sir Francis Grant half-heartedly suggested a space
above the architectural drawings—which would almost certainly
have reduced Sir Edwin to apoplexy. So the picture was not hung,
and Landseer was unrepresented in the Royal Academy's Annual
Exhibition of 1871. His brother Charles, to whom he had left the
final arrangements, could not bear to tell him. The Exhibition
opened, and still none of his family had found the courage to break
the news of the picture's rejection. No doubt they hoped that by
keeping him at home and hiding the periodicals, he would at least
temporarily forget about his lion and his lamb. However, a few days
after the opening, amidst a buzz of speculation, elbow-nudging and
raised eyebrows, the hectic-faced Sir Edwin unexpectedly arrived at
Burlington House and swept upstairs to the Exhibition Rooms. It
was left to the registrar Mr. Eyre to try to head him off, which he
managed to do in the second room where Landseer had gone in
muttering, peering and stamping search of his masterpiece. With
great difficulty he was induced to leave, and his brother Charles was
asked to follow him and explain. But Charles hung back, fearful of
his brother's wrath. As Redgrave rather prissily observed, 'I believe
that it is the continual giving way to him that helps to ruin his
health, and I am glad we withstood this infraction of the rules'.

One can appreciate Redgrave's point of view, though the Committee might at little cost to its pride have bent the regulations a little.
Landseer, after all, had an almost unique record of year by year
contributions to the Academy; at his death he had missed only seven
annual shows and had exhibited 171 pictures there. To one still in his
right mind the lesson that no painter, however distinguished, could
circumvent the rules or expect to be hung automatically might have
been a salutary one. But if the idea was to induce Landseer to mend
his ways or improve his character, they had surely left it a little late
in the day. To Sir Edwin's palsied imagination it was but one more
slight, one more piece of persecution, one more betrayal. And, as
Leslie predicted, the rejected canvas would stand on the easel for one
more year, being slowly worked to death, until it had achieved at
least some semblance of a 'finished picture'. In the final analysis, *The*

Lion and the Lamb suggested less romantic origins than those put about at the time—it looked for all the world like an oil study of one of the recumbent Trafalgar Square lions to which the artist had added a lamb (and, of course, several deadening layers of paint).

Sir Edwin's social outings were becoming increasingly rare. His family would vet his letters, answering approved invitations for him after he had scrawled across them an increasingly shaky YES or NO. The last time the Queen saw him was in 1871, 'at Chiswick, at Bertie's garden party'. She found he was 'hardly fit to be about, and looked quite dreadful'. When he was even more indisposed than usual she sent him flowers, as well as polite congratulations that 'you are gaining health so steadily'—a message that can hardly have cheered Landseer, since it contained the words no hypochondriac likes to hear.

By 1872 the painter was living in a physical and mental twilight. In spite of it, he sent three paintings to the Royal Academy that year, apparently determined to resume his contributions to the shows he had dominated for a lifetime. His family and his friends encouraged him, helpfully adding their suggestions and no doubt their own moiety of paint to his canvases. Their concern can hardly be wondered at. The presence of Landseer pictures in the Exhibition was in the nature of a reassuring despatch from the front, a tangible proof that the Master was far from being the palsied wreck of popular rumour. But the attempts in the long view were well-meaning rather than enlightened. As the Catalogue tartly remarked:

> One observation will apply to the whole of the pictures exhibited by Sir Edwin (or his friends) this year. They are all large—and all *unfinished*—said to have been painted (so far as they *are* painted) some years since, alas! never to be finished by his hand. All promised to have been *good paintings* if finished, as to *subject* quite another matter.
> They are not to be criticised.

It was perhaps the limbo-like backgrounds that most contributed towards the unfinished aspect of the paintings—backgrounds that reflected the mental and ocular haze in which Sir Edwin now lived.

The three pictures were the previous year's reject, *The Lion and the Lamb, The Lady Emily Peel with her favourite dogs* and *The Baptismal Font*. In November 1860 Lady Peel had already confided her regrets that she was deprived, through living abroad, of 'the opportunity . . . to sit to you for the completion of myself and funny dogs this winter'. Lady Peel had an evident soft spot for Sir Edwin.

Her letter from Geneva hopes that he 'might fancy a little visit here? I have entirely hung up my own private room with engravings from your pictures'. In February 1862 she was writing: 'I am miserable at not seeing you. I made an attempt last week but unsuccessfully and went away in despair'—a few days later she declared herself 'your slave whenever you wish to summon me'. 'Kind Lady E. Peel keeps on writing for me to go to Villa Lammermoor and says she will undertake my recovery' wrote Landseer to Jessy during one of his bouts of depression. Even in 1870, when others were describing Sir Edwin either as a revolting or pathetic spectacle, he had clearly lost little of his fascination for the handsome Lady Peel, one of whose visits to him was prefaced with the coyly feminine warning, 'I fear I shall be looking horrid but this you will judge for yourself'. She was clearly charmed and excited when her annually-expressed wish to see herself and her borzois on the walls of Burlington House was finally realised. The critics were less enthralled. It was a subject-portrait of some obviousness; one of the dogs having overturned and broken a garden pot, Lady Peel wags an admonitory finger as the animal looks suitably contrite. The Catalogue, whilst praising the dogs as 'wonderfully brushed in' found in Lady Peel's flesh and clothing 'little more than dead colouring, and the background is an incoherent haze'. However, the *Art-Journal* thought it 'as graceful as anything that bears his name'—though there was surely little more than macabre irony in the reaction of one commentator who saw in it the possibility of Landseer's return to power.

The Baptismal Font reflected the same apparent search for a kind of universal tenderness as had *The Lion and the Lamb* and the much earlier *Shepherd's Prayer*. It showed lambs and doves gathered round a font which, in the picture's unfinished state, appeared to be miles from nowhere. Landseer's anthologist, C. S. Mann, was frankly puzzled by it: 'I suppose there is love and gentleness and purity and innocence and—anything else of the sort that occurs to you'. The *Art-Journal*, though deeming the picture 'inexpressibly rich in Christian allusion', went so far as to doubt the authenticity of 'a divergence so wide from his known course'; whilst the *Graphic* found the conversion of church font into animal drinking-fountain 'sacrilegious'. It was the philanthropic Baroness Burdett-Coutts who had suggested to Landseer that he paint an altar-piece for one of her benevolent institutions. The painting was the outcome of this wish, though it was subsequently admired and bought by the Queen.

Landseer had painted much of *The Baptismal Font* at Eastwell Park, the Abercorn's Kentish home. To the Duchess's son, Lord Frederic Hamilton, it was 'a perfectly meaningless composition . . .

for whatever allegorical significance he originally meant to give it eluded the poor clouded brain'. The painter had also evidenced some ominously odd behaviour, sending for some sheep from the Home Farm for use as models, which he then wanted driven upstairs to his bedroom. The housekeeper, of course, furiously protested that it was impossible to keep a house in good order if sheep were allowed in the best bedrooms, and Landseer, his easels, his colours and his flock were unceremoniously consigned to the garden.

Such eccentricities of behaviour were, however, mild compared with the brainstorms that now frequently beset the elderly painter. Lord Frederic Hamilton* went so far as to describe him as 'hopelessly insane, and during his periods of violence, a dangerous homicidal maniac'. The great affection of the Abercorns for the friend they had always called *Lanny* died hard, and they were the last of the great landed families to tolerate the completely unpredictable behaviour of the seriously deranged artist who continued to visit them for long periods at a time:

> He had necessarily to bring a large retinue with him: his own trained medical attendant; Dr. Tuke, a celebrated Alienist in his day; and above all, Mrs. Pritchard. The case of Mrs. Pritchard is such an instance of devoted friendship as to be worth recording. She was an elderly lady of small means, Landseer's neighbour in St. John's Wood, a little shrivelled dried-up old woman. The two became firm allies, and when Landseer's reason became hopelessly deranged, Mrs. Pritchard devoted her whole life to looking after her afflicted friend. In spite of her scanty means, she refused to accept any salary, and Landseer was like wax in her hands. In his most violent moods, when the keeper and Dr. Tuke both failed to quiet him, Mrs. Pritchard had only to hold up her finger and he became calm at once. Either his clouded reason or some remnant of his old sense of fun led him to talk of Mrs. Pritchard as his 'pocket Venus'. To people staying with us (who, I think, were a little alarmed at finding themselves in the company of a lunatic, however closely watched he might be) he would say, 'In two minutes you will see the loveliest of her sex. A little dainty creature, perfect in shape, perfect in feature, who might have stepped bodily out of the frame of a Greuze. A perfect dream of loveliness.' They were considerably astonished when a little wizened woman, with a face like a withered apple, entered the room. He was fond, too, of descanting on Mrs. Pritchard's wonderfully virtuous temperament, notwithstanding her amazing

* *The Days Before Yesterday*, 1937.

charms. Visitors probably reflected that, given her appearance, the path of duty must have been rendered very easy for her.

To the end he never lost his amazing facility with the pencil. However incoherent his speech or befuddled his brain, his hand still obeyed his professional will; or perhaps the old instinct to sing for his supper. As Lord Frederic recalled:

On another occasion there was some talk about a savage bull. Landseer, muttering 'Bulls, bulls, bulls', snatched up an album of my sister's and finding a blank page in it made exquisite little drawings of a charging bull. The disordered brain repeating 'Bulls, bulls, bulls', he then drew a bulldog, a pair of bullfinches surrounded by bullrushes and a hooked bull trout fighting furiously for freedom. That page has been cut out and framed . . .

The Duchess of Abercorn had been Landseer's friend, girl and woman, for fifty years: their letters had always bespoken an easy family intimacy and affection. It is peculiarly ironic that their sophisticated country-house relationship should have culminated in an act of macabre tragi-comedy worthy of a Goya or a Fuseli:

My mother happened to be confined to her bed with an attack of bronchitis when Landseer's visit came to an end, but she felt no hesitation about receiving her life-long friend into her bedroom, insane though he was, so he was shown in, Mrs. Pritchard, the faithful watchdog, remaining on guard outside the door. Landseer thanked my mother profusely for the pleasure his visit had given him, and then added, 'Now, will you allow an old friend of over fifty years standing to take a very great liberty?' 'Certainly, Lanny,' answered my mother, thinking he was asking permission to kiss her. 'Thank you,' said Landseer, and at once sat down on her chest and remained there. He was a very heavy man, and my mother in her weak state had not sufficient strength to move him from his position. His weight was crushing her; she was quite unable to breathe and, suffering as she was from bronchitis, she began to lose consciousness and might have suffocated, had not the watchful Mrs. Pritchard (who, I suspect, had kept her eye constantly glued to the key-hole of the door) darted into the room and raised Landseer to his feet, soundly upbraiding him at the same time for his outrageous conduct. That was the last visit he ever paid to us.

Though he continued to paint sporadically, Landseer had nothing left to give. The schizophrenic nature of his illness was always in evidence: he still 'enjoyed' periods of comparative lucidity that were perhaps more painful than those of his infantile befuddlement. He did not lack for friendly female companions, though it seems likely that the Mrs. Stevens cited by Jessy's friend, Jeanie Adams-Acton, was the same lady as Mrs. Pritchard—a widowed near-neighbour who could easily control him when his professional keeper could not. When Landseer became unmanageable this lady would arrive 'like a ministering angel'. In appearance she was 'very like a small monkey with her bright, blinking eyes and merry mouth'. She became 'indispensable to him'—and it seems improbable, though not impossible, that one mentally unstable old painter should have been blessed with two such 'pocket Venuses'. She was apparently a fellow dog-lover and when Sir Edwin was convalescent would walk with him in Regent's Park regaling him with stories of her dog Jolly in return for which 'he would produce a pencil and draw for her anything of interest she saw'. Jolly was reputedly the last dog that the artist ever portrayed and has been quoted as belonging to a Mrs. *Prickett*, suggesting certain vagaries of memory where the naming of Landseer's pocket Venus was concerned. Ever a romantic, Jeanie Adams-Acton hinted that the unlikely couple might have married but for the neighbourhood belief that 'all the children of a certain peeress were hers by Sir Edwin, and that on the death of the peer, Sir Edwin had married her "to make an honest woman of her", as he was reported to have told his friend, Mrs. Stevens'. It is indeed possible that such a story could have come from the lips of an intermittently mad old painter who, after years of at least nominal discretion, desired to confide his secrets. Whether the embellishments were his, his lady-companion's or Jeanie's is another matter. The tale might even have served Landseer as an excuse if, at some stage of comparative lucidity, Mrs. Stevens/Pritchard/Prickett had endeavoured to back the inveterate bachelor into a corner.

His sisters are only occasionally in evidence in Landseer's last years. John Landseer was the one member of the clan who had ever attempted to criticise or discipline Edwin: his brothers and sisters had consistently pandered to him. Charles was close to him but more in the role of humble guide-dog than masterful keeper: his touch on his wayward brother's arm was light indeed: he feared Edwin's rages and tended to melt into the background in embarrassment when the great painter staged one of his stand-up apoplectic fits over some (usually imagined) slight or insult. He never forgot that he owed his position in life to Edwin without (unlike Tom) having given him much in return, but it was questionable brotherly love merely to stand by 'on call' while Edwin's tantrums progressed from the

petulant to the monomaniacal. In his last years Emma, who did have
a mind of her own, would walk her famous brother in the garden at
St. John's Wood. On one such stroll Edwin stopped and said to his
youngest sister, 'I shall never see these green leaves again!'. But he
lived through a further spring.

It was very much a borrowed spring. Landseer was by then almost
entirely housebound. When the weather was mild he tottered
occasionally round the grounds of his mansion which had grown un-
kempt and dilapidated, partly because he could not abide workmen
around the place. That year, 1873, he sent two pictures to the Royal
Academy Exhibition. One was of the Queen as a young woman on a
wall-eyed white horse. She had not sat for the portrait, and the pose
was depressingly familiar, as were the other inevitable ingredients—
two dogs, one with a glove in its mouth, their eyes uplifted to their
mistress with looks of adoring supplication. The other picture was of
his own dog, *Tracker*. Though travesties of his former skill, both were
symbolic verses in his swan-song—the dog representing the basis of
his reputation; her Majesty, the high place he had gained in society
largely through that reputation. Victoria had doubtless been one of
the super mother-figures in Landseer's life. 'It is well-known,' wrote
Lady Richmond Ritchie, 'that he appealed to her once, when haunted
by some painful apprehensions, and that her wise and judicious kindness came to the help of his nurses. She sent him back a message:
bade him not to be afraid, and to trust to those who were doing their
best for him, and in whom she herself had every confidence.' Despite
Landseer's occasional annoyance over his carefully-filed *Royal
Fusseries*, she had certainly shown him a good deal of loyalty, expressing interest in and buying his pictures almost to the end. Some
of the later commissions and purchases had mainly been acts of
kindness: they were also, no doubt, acts of nostalgia for the happy
days she and Albert had shared with the artist in her 'Dear Paradise'
north of the Tweed. Her constancy was greater than that of the
generality of the *haut ton*, who deserted him in their droves as he
became more of a social liability than an asset.

Ironically it was in those last impotent months that Landseer
developed a strong emotional loyalty to the art he could no longer
practice. He expressed a repeated wish to die in his studio, which he
could hardly be persuaded to leave—the same studio from which, in
his prime, any suitably-monogrammed invitation could almost
instantly summon him. Day after day he lay on the couch, looking
dim-sightedly around him at the half-finished canvases, fingering his
brushes, picking up his palettes—discovering all too late, it seemed,
where his loyalty ought to have lain.

In 1873 Millais had painted a portrait of Landseer's mentor, Thomas Hyde Hills: to his late summer letter of thanks the business-man added a note of warning: 'I am sorry to say our poor friend Sir Edwin will never see it, for I fear he is dying, and will be but a very short time with us'. The painter died at eleven o'clock on the morning of October 1st; not in his beloved studio, but in his bedroom. His brother Charles was with him. The death certificate gave *cerebral disease* as the general and *cerebral effusion* as the immediate cause of death. The news was at once conveyed to the Queen, whose diary-entry of the same day on her 'kind old friend' was a characteristic blend of *in memoriam* and inventory:

> A merciful release, as for the last three years he had been in a most distressing state, half out of his mind yet not entirely so . . . I cannot at all realise it. How many an incident do I remember, connected with Landseer! He kindly has shown me how to draw stag's heads, and how to draw in chalks, but I never could manage that well. I possess thirty-nine oil paintings of his, sixteen chalk drawings (framed), two frescos, and many sketches.

On the 11th of October the painter was buried in the crypt in the south-eastern corner of St. Paul's Cathedral, being laid between the sculptor Sir J. E. Boehm, R.A. and George Dawe, R.A.—it may be some consolation to Landseer's shade that his name has at least outlived those two immortals! Other near-neighbours, however, were Turner, Reynolds, Lawrence, Fuseli and Wren. Several years later his memory was enshrined there in a sculptured white marble slab by Thomas Woolner, R.A.

October 11th was a day of incessant rain. The Rev. J. A. Hessey, D.D., the Preacher of Gray's Inn delivered an apt discourse based on the eleventh chapter of Ecclesiastes—'He hath made everything beautiful in his time'. Predictably, the chaplain praised Landseer's art for being 'pure and inoffensive. It was impossible to mention one against which the most fastidious mind could raise an objection'. He cautiously described Landseer as 'a moral painter', and commended the influence exerted by his pathos 'which might second the efforts of the Society for the Protection of Animals, if, indeed, it had not mainly conduced to the establishment of it'. Looking out over the crowded pews, he cleverly balked the issue of Landseer's own well-known dislike of formal worship, having left himself 'little room to speak of Landseer's private character, of his genial tone in society, his unambitiousness, his lack of self-seeking, and of his attitude to God and his Saviour. Some of these things were patent to all, some of them were known only to his intimate friends, and into this last no stranger might intrude. "What man knoweth the things of a man save the spirit of a man, which is in him?".'

Among the listeners to the Reverend Hessey's peroration was an almost full turn-out from the Royal Academy. Literature was represented by Browning and Politics and the Army by Lord Granville, Lord Westminster, Lord Hardinge and Sir William Codrington. Queen Victoria and the Prince of Wales sent wreaths. On the day of the funeral an unknown mourner hung wreaths in the jaws of the four Trafalgar Square lions, where they remained for over a week. *The Times*, however, noticed one yawning gap in the ranks of those who had gathered to pay their last respects—'With one or two distinguished exceptions, the world of fashion . . . was conspicuous by its absence'. The stately homes up and down the country were bedecked with Landseers, obtained in many instances for knockdown prices; but their personal enchantment with the painter had ceased with his conversion from one of the beautiful people to a bumbling old near-lunatic with a purple-veined nose and food-stains on his waistcoat.

If there was one thing that might have saved Edwin Landseer from dilettantism and for his art, it might have been a previous peep, by some magic long-range insight, into the list of attenders at his own funeral.

CHAPTER TWENTY

AFTERMATH

Landseer! If I had had Landseer through my hands for six months, I could have made a man of him!
—William Huggins of Liverpool, animal painter

IT WASN'T long, of course, before the verse-mongers sprang into print. 'Mourn, all dumb things, for whom his skill found voice,' *Punch* ordered all its animal-readers, before trumpeting, 'We cry "Queen Art is dead—Long live Queen Art!"' There followed a steep descent into McGonagallese:

> Few have lived busier lives than he
> Whose Art, plied with delight, delight still gave
> And if at last a cloud fell o'er his glee
> It hung not long between him and the grave.

Other poets, too, had been at work:

> . . . He showed the desolation of the goal
> Which men must dare who seek the icy pole,
> And how the king of brutes was subject made;
> But never showed he ought which would degrade
> The hand that painted or the eye that saw
> A prince of painters, he obeyed the law,
> And put his talents out to good account
> To render up his Lord the full amount.
> He has not lived in vain whose magic art
> Portrayed God's creatures in the nobler part;
> He has not lived in vain whose teaching tends
> To human sympathy with our dumb friends.

Landseer's will was a final testimony to his lack of faith in his own powers. His apparent intention to bestow the major part of his store on his favourite brother Charles went characteristically awry. Charles was left £10,000, and the remainder of the estate, after minor legacies, was to be divided equally among his brother Tom and his two sisters (Anna Maria having died in 1871). However, his will was proved in the year after his death for £160,000, and two years later was re-sworn at over £200,000. To Jessy he also left the jewellery and other gifts given him by the Queen. His physician got £250. His prosperous business manager T. H. Hills was left £5,000, whilst his manservant for at least thirty years received only £100 (the non-religious Landseer seeming to subscribe to at least one biblical text, 'To him that hath shall be given').

The sale of Landseer's works of art, some 1,400 of them, took place over seven days beginning 8th May 1874 at Christie's, the last sale personally conducted by Mr. Christie himself. The paintings and drawings realised £69,709. 9/–, considerably less than some experts had forecast. Some alleged old masters were also included, among them two Cuyps, a Wouverman, a Snyders, a Fyt, a Velasquez (*The Betrothal of an Infanta*) and a Murillo (*Head of an Old Woman*); as well as several works *after* the masters.

A final sale of the remainder of Landseer's effects was conducted over three days beginning 28th August 1874. These included some engravings, his furniture, his billiard table, china, bronze, books, stuffed animals, casts, lay figures and other contents of the studio. There was at least one indication that personal interest in the great painter had already begun to wane—his favourite easel, specially designed for him by his next-door neighbour, the portrait-painter John Lucas, was knocked down for a mere three guineas, although there were several artists present. What *The Times* described as 'the quaint rambling old house' was sold in that same summer for £6,850: it was demolished in 1894 and flats erected on the site.

Amongst other uncompleted work, Sir Edwin left behind three large unfinished canvases particularly dear to his heart, with the dying wish that his friend Millais, and no one else, should complete them. Besides their reputation as child prodigies, Landseer and Millais had shared an interest in blood sports. Although they had started on different sides of the pre-Raphaelite fence, Millais had always spoken warmly of Landseer's encouragement over pictures of his which were misunderstood or unpopular. His wife Effie sent Landseer a bouquet every year on his birthday, and was one of the women who could always be relied upon to listen sympathetically to the old painter's complaints about his health. The fact that she had abandoned her first husband Ruskin no doubt endeared her further to Landseer.

The three unfinished pictures were subsequently known as *Nell Gwynne, The Dead Buck* and *Digging Out the Otter*. The first was completed in 1883. There had been nothing on the canvas except a highly-finished white horse, the space for a dog and the background suggestion of a lake and swans. Millais' daughter Effie posed for the life-size figure of Nell, lending an unlikely appearance of virginal modesty to the ribaldly amorous mistress of Charles II. Even this Nell in her own way substituted for a queen: the horse and its trappings were an almost exact replica of those made for a portrait of Victoria in 1839. It was, however, the added dog that most tickled Millais' vanity, especially after a knowledgeable art critic peered at the finished canvas and said, 'Ah, to be sure; how easily one can recognise Landseer's dogs. Wonderful, isn't it?'. 'Yes, wonderful,' agreed Millais, smugly lighting his pipe, 'I finished painting that dog yesterday morning, and have done the whole of it myself.' Millais' animals could certainly be good: his dog in *The Order of Release* is admirably done, though his horse in *St. Isumbras Crossing the Ford* proved both tragic and troublesome, as he elongated it into a kind of equine daschund in his attempts to accommodate three people comfortably on its back.

In *The Dead Buck*, which subsequently went to America, Millais added a background of hills and trees to Landseer's foreground of a dead fallow buck with Scotch terriers. *Digging Out the Otter*, however, was almost two-thirds unfinished, much of it only indicated by charcoal lines. Millais cleverly finished it in the manner of Landseer —and to some effect. Though it had made only 630 guineas at the artist's sale, it sold for 2,950 guineas after completion by the one time pre-Raphaelite.

Several Landseer pictures realised much more than this, though mainly after the artist's death. However, the colossal *Braemar* made £4,200 in 1868 (and almost a thousand pounds more twenty years later); whilst *A Midsummer Night's Dream*, bought by the engineer I. K. Brunel for 400 guineas sold nine years later in 1860 for £2,940. *The Monarch of the Glen*, bought of the artist for a possible 350 guineas, realised £6,510 in 1884 and changed hands again eight years later for £7,245. Four years after the painter's death Agnews paid £5,932 for *The Otter Hunt*. The dog and deer picture known as *Chevy* for short realised £5,985 in 1895. Some big prices were paid at the sale of the collection of Landseer's friend and patron E. J. Coleman in 1881—Thomas Holloway paid £6,615 for '*Man Proposes, God Disposes*', which now hangs in the Royal Holloway College; *The Chase* (or *Stag Pursued by a Greyhound*) and *Well-Bred Sitters* went for £5,250 apiece. At the Wells Sale in 1890 *None But the Brave Deserve the Fair* made £4,620 and *Honeymoon of the Roebucks*, £4,042. Even such a lamentable affair as *Lady Godiva's Prayer* could fetch £3,360 in the year after Landseer's death, no doubt on account of its nudity. Before the end of the century some twenty Landseers had changed hands at prices over three thousand pounds. With the beginning of the present century their value began to decline; and in 1901 what should have been a valuable memento, Sir Edwin's palette on which was sketched in oils the head of a dog, sold, along with an easel, for only £3. 5/–. The twentieth century, in fact, almost disposed of Landseer. Several of his works have changed hands in recent years for pitifully small amounts, though some of these were of doubtful authenticity. There have been some recent glimmerings of hope. An album of his drawings made over £3,000 at auction in 1972. A small 8″ × 10″ Highland landscape that had sold at Christie's in 1910 for 10 guineas fetched 10,000 guineas in the same auction rooms in 1974; but the record price remains the £13,650 paid in 1966, also at Christie's, for *Queen Victoria and the Duke of Wellington reviewing the Life Guards.*

It is perhaps fortunate that the mentally unstable painter was spared the gall of seeing the inflated figures for which many of his works changed hands in the last quarter of the nineteenth century—often ten times more than he himself had been paid. Obviously, the greater part of his fortune had come from engraving rights. One publisher alone, Henry Graves, paid him £60,000 in copyright fees. For the twin-pictures *Peace* and *War* Landseer was paid £1,500; but the sale of the engraving rights brought this figure up to £4,500. The rights of *A Dialogue at Waterloo* are said to have brought the artist £3,600, and those of *The Stag at Bay* and *Refreshment* almost twice that.

It is not, of course, unusual for a painter's death to signal a boom in the popularity of his work. The Landseer Exhibition at the Royal Academy in 1874 was accounted a great success, drawing 105,000 paying visitors, with the receipts, including the sale of 30,000 catalogues amounting to almost £6,000. The Royal Academy mounted a further one-man Landseer exhibition in 1961, and the Mappin Art Gallery, Sheffield, yet another in 1972. Sir Edwin was, naturally, represented by more pictures than any other artist in the exhibition of *Animal Painting* at the Queen's Gallery, Buckingham Palace in 1966–67. Yet none of these well-presented shows has significantly reversed the trend of neglect (deserved or otherwise) which has been the twentieth century's homage to Landseer.

It is perhaps significant that after the death of Landseer—and, of course, of Winterhalter who had died earlier in the same year—no painter was admitted to the royal circle. Some time before he was accepted at court, Landseer had complained to his intellectual friends of how writers and artists were excluded from royal favour. He himself was to be virtually the first and the last so honoured. Under normal circumstances, he would obviously have been due for further distinctions. In June of 1885 Gladstone wrote from 10 Downing Street to the Queen that 'when he had first the honour to serve your Majesty in his present office, he would certainly have submitted the name of Sir E. Landseer for a Baronetcy, but for the mental calamity which at that time overtook him'. After the Prince Consort's death Millais and Watts were only two among several painters who were refused sittings. The camera, anyway, had already begun to take over. The Queen had earlier expressed her fears for art to her miniature painter Alfred Chalon, who had dismissed them—'Ah, non, Madame; photographie cannot flattère!'. This was possibly true of the early portrait photographs which often gave a grainy plucked-chicken look to Victoria's skin and on one occasion revealed her in such a state of trembling nerves that, though others in the picture were perfectly defined, her own likeness was a blur. However, later inventions like the soft-focus lens and studio-lighting would prove the camera's ability to lie almost as effectively as the paint-brush.

Landseer's death moved his artist-friends in different ways—Millais to complete faithfully the unfinished canvases, Frith to wear a gold and blue enamelled mourning-ring inscribed with Landseer's name. Its most immediate effect was, of course, on his own family. For the first time, according to Jeanie Adams-Acton, Jessy found herself financially able to breathe: she 'left off Paisley shawls and poke bonnets and went into a large house, setting up her own carriage'. Tom Landseer survived his famous brother by almost seven years, dying in 1880 at the age of eighty-five. Some time before his death he suffered a crashing fall down a river bank sustaining head injuries which, Mr. Algernon Graves perversely declared, were the means of *prolonging* his life. In his seventies, his considerable powers as an engraver had already begun to falter. In the years of Edwin's death he published plates from three of his brother's works—*The Font, Death of a Wild Bull* and *The Arab Tent*. None was in any way distinguished, and the last two were commercial failures. Queen Victoria considerately gave him *Islay*, the study of a one time favourite dog, to engrave. 'A wonderful production for a man over 80 years old,' she declared; but her beneath-the-breath comment was 'feeble in execution'—as, indeed, was *The Lion and the Lamb*, published in 1877. In all he had engraved 103 of Edwin's pictures. His tardy recognition by the Royal Academy in 1868 twelve years before his death had perhaps applied a spur to his ageing flanks, resulting in work that he would never have passed in his prime. Until Edwin's death he could, of course, plead financial necessity, but hardly afterwards. There may have been some desire to escape his domestic worries; an unfaithful wife and a son who was not his own. George, born about 1834, had become an artist. In his early twenties he went to India where he painted portraits of rajahs and made a large series of water-colours of Cashmere and the hill country. After his return to England around 1870, he did little or no further work, and seems to have been an invalid. He died in London in 1878, two years before the kindly Tom who no doubt mourned the man to whom he had given his name.

The question of legitimate progeny must at times have given the Landseer clan pause for thought. After John Landseer's vigorous attempts to found a dynasty, the final score remained a decided anti-climax—one or perhaps two extra-mural progeny for Edwin, none at all apparently for the bachelor Charles and Tom's son by another man. Of the four girls who survived into adulthood the eldest Jane had died during the birth of her first child, another two—Jessy and the very deaf Anna Maria—had remained spinsters, and only one, Emma, or Mrs. Mackenzie, had been able to present John Landseer with a grandson, Edwin John Landseer Mackenzie. Emma outlived the rest of the brothers and sisters, and eventually inherited most of Edwin's fortune.

Charles lived till the age of eighty (or seventy-nine if the birth-date on his baptismal record is correct). He had become not only stone-deaf but blind to the glazed reactions of those whom he bombarded in loud staccato tones with his endless puns and conundrums. He died in the year before Tom, on July 22nd, 1879, having by that time acquired some wealth as the residuary legatee of his brother. He bequeathed £10,000 to the Royal Academy to found four scholar-ships for art students, two in painting and two in sculpture, each worth £40 and tenable for two years. His other bequest to the Academy was a collection of drawings by George Stubbs made for his book *The Anatomy of the Horse* and given to him by his younger brother. Edwin revered the drawings and during his lifetime had turned down many tempting offers for them. They certainly could not have been in more appreciative hands: a few of his own ana-tomical drawings, like the *Flayed Dog*, were on a comparable level of excellence.

Comparisons are inevitable between Landseer and Stubbs, who had died when Edwin was four years old. The difference in their approach to their art was nowhere more apparent than in the *Ana-tomy of the Horse* itself. Stubbs was engaged for seven years on this labour of extreme unselfishness, for which he could hope to reap little reward. It involved working day after day on the putrefying carcases of horses, exposing himself to the risk of the *miasma* that later killed poor William Duffield. Every horse painter since, from Landseer to Munnings, has acknowledged his debt to this great work. One wonders if Landseer ever paused for thought over the precious drawings. Stubbs, too, had been an animal painter and a portraiturist of genius. He, too, had depended on the patronage of the nobility. He was a painter of considerably more anatomical insight but substantially less imagination that Landseer, repeating his decorative ideas over and over. Yet he remained resolutely his own man, and in his seventy-fifth year painted, in *Hambletonian*, arguably the best horse portrait of all time. After two centuries of neglect Stubbs' reputation has emerged into the sunlight. Landseer's shade, however, awaits a call that may never come. Few painters are remembered more for their execrations and less for their excellencies. The question mark over Landseer's reputation is whether the best of his work can yet separate itself from the worst—or whether the two are doomed to perish together, like the death-locked stag and deerhound in one of his own Highland torrents.

ACKNOWLEDGEMENTS

My grateful thanks are due to Mr. K. J. Lace, F.L.A. Librarian of the County Council, Chelmsford and his staff, for so patiently digging out Victorian books and other publications of the time. I am equally thankful to the Librarian and staff of the British Museum Library, and of the Victoria and Albert Museum Library, with its sizable (and helpfully transcribed) collection of Landseer letters. I should like to express my appreciation also for the help given by Mr. Reginald Williams and the staff of the British Museum Department of Prints and Drawings, where the very useful *Algernon Graves Illustrated Catalogue* is housed.

I am grateful to her Majesty the Queen for permission to view the unusual Landseer collection at Windsor, and to reproduce pictures from the royal collection. My thanks are also due to Sir Oliver Millar, Surveyor of the Queen's Pictures, and to Miss Jane Low, Curator of the Print Room at Windsor Castle.

Many of the best Landseer pictures, of course, remain in the stately homes, and I am most grateful to the Duke of Devonshire for access to correspondence, diaries and pictures: I should also like to thank the Librarian at Chatsworth, Mr. T. S. Wragg, MBE, TD and Mr. Peter Day. My thanks for their co-operation and kindness are also due to their Graces the Duke of Abercorn, the Duke of Argyll and the Duke of Northumberland; to the Countess of Sutherland; to Mr. David C. Mansel Lewis, H.M. Lieutenant for Carmarthenshire, Mr. L. Stevenson of Shipley, Yorks., Mr. Pierre Jeannerat, Mrs. A. Conran and John Dewar & Sons, Ltd.

My thanks are due to the staffs of numerous city and municipal art galleries up and down the country including the Director and his Assistant, the Wallace Collection, London; Mrs. Judy Egerton and Miss Ruth Ranking of the Tate Gallery, London; Miss K. R. Poole, the Department of Film and Photography, National Portrait Gallery, London; Miss C. J. Baker of the Royal Albert Memorial Museum, Exeter; Mr. Trevor Jones, City Museums and Art Gallery, Birmingham; Mr. Julian Treuherz of the City Art Gallery, Manchester; Mr. Hugh McNamara of Wolverhampton Art Gallery; Mr. Martin Hopkinson of the Walker Art Gallery, Liverpool; Ralph Fastnedge, Curator, the Lady Lever Art Gallery, Port Sunlight; G. L. Taylor and R. I. Charlton of the Ashmolean Museum, Oxford; Mr. Julian Spalding, Keeper, the Mappin Art Gallery, Sheffield; the Director, the Graves Art Gallery, Sheffield; Miss Pamela Murray, BA, AMA of Shugborough; Mr. Michael Millward, Art Gallery and Museum, Bury; the Director, Art Gallery and Museum, Cartwright Hall, Bradford; Mr. Hugh L. Stevenson of the Glasgow Art Gallery; Mr. R. E. Hutchison, Keeper, Miss Sara Stevenson, Miss J. Heron and Miss C. A. Robertson of the Scottish National Portrait Gallery.

I should like to thank also the Librarian and staff of the Royal Academy of Arts, London; Miss Esme Gordon of the Royal Scottish Academy; Mr. Robert Key of P. & D. Colnaghi & Co. Ltd., London; Mr. J. L. Naimaster, Managing Director, the Fine Art Society Ltd., and Tom Scott of Edinburgh.

Several people with access to public and other records rendered me great assistance, among them Mr. W. J. Smith, MA, FR Hist S, Head Archivist and the staff of the County Hall, Greater London Council; the staff of the Census Department of the Public Records Office and of St. Catherine's House, London; Mr. Kirby of Highgate Cemetery, London; Mrs. M. Wilford of the Lincolnshire Archives Committee and Dr. M. O'Sullivan of the Staffordshire County Council, and Mrs. P. New of the Royal Holloway College

While in the throes of preparing this biography I owed much to the personal help and forbearance of several kind souls, among them Tom and Alice Langhorne of Balmore, Stirlingshire, Mrs. Elizabeth Paton of Dunfermline and Ian and Christine Stuttle of Silver End, Essex. My particular thanks go out to my wife, Isabel, in whom I was fortunate enough to have a ready-made research assistant, and for whose enthusiasm and encouragement (not to say voluminous letter-writing) I am deeply grateful.

CAMPBELL LENNIE
Hampstead 1976

BIBLIOGRAPHY

AMES, Winslow *Prince Albert and Victorian Taste* 1967

ASPINALL, A. Ed. *Three Early Eighteenth Century Diaries* 1952

BALLANTINE, James *The Life of David Roberts* 1866

BECKETT, R. B. Ed. *John Constable's Correspondence*, Vols. III, IV 1966

BEDFORD, John, Duke of, *A Silver-Plated Spoon* 1959

BESANT, Walter *Fifty Years Ago* 1888

BLAKISTON, Georgiana *Lord William Russell and His Wife, 1815–1846* 1972

BLYTH, Henry *Skittles The Life and Times of Catherine Walters* 1970

BOASE, T. S. R. *English Art 1800–1870* 1959

BORER, Mary Cathcart *Two Villages* 1973

BUCKLE, George Earle *The Letters of Queen Victoria* Vols. I (1908) II (1926)

CONRAD, Peter *The Victorian Treasure House* 1973

COOPER, Thomas Sidney, RA *My Life* 1890

COPE, Charles Henry *Reminiscences of Charles West Cope, RA* 1891

CREALOCK, Lt.-General H. H. *Deer-Stalking in the Highlands of Scotland* 1892

CULLEN, Tom *The Empress Brown* 1969

CUNNINGHAM, Allan *Lives of the Great Painters* 1892

DAVIS, Frank *Victorian Patrons of the Arts* 1963

DUFF, David *Hessian Tapestry* 1967

DUFF, David *Albert and Victoria* 1972

FLEMING, G. H. *That Ne'er Shall Meet Again*, 1971

FONBLANQUE, Albany *The Life and Labours of Albany Fonblanque* Ed. E. Barrington de Fonblanque 1874

FORSTER, John *The Life of Charles Dickens* 1928

FRITH, W. P., RA *My Autobiography and Other Reminiscences* 1887

FULFORD, Roger Ed. *Your Dear Letter: Private Correspondence of Queen Victoria and the Crown Princess of Prussia 1865–1871* 1971

GAUNT, William *The Restless Century* 1972

GIBSON, Colin *Highland Deer Stalker* 1958

GILBEY, Sir William, Bart. *Animal Painters of England* 3 vols. 1900–1911

GOODALL, Frederick, RA *The Reminiscences of Frederick Goodall, RA* 1902

GORDON, Mrs. *The Home Life of Sir David Brewster* 1869

GORDON, W. J. *The Horse World of London* 1893

GOWER, Lord Ronald, FSA *My Reminiscences* 1883

GRAVES, Algernon *Catalogue of the Works of the Late Sir Edwin Landseer RA* 1876

—— *The Royal Academy Dictionary of Contributors* 1905–6

—— *The British Institution 1806–1867* 1908

GREIG, James. Ed. *The Farington Diary* 8 vols. 1922–28

GREVILLE, Charles C. F. *The Greville Memoirs 1837–1852* 1888

HAMILTON, Lord Frederic *The Days Before Yesterday* 1937

HARDIE, Martin *Water-Colour Painting in Britain* Vol 3 1968

HAYDON, B. R. Ed. M. Elwin *The Autobiography and Journals of Benjamin Robert Haydon* 1853

—— Ed. William Bissell Pope *The Diary of Benjamin Robert Haydon* 5 vols. 1963

—— *Correspondence and Table Talk: with a Memoir by his son Frederic Wordsworth Haydon* 1876

HEATH, Vernon *Recollections* 1892

HORSLEY, John Callcott, RA *Recollections of a Royal Academician* 1903

HUXLEY, Gervas *Victorian Duke The Life of Hugh Lupus Grosvenor* 1967

HUTCHISON, Sydney C. *The History of the Royal Academy 1768–1968* 1968

KEPPEL, Sonia *The Sovereign Lady* 1974

LANDSEER, Thomas, ARA Ed. *Life and Letters of William Bewick* 1871

LESLIE, Charles Robert, RA Ed. Tom Taylor *Autobiographical Recollections* 1860

LESLIE, George Dunlop, RA *The Inner Life of the Royal Academy* 1914

LEVEY, Michael *Painting at Court* 1971

LEY, J. W. T. *The Dickens Circle* 1919

LUCAS, Arthur *John Lucas* 1910

MAAS, Jeremy *Victorian Painters* 1969

MANNING-SANDERS, Ruth *The English Circus* 1952

MANSON, James A. *Sir Edwin Landseer, RA* 1902

MARTIN, R. B. *Enter Rumour: Four Early Victorian Scandals* 1962

MAXWELL, Sir Herbert *The Creevey Papers* 1904

MILLAIS, John Guille *The Life and Letters of Sir John Everett Millais* 1899

MILLS, A. R. *Two Victorian Ladies* 1969

MONKHOUSE, W. Cosmo *The Studies of Sir Edwin Landseer, with a History of his Art Life* 1877

MORLEY, John *Death, Heaven and the Victorians* 1971

NEVILL, Ralph *London Clubs: Their Histories and Treasures* 1911

PALMER, A. H. *The Life of Joseph Wolf* 1895

PENDERED, Mary L. *John Martin, Painter: His Life and Times* 1923

PREEST, John *Lord John Russell* 1972

REDGRAVE, F. M. *Richard Redgrave, CR RA* 1891

REDGRAVE, Richard, RA, and Samuel *A Century of Painters of the English School* 1866

ROE, F. Gordon *Victorian Corners* 1968

RUSKIN, John *Modern Painters* 1898 Edition

SADLIER, Michael *Blessington-D'Orsay: A Masquerade* 1947

SANDBY, W. *A History of the Royal Academy of Arts from 1768 to the Present Time* 1862

SCOTT, L. *Sir Edwin Landseer* 1902

SCOTT, Sir Walter *Journal* Ed. W. E. K. Anderson 1972

SHERRARD, O. A. *Two Victorian Girls* Ed. A. R. Mills 1966

SMITH, Charles Eastlake Ed. *Journals & Correspondence of Lady Eastlake* 1895

ST. JOHN, Charles *Wild Sports of the Highlands* 1846

STEEGMAN, John *Consort of Taste: 1830–1870* 1950

STIRLING, A. M. W. *Victorian Sidelights* 1954

STOREY, G. A., ARA *Sketches from Memory* 1899

STORY, Alfred T. *The Life of John Linnell* 1892

SWEETSER, M. F. *Landseer* 1879

THACKERAY, W. M. *Letters/Private Papers* London University Press 1945
—— *The Uses of Adversity 1811–1846*
—— *The Age of Wisdom 1847–1873*
—— *Critical Papers in Art* 1904

UWINS, Mrs. *A Memoir of Thomas Uwins, RA* 1852

QUEEN VICTORIA *Leaves from the Journal of Our Life in the Highlands* 1868

WALFORD, LB. *Memories of Victorian London* 1912

WALKER, Stella A. *Sporting Art: England 1700–1900* 1972

WHITEHEAD, G. Kenneth *The Deer Stalking Grounds of Great Britain and Ireland* 1960

YOUNG, G. M. *Early Victorian England* 1934

Other sources

Photographic record of Sir Edwin Landseer's work, with commentaries, compiled by Caleb Scholefield Mann (Victoria and Albert Museum)

Manuscript letters to Sir Edwin Landseer, transcribed by R. E. Mitchell (Victoria and Albert Museum)

Christie's Sale Catalogues (Various)

Art-Journal (Various)

Sir Edwin Landseer by Lady Richmond Ritchie: *Cornhill Magazine* 1874

Sir Edwin Landseer: Illustrated Catalogue of the Royal Academy of Arts Landseer Exhibition, 1961

Animal Painting: Van Dyck to Nolan: Illustrated Catalogue of the Exhibition at the Queen's Gallery, Buckingham Palace, 1966–67

Landseer and his World: Illustrated Catalogue of the Exhibition of Landseer works at the Mappin Art Gallery, Sheffield, 1972.

INDEX